# take a hint from the heavens ...

**1986** is packed with promise. Make the most of it with the predictions, insights, clues and suggestions America's most popular astrologer, Sydney Omarr, has prepared for you!

Learn about the "geometry" of relationships—who you get along with, and why . . . pore over celebrity sun signs and personality profiles . . . discover how and why the movements of the zodiac affect men and women so differently . . . and much, much more. Whatever your desire, whatever your dilemma, let Sydney Omarr's time-tested wisdom guide you through 1986, and watch your dreams become exciting realities!

For Expanding Your Personal Knowledge of
Astrology, SIGNET Brings to You

## SYDNEY OMARR'S
## ASTROLOGICAL GUIDES
## FOR YOU IN 1986

# SYDNEY OMARR'S
## DAY-BY-DAY ASTROLOGICAL GUIDE FOR

# *Sagittarius*
### (NOVEMBER 22–DECEMBER 21)

# *1986*

Ⓞ
## A SIGNET BOOK
## NEW AMERICAN LIBRARY

NAL BOOKS ARE AVAILABLE AT QUANTITY DISCOUNTS
WHEN USED TO PROMOTE PRODUCTS OR SERVICES.
FOR INFORMATION PLEASE WRITE TO PREMIUM MARKETING DIVISION,
NEW AMERICAN LIBRARY, 1633 BROADWAY,
NEW YORK, NEW YORK 10019.

SIGNET, SIGNET CLASSIC, MENTOR, PLUME, MERIDIAN AND NAL BOOKS
are published by New American Library,
1633 Broadway, New York, New York 10019

First Printing, July 1985

1 2 3 4 5 6 7 8 9

PRINTED IN THE UNITED STATES OF AMERICA

# CONTENTS

# 1

## Defining Terms

## What Are Those Astrologers Talking About?

Everyone knows it is more fun to visit another country if you know a bit of the language, and it's a lot easier to find your way around, too. The same idea applies to astrology, which is still foreign territory to many people. Astrology has its very own language, but it really isn't difficult to get a handle on it as long as you understand a few important terms. What follows is a kind of "Astrological Phrase Book," a brief compendium of the most basic words and concepts in the astrological language. Once you've learned them, you'll find you know a lot more about the why of your sun sign as well as information that will help you understand other astrological factors that make you what you are. Best of all, your new language can help you enjoy and explore one of the most exciting, underdeveloped territories under the sun—modern astrology!

### Astrology Is an Ancient and Practical "Science"
The first definition of astrology in the standard dictionary is "astronomy," and at one time in history the two studies were synonymous. The word astrology derives from Greek and literally means "the science (or study) of the stars." However, even in earliest times astrology has had much less to do with the "fixed" stars, which appear to remain in one place, than the planets, which move. (The word "planet" means wanderer.) Early man noticed that, as these heavenly bodies moved, their movements coincided with certain earthly events—mainly the changing of the seasons. Gradually, the movement

of the planets was observed to coincide with other important worldly events, such as wars, and the science of "divination" (prediction) by the planets was born. Astronomy and astrology lived happily together until the Christian church banned the latter in about 1550, condemning it as mere superstition. Astrology bounced back in the 1700s, when it came into use as an indicator of human personality, as well as a way to foretell future events. However, this so-called modern astrology is based on the same premise the ancients set down thousands of years ago: "As above, so below." Simply put, what it means is that the positions of the planets, which represent the cosmic order, are related in a significant and observable way to both human behavior and events in human life.

## The Zodiac Is a "Circle of Signs"

The zodiac ("circle of animals") is an invisible band in the sky which corresponds to the apparent yearly path of the sun, moon, and the major planets around the earth. It is the "apparent" path in the sense that it is what we *observe* from here on earth. Obviously we know that the earth and other planets revolve around the sun, but the study of astrology (and astronomy) takes earth as the reference point.

The 360-degree circle of the zodiac around the earth is divided into twelve thirty-degree segments—the twelve astrological signs. Throughout the year, as the sun appears to move, it passes through each of these segments in about thirty days. Zero degrees Aries, the vernal equinox or beginning of spring, is the beginning of the zodiac and the start of the seasonal year. It is at that point, on or about March 22, that the sun crosses or intersects with the *ecliptic*—another imaginary band that is (in the mind's eye) the extension of the earth's equator. Another major intersection of the sun's path and the ecliptic takes place at the fall equinox about September 22, the beginning of the seventh sign of the zodiac, Libra. (Equinox means equal days and nights, which is what we experience briefly in the early spring and early fall.) The zodiac "finishes" with the end of the twelfth sign Pisces, about March 21, then begins again with Aries.

Though the segments of the zodiac (the astrological signs) are *named* for the constellations of stars in the sky, they do not correspond with them. The constellations served as convenient visual markers for the ancient astrologer/priests, but the zodiac—and astrology—has always been based on the seasonal year, which never changes. The position of the constellations have changed with reference to our point of view here on earth, however, due to the slipping of the earth's axis. The constellations return a couple of degrees every year and have been doing so for centuries. That's why when the modern *astronomer* says "Aries," he is referring to a group of stars that is in a different position in the sky than the segment of the zodiac the *astrologer* calls "Aries."

## Your Sun Sign is Determined by the Month and Day You Were Born

The twelve segments of the zodiac are the twelve astrological signs, from Aries through Pisces, and it takes the sun exactly one year to pass through all twelve signs. A person born when the sun is passing through a particular segment of the zodiac is said to be born under that sign, and it is his/her sun sign. For example, a person born October 14 is said to be born under the sign of Libra. Your sun sign is the most important component of your astrological personality, it is the "real you." However, there are nine other planets besides the sun, and at the moment of a person's birth, those planets are passing through certain segments of the zodiac, or signs, as well. You will learn about some of these lesser influences on your personality in this book later on.

## An Element Is Part of a Sign

Obviously your sun sign is a lot more than simply a piece of the sky, or it wouldn't have any meaning. The meaning it has is based on two ancient astrological concepts, the *four elements* and the *three modes*. When these two factors are combined they form the basis of all astrological descriptions of human personality. You can't *see* an element or a quality; they are only to be under-

9

stood in terms of analogy, but they are fundamental to everything else in astrology, so it is important to understand them.

The four elements, defined by ancient philosophers as the basic components of everything and everybody, are *fire, earth, air,* and *water.* It is doubtful that even in earliest times this breakdown was to be taken as a physical reality: The elements are really four different ways we experience both things and people. For instance, if a thing or a person was experienced as hot rather than cold, sharp rather than dull, active rather than passive, it was said to partake of the *fire* element. And it's easy to see the connection.

Later on, during the Renaissance, the four elements were called "humors," starting a whole new way of typing people. *Fire was the humor choler*, and people who were said to have too much of it were those angry, impatient types who are subject to modern-day diseases like high blood pressure and heart attacks. *The earth element was called black bile* and could cause extreme melancholia (depression) in a person who had too much of it. *Air was the sanguine or rosy humor* and meant a lighter personality. *The water element was the humor phlegm*, and people with too much of it had rather "soggy" personalities and tended to be fat, as well. If the relationship between the elements (or humors) and the signs of the zodiac is beginning to ring a bell, it should. Here's the way the twelve signs break down into elements:

*Fire signs:* Aries, Leo, Sagittarius
*Earth signs:* Taurus, Virgo, Capricorn
*Air signs:* Gemini, Libra, Aquarius
*Water signs:* Cancer, Scorpio, Pisces

The four elements as four primal types of being exist today in the way many psychologists categorize people's thought processes. Once again, the relationship to the ways in which the twelve astrological signs really do perceive and react to the world is uncannily correct:

*The fire signs* are instant reactors who put it all together very quickly; things rarely have to be spelled out for a fire sign. These types of people also see the future possibilities inherent in the present and want to bring them about *now*. Obviously, fire signs tend to be impatient, but they have strong wills. Fire is the principle of *action*.

*The earth signs* are more pragmatic and slower to react. If they can't literally see something or touch it, they have difficulty visualizing it. They operate out of *sense perceptions* and are the realists of the zodiac—the builders who provide stability and continuity. Earth is the principle of *sustenance*.

*The air signs* see everything as connected to everything else. They are sequential thinkers for whom there must be a beginning, a middle, and an end to everything. For the most part these people operate on *logic* and act only when they can see the sense of their actions. The air signs are endlessly curious and represent the principle of *connecting and reasoning*.

*The water signs* tend to feel their way through life. What is most real to them is what their emotions tell them; they do what their emotions tell them to do as well. They are imaginative thinkers, the poets and artists of the zodiac. The water principle is that of *caring, nurturing, and protecting*.

## A Quality Is Part of a Sign

There are only four elements, but there are twelve signs. In astrological arithmetic, the *three qualities* which divide the *four elements* make up the difference. It isn't easy to grasp the concept of the elements, but the qualities (or "modes" as they are sometimes called) help a lot, because they make the elements a lot more tangible. Called *cardinal*, *fixed*, and *mutable*, the three modes can best be understood as *kinds of motion*.

*Cardinal motion is start-up movement.* It is the principle of bringing into being. Cardinal goes forward, so, the cardinal signs are *initiators*.

The four cardinal signs are those that start the four seasons:
Aries (*spring*)
Cancer (*summer*)

11

Libra (*fall*)
Capricorn (*Winter*)

*Fixed motion means staying in place.* Fixed things have come into being, and now simply are. The fixed signs represent stability, and are difficult to move. The four fixed signs represent the middle of each season:

Tarus (*spring*)
Leo (*summer*)
Scorpio (*fall*)
Aquarius (*winter*)

*Mutable motion means flexible motion.* Things that are mutable are changing, able to turn into something else. The mutable signs represent the *ability to adjust, and to accept change.* The four mutable signs are those that end the seasons:

Gemini (*spring*)
Virgo (*summer*)
Sagittarius (*fall*)
Pisces (*winter*)

## Elements and Qualities Together Add Up to Signs

When you put elements and qualities together you begin to get a picture of what they add up to—the twelve astrological signs. Here is how each quality modifies each element.

### *Fire element/Cardinal quality* = **Aries**

This get-up-and-go sign has all the flash and dash of fire plus an added dose of a pioneering spirit by virtue of its cardinal quality.

### *Fire element/Fixed quality* = **Leo**

Leo burns with the ardor and enthusiasms of fire, but gives off very steady heat due to its fixed quality.

### *Fire element/Mutable quality* = **Sagittarius**

Sagittarius represents the kind of fire that spreads, igniting everything and everybody in its path—which is rather erratic because of Sagittarius's mutable quality.

### *Earth element /Cardinal quality* = **Capricorn**

Capricorn is the most active builder of the earth signs because of its cardinal quality. Capricorn's brand of reality demands that something be brought into being.

***Earth element/Fixed quality*** = **Taurus**
This strong sign stands and waits, holding things and people together. Taurus is the warmest and most nurturing of the earth signs, and is always "there."

***Earth element/Mutable quality*** = **Virgo**
Virgo's practical sense knows that all things must change. This mutable sign represents the principle of stability with flux; that is, permanence in the face of change.

***Air element/Cardinal quality*** = **Libra**
Libra's air nature moves forward, actively connecting people and things into partnerships via its cardinal quality of initiation.

***Air element/Fixed quality*** = **Aquarius**
Aquarius is the most immovable of the air signs, representing the permanance of ideas and their practical application.

***Air element/Mutable quality*** = **Gemini**
This very movable sign represents changing thoughts and opinions, the breaking up of static ideas so that new ones can come about.

***Water element/Cardinal quality*** = **Cancer**
Cancer is the most initiating of the water signs because of the cardinal quality. Though shy, Cancer generally moves quietly but effectively to the forefront.

***Water element/Fixed quality*** = **Scorpio**
Scorpio's powerful self-control comes from the emotional water element that is contained and compressed because of this sign's fixed quality.

***Water element/Mutable quality*** = **Pisces**
Pisces extreme emotionalism—as well as this sign's creativity—comes from feelings that constantly change and move into new areas, creating new outlets.

**Planets Are the Most Important Factor in Astrology**
"Planet" is probably an even more important word in the astrological language than "sign." How can that be?

*Because it is the placement of the planets in various signs which indicates personality and it is the movement of the planets through the zodiac that indicates events.* In other words, without the planets the signs would have no application to people and what happens to them.

As early man noticed that the planets moved in fairly regular patterns, he began to associate certain characteristics with each of the planets, and each planet gradually took on a "personality." In a number of different cultures, certain planets were hooked up with certain gods, because it was the gods who really controlled life on earth. The moon was virtually always a female god—like Diana or Artemis. Jupiter, always a "good guy" planet, was known as Vishnu, the preserver, to the Hindus. Before he got his Roman name of Jupiter, the Greeks knew him as Zeus, a lusty fellow who had a heart of gold. (You'll get a complete rundown on each of the planets in Chapter 9, "The Planets As Stars.")

From these planetary "personalities" came the idea that each planet caused a certain kind of behavior or event by virtue of its own nature. For instance, Mars, always the war god, is still regarded by modern astrologers as an indicator of strife and conflict. When predicting events, the astrologer looks at what sign and what house Mars will be passing through at a certain point in time to see what kind of influence it is most likely to bring into a person's life.

When looking at personality, the astrologer determines which sign a person's Mars is in at the time of the person's birth to see how that individual is most likely to assert him-/herself. The sun, the most important planet makes us what we are in totality according to which sign the sun is placed in at our birth; i.e., our sun sign's Venus is the planet of relationships, and its placement in a specific sign shows how a person is likely to relate to others.

In short, planets indicate *action*, and the signs in which the planets are placed indicate *the kind of action*.

Since ancient times, astrologers have recognized seven planets. The sun (which is really a star), the moon (which is really a satellite of our own planet, earth) Mercury, Venus, Mars, Jupiter, and Saturn.

With the development of the telescope, thre     .
planets were discovered (although there is so
dence that early astrologer/priests divined the.. ...
tence). Uranus was first spotted in 1781, Neptune in
1846, and Pluto as late as 1930. Some astrologers/astro-
nomers anticipate that there are two more to be found,
so that there would be twelve planets instead of the
current ten.

**A House Is an Area of Life—and a Planet's "Home"**
Just as there is a great circle in the sky called the
zodiac, and it is divided into twelve equal units of *space*,
there is another circle which is based on units of *time*.
As we all know, the earth makes one complete rotation
on its own axis every twenty-four hours. Imagine yourself standing in one place during a twenty-four-hour
period and making a mark on the sky every two hours
while that sky appears to pass by you as the earth turns.
At the end of twenty-four hours, you will have marked
off twelve different units of sky. A "house" is simply
one of those pieces of sky that has passed by during
your day-long vigil. Toward the end of your day of
skywatching, twelve houses will have gone by, and "house
one" will be coming up again.

When an astrologer draws up a natal horoscope—
which is simply a map of the sky when you were born—
he/she does it by drawing a picture of the sky as it
appeared from the exact place of birth, at the exact
time of your birth. What happens is that the twelve
houses are lined up in a very specific way—a very
different way than if you had been born *in another
place at the same time* or *at the same time in another
place*.

What is most important about the particular lineup
of the houses is that each house represents a different
area of human life, and how those areas are positioned
*for you* has a tremendous effect on your astrological
makeup. For instance, the second house is the house
of income and personal possessions and has a lot to do
with attitude toward money and how easy or how difficult it will be to come by in your lifetime. The seventh
house is the house of partnership and offers clues

bout who you are likely to marry. If you know the time of your birth within one hour or so, you can add a very important dimension to your astrological self-knowledge by reading the chapter "Your House of the Sun—Your 'Piece of the Pie,'" because the house of the horoscope into which the sun falls in your horoscope usually indicates what area of life will absorb you during your lifetime.

## Your Rising Sign Is the One that Starts the First House

Your rising sign is sometimes called the ascendant, because it is the sign of the zodiac that was "ascending" on the eastern horizon at the time of your birth, no matter what time your birth occured. It is the "sunrise sign," corresponding to the nine o'clock position on the face of an ordinary clock. The astrologer's "clock" starts at this position and is read counter-clockwise around the circle of the face. If you were born around sundown, your rising sign will be the one 180 degrees *opposite* the sign you were born under. For instance, if you are an Aries born at sundown, your rising sign will be Libra. If you are an Aries born at sunrise, your rising sign is probably Aries as well.

Why is your rising sign so important? Because it starts the first house of personality, or your very individual way of presenting yourself to the world. No matter what your sun sign is, your rising sign will cover it to a greater or lesser degree (which is why it is so difficult to guess someone's Sun Sign when you first meet them). The rising sign has to do with appearances and can actually influence your physical looks.

If you don't know the time of day you were born, you can't determine your rising sign (although some astrologers can by doing what is called a "rectification," based on the events in your life so far). However, even those who do not know their rising sign can have their horoscopes read; what the astrologer does is put your sun sign on the first house, and do an analysis of what is called a solar horoscope. If you *do* know your birthtime within an hour or so, you can use the rising sign chart in this book to determine yours.

## Planets in Signs in Houses Make Up a Horoscope

The whole basis of astrology is that anyone born in a particular moment in time partakes of the qualities of that moment in time. Actually, the same applies for things; for instance, a business that has its beginnings at a precise astrological moment also has a horoscope which can be read, and tells a lot about its potential for success or failure.

An astrologer looks at the particular moment in drawing up a horoscope—or "picture of the hour." A horoscope is basically a map of the sky, showing exactly where the planets were in relation to the signs and the houses, to each other, and from the particular reference point of your birthplace. It is also called a "natal chart" or "natal map."

Everyone's horoscope has ten planets and twelve houses. Those ten planets can be in a variety of signs, and in a variety of houses. Each planet means something different according to its own nature, how that nature operates in a particular sign, and what area of life the planet is most likely to affect by virtue of which house of the horoscope it falls into. Sound complicated? It is, and only a highly trained astrologer can interpret the many factors and put them together for you in a meaningful way. The most exciting part of astrology is the fact that *no two individuals are ever exactly alike*—not even twins, who are born a few minutes apart.

Although you can find out a lot about your astrological personality right in this book, many people like to take the next step and have a personalized horoscope drawn up for them and interpreted by a professional astrologer. There are a number of ways to find a good person to do this for you; in astrology, as in every other profession, there are variations in the level of competence. Two places you can start your search are:

National Astrological
  Society
62 West 39th St.
New York, NY 10018

American Federation of
  Astrologers
Tempe, AZ 85282

## An Aspect Is the Distance Between Planets

Among the more sophisticated factors an astrologer looks for in your horoscope are the *aspects*. Within the 360-degree circle of the horoscope (and the zodiac), planets form certain aspects to each other by virtue of the distance between them. Some distances are considered harmonious, and some are inharmonious, in terms of how those two (or more) planets work together. It's all a matter of mathematics. The soft or harmonious aspects are the sextile (60 degrees apart) and the trine (120 degrees apart). The hard or inharmonious aspects are formed when planets are in square to each other (90 degrees apart) or in opposition, 180 degrees or exactly half a circle apart. These are only the major aspects, and there are lots and lots of minor ones between, but you can get a good picture of interplanetary relationships with only these few.

For example, if your sun sign is Aries, and at the time of your birth the planet Saturn was in the sign of Libra, or 180 degrees away from Aries, you are likely to have a more serious (Saturnine) disposition than the typical "happy" Aries. Depending on your point of view, this can be a positive note in your horoscope, because you will have greater powers of concentration than many an Aries—or a negative note, because you will be less happy-go-lucky. In another example, a person with a Capricorn sun sign may have a horoscope in which Jupiter, the planet of expansiveness, is 120 degrees away from the sun—either in the sign of Virgo or Taurus— and therefore in "trine" aspect to his/her sun. The result: a much more outgoing, giving Capricorn than the run-of-the-mill type. On the other hand, such an easy aspect could expand Capricorn's acquisitive nature too much, and make for a megalomanic (someone who craves worldly goods and power).

The ancients separated aspects into "favorable" and "unfavorable," but psychologically-thinking modern astrologers know that it is not that simple; it all depends on the total horoscope, plus the individual's reactions to the particular vibrations of the planets in that horoscope.

## A Transiting Planet Affects Your Life Now

When someone goes to an astrologer for the first time, he/she usually has *two* readings—separate, but interrelated. The first will be an interpretation of your natal chart or birth horoscope. This tells you about your given personality—the traits, problems, abilities, and advantages you are most likely to have by virtue of the placement of the planets in the sky at the time of your birth. The second reading will have to do with what you can expect in your life at the present time and the near future. Your birth horoscope always remains the same, but the planets in the sky keep changing their relationships to your birth horoscope throughout your lifetime. The astrologer will acquaint you with the current "transit"—or movements—of the planets and how you, the individual, can expect them to affect you. For instance, if an astrologer notes that Uranus, the "earthquake planet," is approaching your fourth house (the house of emotional security, the place where we really live), the astrologer might alert you to the fact that big changes are in the offing: even a total shaking of the foundations, or a pulling up of roots. This is a major transit, and many people change their residence, partners, or jobs when it occurs. Similarly, but on a less critical note, the astrologer may notice that the planet Venus is going to make a transit over the place in the zodiac occupied by Mars in your birthchart. This could indicate a firey romantic interlude or the rekindling of an old flame.

There are two important things to keep in mind about astrological predictions. The first is that your natal horoscope—your "birth imprint"—really determines how you will react to life's events. To put it even more strongly, your innate personality will really *create* the events of your life, because "character is destiny." There is no doubt that the planets create conditions, but we must take responsibility for how we cooperate with those conditions. The second thing is that *there are very few hard and fast rules*. There are guidelines, to be sure, and most of them have ancient roots; a lot of astrological prediction is based on the case history technique. However, since no two sets of conditions—

the one in the sky and the one in an individual birthchart—are ever *exactly* the same, it is virtually impossible for any astrologer to tell you specifically what is going to happen.

# 2

## Your House of the Sun

### Your "Piece of the Pie"

The prime symbol in the very symbolic language of astrology is the perfect circle; it represents the sky around us, the cosmic atmosphere into which we are all born. All astro-math is based on division of the 360-degree figure, which since ancient times has been regarded as having mystical qualities. When thinking about the houses of the horoscope, however, it helps to use a very down-to-earth analogy. Look at that circle as a great "pie in the sky," which is divided into twelve cosmic slices—each slice representing one house and a different facet of human experience.

Just as there are ten planets in everyone's horoscope, there are twelve houses. However, not all those houses may be occupied by a planet; it all depends on where the planets were in the sky at the moment of your birth. The placement of any planet in a specific house is a *very* important factor in your individual horoscope, but the most important is the placement of the sun. No matter what your sun sign, your House of the Sun has a lot to tell you about the life you've been "given" to live on this earth. As your sun sign is the prime indicator of *character and personality,* your house of the sun points to the *area of human affairs* that you are most likely to find yourself concentrating on in your lifetime.

In the sense that it helps define the boundaries of your life, your house of the sun is your "piece of the pie"—that slice of life within which you will live. Does your house of the sun totally box you in? In a way it does, but it is more productive to think of the dimensions of your house of the sun as *guidelines* about where you can most profitably focus your energies.

Here's the way it works:

- The *sun* is the most important planet in your horoscope. It is the planets that do the "acting," and the sun plays the leading role.
- Your sun sign determines *how* your sun (the real you) acts, i.e., the characteristics of the character you play.
- Your house of the sun is the "stage" on which you will play out your role.

For instance, if your sun sign is Scorpio (the great investigator) and your house of the sun is the twelfth (hidden things), you find yourself drawn to some kind of career in which you must "dig" to do your investigating. Ergo, you might make a good psychoanalyst, archeologist, or genetic researcher. Or, your greatest pleasure in life might be reading mystery novels or spy thrillers—or writing or editing them.

In order to figure out which piece of the pie you've been served, you have to know your birth-time within an hour or so. If you were born during Daylight Savings Time or War Time, you have to subtract one hour from your birth time to determine the "real sun time."

Each house is described here from three different angles:

- The matters or principles connected with it
- The people/places/things related to it
- The problems and the possibilities of having your sun in that house.

Birth time, 4 to 6 a.m.: **Sun in First House**

- *First house matters:* Exploration . . . use of the physical body . . . being on the scene . . . breaking new ground . . . independent action . . . emergencies . . . conquest . . . controversy . . . strategy . . . competition . . . being in the vanguard.

22

- *First house people/places/things:* Entrepreneurs . . . acrobats . . . cutting instruments . . . rock music . . . metals . . . satire . . . hardware . . . the head and face . . . opticians . . . adrenalin . . . new products . . . commodities . . . salesmen . . . fighters . . . firemen.
- *Problems and possibilities:* With your sun in the first house, your sun sign personality is quite strong. Regardless of what your sun sign is, you should be able to make clear-cut decisions and have a good sense of your own identity. If you are to gain control over your life, you are going to have to banish fear from it and develop both the moral and the physical courage that is available to you. Though your will should be strong, you will have to keep yourself from a tendency to tyrannize others. When you feel most defeated is the time your first house sun will come to your rescue. The one thing that could keep you from living out the very vivid life this house placement gives you is inflexibility and intolerance. Be willing to listen.

Birth time, 2 to 4 a.m.: **Sun in Second House**

- *Second house matters:* Calmness . . . conservation . . . ability to make grow . . . eroticism . . . collecting . . . comforting . . . administrating . . . luxury . . . stabilizing . . . building up . . . perpetuating . . . patience . . . using . . . making stronger . . . indulging.
- *Second house people/places/things:* Possessions . . . money . . . the voice . . . landscape gardeners . . . brokers and bankers . . . love/passion . . . personal adornment . . . life-sustaining skills . . . buying and selling . . . security needs . . . nurses . . . food and shelter . . . good music . . . creature comforts.
- *Problems and possibilities:* You should be able to establish yourself firmly and securely in whatever you choose to do; self-adjustment should come easily to you. Your economic life could be relatively worry-free but you must resist valuing money and

possessions for their own sake and becoming overly materialistic. You must develop the will that is given you and turn it into willpower, or you could lose self-respect. You are a good manager, but if you allow yourself to become too settled, you will fear to take the necessary risks to make your life less limited. Though things come to you fairly easily, do not let yourself over-indulge in any of them, including rich food.

## Birth time midnight to 2 a.m.: Sun in Third House

- *Third house matters:* Connecting ... associating ... verbalizing ... dexterity ... inquisitiveness ... distribution ... novelty ... thinking and reasoning ... cause and effect ... exchanging ... bringing the news ... being responsive ... "here today, gone tomorrow."
- *Third house people/places/things:* Short journeys ... realatives (especially siblings) ... speech/languages ... high school teachers ... role-playing/entertaining ... computers ... graphic arts ... handwork ... transportation ... the nervous system ... handwriting .. repair men ... gossip ... comedy ... ventriloquists.
- *Problems and possibilities:* You should be an excellent communicator who reports things clearly and accurately. In your desire for information, however, you could become rather superficial and a bit of a talebearer. If you don't focus your mental energies carefully, you may waste the gift of curiosity your third house sun gives you. You must also learn to live with uncertainty, and to keep your opinions flexible. If life scares you, you are likely to become very defensive and locked in to your ideas. Develop your capacity for listening as well as your talent for talking.

## Birth time 10 p.m. to 12 a.m.: Sun in Fourth House

- *Fourth house matters:* Adaptability ... change ... instinctiveness ... fluctuation ... protecting ...

24

imagination ... softness ... the subconscious ...
survival ... enveloping ... integrating ... fertility
... mothering.

- *Fourth house people/places/things:* Dreams ... the past
... roots ... home and family ... physical sensation ... museums ... caterers ... water and other
liquid ... introverts ... obstetrics ... boats ...
domestics ... imagination.
- *Problems and possibilities:* Via your fourth house sun,
you are given the possibility of understanding yourself and your motivations quite thoroughly. If you
handle your life in a mature way, you will establish
a warm and comfortable home for you and your
family. However, you must strive for real self-
knowledge if you are not to become simply self-
absorbed and self-centered. Your imagination is
considerable, and you could be highly creative; the
down side is that you could develop irrational fears
that verge on paranoia. Work to see the world
clearly at all times and try to conquer your tendency to play the introvert. No mater what your
sun sign, the placement of that sun in the fourth
house will make you instinctively avoid the limelight. Get out there and shine!

Birth time 8 to 10 p.m.: **Sun in Fifth House**

- *Fifth house matters:* Being at the heart of things ...
pleasures ... power ... ambition ... generosity/
giving ... "gilding the lily" ... showmanship ...
stability ... management ... territorial rights ...
self-expression ... autocracy ... organization.
- *Fifth house people/places/things:* Philanthropy ... cor-
porations ... impresarios ... holidays and vaca-
tions ... romantic love ... children ... gamblers
... gold ... circuses ... nursery teachers ... fashion and fashion designers ... public life.
- *Problems and possibilities:* Even if you have a "shy"
sun sign, your fifth house placement of the sun will
force you into some form of self-expression that is
possibly very creative. You also have a capability

for approaching life with a joyful, expectant manner; however, your pursuit of pleasure and play could become extreme. Consciously avoid any pleasure that threatens to get out of control. Your affairs of the heart could be many, but it is important to keep alert for anything that smacks of an abusive partner; it's possible you could enjoy the drama of an unhappy situation. Develop your capacity for warmly accepting others.

Birth time 6 to 8 p.m.: **Sun in Sixth House**

- *Sixth house matters:* Competence/skill . . . specialization . . . refining . . . categorizing . . . analyzing . . . obedience . . . realism . . . responsibility . . . purifying . . . invention . . . making things work . . . ministering . . . discriminating.
- *Sixth house people/places/things:* Service . . . critics . . . crafts . . . libraries . . . closets . . . public health . . . the harvest . . . small animals . . . dependents . . . dental hygienists . . . research . . . diagnosing . . . numbers work . . . chemists.
- *Problems and possibilities:* With your sun in the sixth house you have the potential of becoming a true master at something; however, if you allow yourself to get bogged down in life's details, you could possibly end up being a wage slave. No matter what your sun sign, your instincts tell you to be of service to others. While you are capable of great self-sacrifice, you must avoid the temptation to be overly humble and to assume the servant role. You are mentally very keen, and can break things and jobs down into smaller parts in order to accomplish them. Do not let the state of your own health become an obsession. With the sun is the sixth house, your basic constitution should be quite strong. Don't worry!

Birth time 4 to 6 p.m.: **Sun in Seventh House**

- *Seventh house matters:* Sharing . . . comparing . . . give-and-take . . . peacemaking . . . negotiation . . .

making things beautiful ... creating balance ... fairness ... sociability ... gratification ... advocacy ... diplomacy ... aestheticism.

- *Seventh house people/places/things:* Divorce lawyers ... love poetry ... marriage brokers ... the kidneys and lower back ... illustration ... resort managers ... public relations ... fine arts ... receptionists ... boutiques ... jugglers ... tailors ... pianos.
- Possibilities and problems: You have a great need to identify with others, and can create a wonderful rapport with them easily. However, your need for a life partner could make you overly dependent. If you have an independent sun sign, this could create a serious life conflict. With this placement, you are able to adjust to new people and new situations easily, but you must avoid a tendency not to stick with a position when you really believe in it. You have the potential of forming very warm, balanced and intimate relationships; however, if you do not handle this gift in a mature manner, you could develop a fear of intimacy, and shy away from it or become an outrageous and insincere flirt.

## Birth time 2 to 4 p.m.: **Sun in Eighth House**

- *Eighth house matters:* Release of blockages ... probing ... anonymity ... procreation ... rejuvenation ... willpower ... endurance ... controlling ... investigation ... aloneness ... demolishing and rebuilding ... crisis ... elimination.
- *Eighth house people/places/things:* Puzzles ... generals ... political parties ... labor lawyers ... the healing arts ... death and dying ... taxes ... spies ... superathletes ... crime detection ... statesmen ... sex symbols ... geologists ... explorers ... mating instinct ... sanitation engineers.
- *Problems and possibilities:* A light sun sign (like Gemini or Libra), the placement of the sun in this house will add depth to your character. You will feel compelled to investigate things that are hidden or

even dangerous. While it is good to probe, you must beware of a tendency to concentrate on what is morbid. All things being equal, you will be highly sexed; however, with insufficient self-knowledge, your healthy sexual instincts could turn into obsession with the subject—or a total advoidance of it. Learn to live with your dynamic physical body and you will live with others quite happily. Also, encourage your religious or mystical feelings, which are quite real. You have the potential of totally transforming your life at one point or another.

Birth time noon to 2 p.m.: **Sun in Ninth House**

- *Ninth house matters:* Anticipating . . . aspiring . . . moving around . . . expanding things . . . speculating . . . idealism . . . advising . . . unpredictability . . . search for truth . . . search for opportunity . . . taking aim . . . magnanimity . . . excess.
- *Ninth house people/places/things* Casinos . . . ambassadors . . . passport offices . . . luck . . . international transportation . . . trading/high finance . . . dancers . . . aristocrats . . . large animals . . . higher studies . . . lawmaking . . . profiteers . . . veterinarians.
- *Problems and possibilities:* Even if you have a routine-loving sun sign (like Virgo), this placement of the sun will give you the desire and the ability to constantly renew your life, and to adapt to new patterns of behavior. You will feel strongly about one religious or ethical system or another, or at least have a very strong personal philosophy. However, you could become rather dogmatic and rigid in your opinions. Your adaptability is admirable, but a desire for the new and novel could be the "downside" of your openness to new experience. Exercise control. With certain sun signs, there may be a tendency toward inner battles between opportunity-seeking and a firm set of principles. You are a spender—of both your money and your physical resources.

Birth time 10 a.m. to 12 a.m.: **Sun in Tenth House**

- *Tenth house matters:* Realism . . . structure . . . ambition . . . rigidity . . . integrating . . . limitation . . . disciplining . . . reputation . . . social position . . . creating the useful . . . contraction . . . coolness . . . convention.
- *Tenth house people/places/things:* Figures . . . fame . . . common sense . . . property . . . correctional systems and facilities . . . ceramics . . . money lenders . . . efficiency experts . . . the bones . . . the elderly . . . sculptors . . . watches and clocks.
- *Problems and possibilities:* You have the capacity of becoming a respected member of whatever group you move in, because your public image is very important to you. If you play your cards right, you can arrive at a sense that you are fulfilling your destiny. However, if you become obsessed with power and appearances, you could end up living a shallow, meaningless life behind your strong facade. It is most important with this placement of the sun to find the right outlet for you to express yourself and get positive feedback from others. You won't be happy starving in a garret, because both money and recognition are too important to you. This position of the sun often brings fame.

Birth time 8 to 10 a.m.: **Sun in Eleventh House**

- *Eleventh house matters:* Helping . . . experimentation . . . humanitarianism . . . association . . . liberalism . . freedom . . . suddenness . . . awakenings . . . combining . . . freethinking . . . rationality . . . caring . . . breaking through . . . observing coolly . . . predicting.
- *Eleventh house people/places/things:* Paradoxes . . . stunt men . . . electricity . . . zealots . . . divorce . . . fireworks . . . the social sciences . . . reform . . . geniuses . . . aviation . . . weathermen . . . brotherly love . . . magnetism . . . groups . . . friends . . . causes.
- *Problems and possibilities:* If you are a very personal

sun sign (like Cancer), you will gain a lot of objectivity with the placement of the sun in this house. You should have very high aims and goals, and some of them will undoubtedly involve helping the less fortunate in some way or another. Though this is admirable, if you don't set yourself on a definite path in life and stick to a definite plan, you could simply drift along, with only vague ideas about where you can shine. It is important to be quite realistic with the sun in this house. Your own crowd is important to you, but you must avoid becoming such a part of the group that you lose a sense of your own individuality—which is potentially very great. Some people with the sun in the 11th house are downright wacky, but often very achieving people.

## Birth Time 6 to 8 a.m.: **Sun in Twelfth House**

- *Twelfth house matters:* Dissolving ... ambiguity ... disguising ... retreating ... sensualism ... enchantment ... paying dues ... healing spiritually ... insubstantiality ... confinement ... persuading ... comprehending the incomprehensible ... merging ... pretending.
- *Twelfth house people/places/things:* Makeup ... escapism ... alcohol and drugs ... drama and dramatic actors ... films ... advertising ... pastoral work ... fishing ... astrophysics ... con men ... magicians ... hospitals ... alibis ... myths ... prisons.
- *Problems and possibilities:* Yours is not an easy house of the sun to have—especially if you are a very self-expressive sun sign type like Leo. You may feel that life is confining you in some way or another; what you are really sensing is your gift of the ability to transcend self to a much higher spiritual level. You should be an expert at coping with intangibles and sensing the nuances of any situation. In a sense, you have a kind of ESP which can be developed for life success. However, the real down side of the twelfth house sun is that it

can lead to a very confused, unfocussed attitude toward life. It is essential that you give yourself a definite structure to work within if you are to free yourself from the worries and cares of life. By all means avoid any form of escapism that is dangerous.

# 3

## The Geometry of Relationships

### What Signs You Get Along with—and Why

The first thing most people want to know about their sun sign is what other signs they are compatible with. It's a natural question, and a good one to ask an astrologer, because one aspect of astrology, called "synastry" (literally, "stars together") concentrates on the subject of relationships. When practising synastry, the astrologer compares the two birth charts of the two people involved to find what connections there are between them. It is a complicated process, but it provides excellent clues about how two people will relate to each other. What chart comparison does is *describe the nature of the relationship*. Actually, to an astrologer there are no "bad" or "good" relationships; there are just a lot of different kinds and each has a special character. Of course it is true that some relationships end up on the rocks, sometimes devastating one or both parties involved. But, even in such cases, the astrologer looks at it as a "karmic" relationship—one in which people *had* to come together in order to learn some life lessons.

While comparing two complete horoscopes is the ideal way to look at a relationship, there is a very simple method of looking at two sun signs, and coming up with an overall prediction of how two people will relate to each other. This method goes back to the great circle of the zodiac and to the division of the twelve signs into four elements: fire, earth, air, and water.

Here's the lineup of signs in each element:

**Fire:** Aries, Leo, Sagittarius

**Earth:** Taurus, Virgo, Capricorn
**Air:** Gemini, Libra, Aquarius
**Water:** Cancer, Scorpio, Pisces

The general rules of thumb for element-mixing are as follows:

| Great | Good | Semi-tough or Difficult |
|-------|------|-------------------------|
| Fire and air | Fire and fire | Fire and water |
| Water and earth | Earth and earth | Earth and air |
| | Air and air | Fire and earth |
| | Water and water | Air and water |

Here's the way it looks mathmatically:

If you divide the 360-degree circle of the zodiac by the twelve signs, you find that each sign is 30 degrees away from the next.

- Signs that are 30 degrees apart—or next to each other—are semi-tough.
- Signs that are 60 degrees (two signs) or 180 degrees (six signs) away from each other are the best combinations. (The latter, 180 degrees away from each other, makes these signs polar opposites, and in astrology polar opposites attract.)
- Signs that are 120 degrees apart—four signs away from each other—are in the same element, and their relationship is good, but far from perfect.
- Signs that are 90 degrees or three signs away from each other have the most difficult relationships of all. They are said to be in "square aspect" to each other.

When you look at the four elements in terms of what they signify in the physical world, you get a good idea why some elements get along more easily.

*Fire turns water into steam* (hot air).
*Water puts fire out.*
*Fire scorches earth.*

*Earth smothers fire.*
*Air fans fire and makes it brighter.*
*Fire warms up cool air.*
*Water softens up hard earth.*
*Earth makes water keep its shape.*
*Water and air do nothing* (unless you add heat).
*Air blows earth around.*

What about combinations of the same element, such as fire with fire? In effect, they tend to neutralize or cancel each other out. Or, they can simply be too much of one element for comfort.

- Two fire signs together could experience "burn out" fairly quickly.
- Two air signs might analyze each other to the death of the relationship.
- Two earth signs could depress each other a lot.
- Two water signs could make for an overly "heavy" relationship.

# 4

## Twelve Places at the Table

### A Mini Astrodrama in Which the Twelve Signs Play Themselves

No matter how accurate or colorful any description of a zodiac sign may be, it is still a description—not the real thing. A sign is simply an abstract concept until it takes form in a living, breathing human being. There are obviously as many different types of people as there are individual horoscopes, and no two are exactly alike. However, the twelve signs of the zodiac are still the best guidelines we have for sorting out human behavior into broad but meaningful categories. There are even fiction writers who use the zodiac signs as prototypes for characters they create because it makes them more realistic, i.e., more like people you are likely to meet.

What follows is fiction, but it gets closer to the truth about each zodiacal sign than a general description ever can. The twelve characters in this docudrama are obviously caricatures, because their behavior is highly exaggerated. But it is exaggeration for emphasis, and for the purpose of bringing to life the twelve signs of the zodiac, which don't really exist except as real people. Like real people, these twelve characters have foibles; but they have fine points too. As you read this drama, you may find yourself drawn to some signs and put off by others. Make mental notes of which signs you find yourself most sympathetic with and check out your findings in the parts of this book about astrological compatibility. It could prove very interesting—

and very revealing. As each sign of the zodiac has a sex or gender, they are portrayed here as male or female accordingly. But the basic behavior pattern is applicable to both sexes.

The twelve signs of the zodiac are invited to dinner at that great dining room in the sky. When they arrive, they find that their host (who shall remain signless) has slipped up, and there are only eleven places set at the table. Since it is a fancy affair, each sign is trying to be on his/her best behavior. However, the situation is a bit unsettling, so in the course of trying to resolve it, they all relapse into their natural zodiacal characteristics.

*Aries*     An energetic young man, he comes bounding into the room, almost tripping on an untied shoelace. He is dressed rather casually for the occasion, and looks as if he got dressed rather quickly. When he realizes what the situation is, there's no doubt in his mind how to handle it.

"Only eleven places? Don't worry; Pisces will probably never show anyway. But, I got here before anybody else (the doorman will prove it) so I should definitely get a seat. In fact, I should sit down *first*. No, I don't need to wash my hands or anything. I'm *starved*, so I hope you aren't having anything like the gooey mess with the French name you had before. A hamburger will do just fine. And don't serve it cold like you did the last time. Hey, there's a great-looking dish over there, ha ha! Seat me next to her, will you Cancer? Well, she looks like a nice warm type, so I think I'll go let her warm me up. By the way, I'm organizing a sky-diving club. Want to join? Seriously, if you can't afford the membership fee, I'll put it up for you, because I'd love to have you join. Oh, you're doing okay now? Glad to hear you're off the rack. Got any pretzels?"

*Taurus*     An attractive young woman with faint dimples in her roundish cheeks and a slightly unruly but pretty mass of curly hair comes sauntering into the room. She is dressed in a soft and pretty outfit that looks expensive, and has her handbag clutched tightly under her arm. She looks around the room with moderate curiosity. As the host walks up to her, she gives him a warm smile; when she speaks, her voice is low and melodious—but firm.

"Only eleven places? You mean, only eleven *chairs*. All you have to do is set another place and give me a pillow to sit on. I don't mind, as long as I'm comfortable. And I smell something wonderful, so I know the food is going to be delicious. To be honest with you, that's really why I came. I don't like to go out much, you know. What I really like is curling up in my warm and comfy bed—with someone warm and comfy, of course. (Are you busy later on?) But, now that I'm *here*, there's no way I'm not going to eat. What's for dessert? Who's that nervous-looking lady over there? Virgo? I'll go try to make her feel comfortable."

**Gemini**    It's hard to tell just how old this fellow is as he springs in the door; he could be any age, though he looks about eighteen. He is dressed in the very latest style, though nothing he has on is really extreme. His eyes dart all over the room, and he is carrying a notebook under his arm. When the host tells him about the eleven places, he is so busy listening to another conversation, he almost misses it. When he reacts, it is in a typically casual way.

"Don't worry about me; I don't need a place. I'll just float around the room, because what I really came here for is the conversation. I'm writing a book, you know—it's called *1001 Opening Conversational Gambits* and tonight I'm researching. I see you've got some really fascinating types here. How did you make up the guest list? Are they all married? Why did they come alone? What's the menu? Who's the chef? Can I see the wine list? Who's that blowsy-looking type over there? Taurus? I'll bet *she's* got a story. Where's the telephone? I've got to make a call."

**Cancer**    A sexy, voluptuous woman of indeterminate age pauses at the door; she seems shy, but conscious of the impression she is making. Her clothes are a bit unusual, and some things are from the thrift shop. However, her antique jewelry is genuine, and the whole effect is glamorous. When she discovers there are only eleven places, she is visibly upset, and there is a touch of a whine in her voice as she speaks.

"I wish I'd known; I could have stayed home with the children. They have colds, you know. If you want, I'll simply leave; but I really don't want to go home by myself; I'll get scared and have bad dreams. Upset? Yes, I am upset, and when I get upset I can't eat. Unless it's really soothing and nourishing. Did you know that a touch of heavy cream in mashed potatoes is simply heavenly? Chicken soup? I make it by the gallon. Say, you look as if you could stand a little fattening up. Well, all right. I *guess* I'll stay—unless I change my mind, of course."

**Leo**     This is a fine figure of a man—fairly tall, rather muscular, and with a thick crop of curly hair that is somewhere between blond and red. He is elegantly dressed and his gold cufflinks probably put a real drain on Fort Knox. His grand entrance is smooth and practised, and his handshake is hearty and warm. When his host tells him the news, he takes it very personally.

"Well, let me tell you, this is embarrassing! I mean, all these people here to see me, and I may have to stand? I've given bigger parties than this, and they've always gone off without a hitch. Let me handle things for you the next time. For now, just get that chair over there and squeeze someone in—Virgo won't mind. No, *here*; not *there!* While we're all waiting I guess I can entertain everyone with my tantrum act. What? No, I'm only kidding—though I am mad. I'll do my Hamlet number instead. Like my cufflinks? They match my Gold Card. I've ordered another pair with sapphires, too."

**Virgo**     A rather prim woman stands quietly at the door looking as if she would like to blend into the woodwork. She is dressed very neatly, but conservatively, with flat-heeled sensible shoes. In her handbag she carries a surgical mask to wear in case any of the other guests has a cold. Her reaction to the news that there are only eleven places is swift and shrill.

"Well, it certainly isn't *my* fault. I answered the invitation the minute I got it. I *always* do! Why didn't you check on things more carefully? If you had, this wouldn't have happened, and you wouldn't have all these people standing around thinking terrible things about you. I don't mind for myself, you understand, I don't eat much anyway; you never know what you're going to get. I'll stay in the kitchen and help the cook clean up. You can't be too careful about these things, you know. You wouldn't believe the sanitary conditions I've found in *some* kitchens. Not mentioning any names, of course. Oh, *why* did you mess things up this way; you are simply impossible. . . ."

*Intermission:* Our host walks away as Virgo continues to complain. As he checks on the guests, he discovers that Libra has just arrived. Sagittarius and Pisces are nowhere to be found, but Scorpio, Capricorn, and Aquarius are waiting to greet him. Because he looks like he's a bit uncomfortable, the host talks to Libra first.

*Libra*    A very attractive male, wearing all the right things, walks tentatively into the room, looking as if he is searching for someone. He is visibly uncomfortable alone. His gaze scans the room, quietly appraising everything and everybody in it. He seems to approve, but in his nervousness, he approaches the table, and starts rearranging one of the settings, then rearranging it again. All this is done very tactfully and gracefully. In fact, he looks as if he couldn't make an awkward gesture if he tried. His host approaches him and breaks the news. Libra's reaction is smooth and unruffled.

"Oh, how *clever* of you to arrange this little puzzle for us. It will make things so much more fun. Of course, we've got to make things absolutely fair; we wouldn't want to hurt anyone's feelings. I could leave if it would help, but . . . Oh, how nice of you to tell me I'll definitely have a place; it makes me feel a lot less awkward. I rarely go places alone, you know. Who would I like to sit next to? Well, the Capricorn lady looks like a sturdy and sensible type. But on the other hand, Scorpio is a *knockout*. Is she attached? Hmmm, Taurus looks like she'd like to chat, but oh, that Cancer! Decisions, decisions; I'll make up my mind later on. Where did you get that *great* painting?

*Scorpio*     A slim and sexy woman dressed totally in black comes slinking into the room. Her style and movement are absolutely magnetic, and every eye turns to look at her. But she gives no visible response that she is aware of it. She doesn't seem to be feeling anything at all, but when her host approaches and tells her what is going on, she is seething with quiet rage.

"Do you really think you are going to get away with this? I suspected something when I got that weird invitation. Who in the world would ever come as they are and let everybody else know what they're really like? No matter how many times you tell me it was an innocent mistake to set only eleven places, I'll never believe it. Nothing in this world is innocent. And when it comes to drawing straws, just remember you owe me one from the last time. You know, the *last* time! Who's that wimpy looking guy over there? Gemini? Maybe I'll amuse myself with him for a while. I need a new conquest; I'm getting out of practice."

*Sagittarius*     While Scorpio has been talking with the host, a tall rather rangy male has come loping into the room carrying a suitcase. He is a bit disheveled because his flight was late. He throws the suitcase in a corner and starts putting himself back together—a bit absentmindedly because he is looking around the room with a big smile and a lot of anticipation. He moves toward the host and gives a slap on his back that is almost *too* hearty.

"Only eleven places? Why worry? We'll work it out somehow. Life's too short to get uptight anyway. Had the greatest trip, and I'm turning right around tomorrow and going to the Orient so I can practice my Chinese. Say, are you serving Chinese food? I love Chinese food—and a good beer to go with it. At least I hope you're serving better wine than you did last time. You're looking a little pale . . . been partying too much lately? Ha ha, only kidding. Who's that guy over there with the flashy cufflinks? And the mouse with the sensible shoes? Think I'll see if I can loosen her up a bit. Did you hear I'm going to win the lottery again? What do you mean, how do I know? I just *know*. And I've got a great idea for an international fast food chain I'm going to bankroll with my winnings. I'm gonna call it 'The Great Gobler' and serve only turkey sandwiches. Hey, I'm thirsty. Where's the bar?"

**Aquarius**    An intellectual-looking gentleman—sort of an absentminded professor type—has been standing in the doorway quietly puffing his pipe and scrutinizing the crowd. His jacket and pants don't match, but he isn't aware of it. An even stranger—but typical—sartorial note is his electric blue tie with orange stripes. He's got his earphones with him; if things get too dull, he'll listen to some hard rock or electronic music and be in seventh heaven. When he finds out about the missing place, he gives a thoughtful answer and makes an impractical suggestion.

"Oh, well, rather than make anyone feel left out, we could cancel the whole dinner and bring the food to the local shelter for the homeless. Ah, you don't care for that idea. Too bad; I'm becoming more and more concerned about poverty in our own backyard. Of course, I'm no bleeding heart like Pisces, but fair's fair. Want to hear about a new invention I'm working on? It's an electronic stamp sorter that will revolutionize the whole philatelic world. Huh? Oh, that's stamp collecting. Glad you asked me to come alone, since I'm free as a bird now. My last attachment got so *sticky!* I've sworn off. At least off those emotional types who want you to get so involved. No, I never get lonely—I've got too many friends for that. By the way, I can just sit on the floor in the lotus position, and get some meditating in at the same time."

**Capricorn**    A rather handsome, perfectly put together woman has been quietly observing the crowd and the room, mentally putting a price tag on everything. What she has on is very expensive, but understated and in excellent taste. In her handbag she carries a petition with her name on it. She wants to run for local office, and is hoping to pick up some supporters tonight. If they are "her kind of people," that is. Her reaction to the host's situation is sober but logical.

"Well, it's obvious someone will have to go, but I

41

trust your judgment to decide who is most important—if you know what I mean. Your appointments are in excellent taste; I see you like Tiffany as much as I do. Who's that rather tacky looking type over there? Cancer? Where *does* she get her clothes? I have little sympathy for people who can't get their act together and run their lives successfully. She's probably a poet. Ah, well, different strokes for different folks; fantasy has no place in *my* life, you know. By the way, I have some excellent ideas about how to shape things up in the community; will you sign my petition? At dinner, are we going to discuss great books? I just bought a whole series . . . all leather-bound, of course. They look smashing in my living room."

*Pisces*     Meanwhile, a rather wispy but very pretty woman has been wandering in and out of the doorway, looking as if she isn't quite sure she is in the right place. She is dressed in a misty fabric of very pale colors; there doesn't seem to be a clear-cut edge anywhere. In fact, if you don't rub your eyes, you might think you are seeing an apparition. The host knows it's Pisces and catches her just as she's about to drift out the door again. He doesn't bother telling her about the missing place, because he knows she wouldn't understand why that was important.

"Late? Am I late? I lost my watch two weeks ago. Or was it three? Oh well, what's time anyway in the larger scheme of things? Hungry? Not really, though I can't remember the last time I ate. *Love*—it's *love* that's food for the soul, and that's what I care about nourishing. I wonder if any of these people have had any *real* soul food lately. No, don't worry, I won't try to convert anyone tonight. I'm too, too drained because of my current work. What kind? Well, it really isn't a job-job, I mean where you make money, and all. I've started a shelter for homeless animals in my apartment; I cry so much when I see a stray that I can't stand it. Who? Ho, he left some time ago. Something about there being 'other fish in the sea.' What in the world do you suppose he meant by that? By the way, I'm a little short of cash. Do you think you could lend me . . .?"

At this point, things are at a stalema
tion will quickly resolve itself in one o
Take your pick: This time *you* can choose
you like—and the one you think makes best a
sense.

A. Aries gets in a fight with Leo and has to go to emergency room.
B. Taurus gets really tired and hungry and decides to go home, cook a hamburger, and go to bed early.
C. Gemini runs out of note paper and gets laryngitis at the same time.
D. Cancer gets a call from the babysitter and is so worried she goes home to take care of her children.
E. Leo gets so irritated that no one is paying attention to the bruises Aries gave him that he leaves in a huff.
F. Virgo gets a stomach ache and decides to leave. Besides, it's time for her mineral bath.
G. Libra isn't able to make up his mind and gets a headache in the process.
H. Scorpio decides it's definitely a plot to humiliate her, and bows out less than graciously.
I. Sagittarius gets a little drunk and leaves early to get the plane.
J. Capricorn leaves as soon as she gets her petition filled up because there isn't anyone there *really* worth knowing.
K. Aquarius decides to go teach people at the shelter to use his stamp-sorting machine so they can get jobs.
L. Pisces remembers she has a date with her spiritual advisor and that she forgot to feed the animals.

# 5

## s of the Moon

### How to Successfully Navigate
### Its Day-by-Day Changes

Never underestimate the power of the moon. It is the closest planet to earth, and the only one whose effect on human life can actually be measured. Even the most skeptical antiastrology person has to admit that the moon rules the tides. If you stand on the beach for even a half hour or so, you can literally *see* how the moon works its magic as the water flows higher or lower, according to the time of day. There are places in the world where the tide rises as much as forty feet from its lowest to its highest point—that's *power.* If you think about the fact that humans are about 98 percent water in our chemical makeup, it's much easier to accept the fact that the moon has the same powerful effect on us as it does on the tides.

Like the "female" she symbolically is, the moon also changes her mind—or her sign—more quickly than any other planet. If you look at the day-by-day predictions in this book, which gives the position of the moon for every day, you will see that this changeable planet moves into a different sign about every two days.

As it moves from sign to sign, the moon brings a different kind of energy to the earth's atmosphere. Those who are particularly sensitive—like Cancers—feel it most strongly. But even the most stolid types are often moved by the effect of the particular sign the moon occupies on any given day, though they may not want to admit it.

Are we then slaves to the moods of the moon? Not if we understand its energies and cooperate with them. If you work *with* the moon and not against her, you can actually make life a lot easier for yourself. For instance, there are certain activities that go more smoothly when the moon is in a particular sign, just as other activities are more difficult to accomplish. Scheduling things accordingly could prevent a lot of frustration. You don't have to become a complete "lunatic" (ancient meaning, "one ruled by the moon") to benefit from its positive vibes, but simply go with the flow. Keep in mind, however, that the moon's effect will be *modified* by your sun sign, so be sure to check out your individual daily prediction. For instance, for *any* sun sign, the days when the moon is in that sign should bring a surge of energy. Whether you handle that energy positively or negatively is up to you.

Here's a rundown of the moods of the moon and the human activities that go with them.

*When the Moon Is in Aries*       There is a very *physical* tone to this day. People may be throwing their weight around in more ways than one. Impatience, independent action, and quick tempers can sprout up all over the place. The good news is that most people will be feeling rather decisive, so some things can be completed. The bad news is that decisions may be totally unilateral; what *you* want may be exactly what someone else *doesn't* want. Similarly, people may be invading each other's territories; "keep off the grass" signs won't mean much today. Rule-breaking is the order of the day, and so are the consequences that go along with it. However, if there's a big mountain to scale, today's the day to begin the climb. If there's a formidable task that requires a lot of get-up-and-go to accomplish, today's the day to plunge in with both feet. If there's something you've been hesitating to tell someone, today you'll get the nerve to say it, but it may be difficult to be tactful. Try, anyway. On the up side, people will be feeling in the mood for some fun and frolic—practical jokes are very "moon in Aries." Even the boss may get in the spirit of things. It's a good day to:

| Make a sale | Sharpen knives |
|---|---|
| Do heavy housework | Stop worrying |
| Do some baking | Make a clean break |
| Start a diet | Start an exercise class |
| Buy a lottery ticket | Do something on your own |
| Get a haircut | Try a new recipe |
| Have your eyes checked | Throw a last-minute party |

***When the Moon Is in Taurus*** Today, the amber light goes on, and people start to proceed with more caution. Rather than being adventurous, most people will feel like sticking with routine tasks. It is not a good day to try something new. In this more conservative mood, people will tend to hold on to what they have; don't try to borrow money from a friend today. Concentrate on making your own money grow, instead. Speaking of increase, this is an excellent day to "make your garden grow" in every sense of the phrase. Along with a quieter mood of the day, you may feel like pampering yourself a bit; allow yourself at least one luxury. Chocoholics, beware, however; this is a day for food binges and all forms of dietary excess. Creature comforts are a lot on everyone's mind; in fact, it may be difficult to crawl out of that comfortable bed in the morning. And more than a few people will be crawling back into it fairly early—with their favorite person. Sexual cravings are high on the list of "moon moods" today. Enjoy!

It's a good day to:

| Put something off until tomorrow | Put up preserves |
|---|---|
| Buy clothes or jewelry | Have a massage |
| Get your teeth filled | Start singing lessons |
| Start a savings account | Sell high on the market |
| Stick to your guns | Buy a plant |
| Buy candy | Buy real estate |
| Stay home and watch television | Hug somebody |

***When the Moon Is in Gemini*** There's a touch more energy in the air today, and people will begin moving around a lot more. For some, there will be a lot of nervous energy and the scattery feeling that goes along with it; don't force yourself to concentrate if you can avoid it. It's a day to make connections—call, write, or bump into both new and old friends. Wits are generally sharp today, and people could be cracking jokes all around you. On the other hand, they may also be spilling some secrets. Gossip is easy to start today, and it could spread like wildfire. Mind your mouth! Anything requiring manual dexterity can easily get done today; even those who are usually clumsy may find they have nimble fingers. The tendency today is to do things quickly, if a bit superficially. If there are a couple of things that require a once-over-lightly treatment, get them out of the way now. If you haven't been invited to a party, give your own—or at least plan to get together with some buddies for a little socializing; the time is definitely right.

It's a good day to:

| | |
|---|---|
| Get your hair cut | Use your hands |
| Join a club | Pay bills |
| Have a tooth pulled | Eat out |
| Sign up for a new course | Take a walk/drive |
| Send a letter | Call your brother/sister |
| Try something new | Tell a fib |
| Learn a language | Do two things at once |

**When the Moon Is in Cancer**     In Cancer, the moon is in her very own sign—and you'll know it. All those "moon" characteristics—like changeableness, sensitivity, and the desire for security—will be heightened. Cancers, of course, will feel it most strongly; and the other water signs, Scorpio and Pisces, may be even moodier than usual. The general tendency today is to do things that make you feel comfortable and feel good. For some, that means eating a lot of food; for others, it could be hitting the bottle a bit. People tend to feel a bit sorry for themselves during the transit of the moon through Cancer. When two people who live together are both feeling that way, the result can be a rather touchy day—and evening. As much as you want the comfort of others, you are better off on your own and working off those anxious feelings by yourself. Not for safety, but for comfort's sake, the best place to go today is no farther than your own backyard. You'll probably

47

be feeling very stay-at-home anyway. However, it's an excellent day for memories. Reminisce with somebody you love, or get out that old photo album by yourself. You might find yourself shedding a tear or two, but it's all in a good cause.

It's a good day to:

| | |
|---|---|
| Bake something delicious | Hug your children |
| Buy something old | Take care of somebody |
| Put up preserves | Go without makeup |
| Buy property | Call your mother |
| Start a habit | Buy something for the house |
| Plant something | Entertain at home |
| Pamper yourself | Give your hair a treatment |

**When the Moon Is in Leo**    Today, everyone feels like "coming out of the woodwork." Just as Cancer moon makes you want to hide, Leo moon makes you want to get out there and be seen. Nothing but the best will do on this day, so it could be a rather expensive one. Most people will be more generous than usual—both with their money and their affections; many a new romance has started under a Leo moon. Leo is also one of the more playful signs, so a lot of you will be in the mood for fun and games. Eating out is very Leo moon—and so is picking up the check. Today, you may have to fight for it. However, the boss may be a lot stricter than usual, and even those with nobody to "boss" will try to push somebody around. If you've got children, today you will appreciate them very much—no matter what they do. Most people find themselves reaching for the newest thing in the closet under this transit of the moon. If they don't have anything new to wear, they'll probably go out and buy it—on credit. No matter what time of the year it is, you'll be looking for a little sunshine or at least a warm place. On the beaches or by the fireplaces are where most people would like to be today—wishing life were one long vacation.

It's a good day to:

| | |
|---|---|
| Borrow money | Buy jewelry |
| Get a new hairstyle | Invest in the market |
| Start building something | Do something creative |

Follow a hunch              Prepare a gourmet meal
Steal the spotlight         Dress up
Be brave                    Kiss somebody new
Be waited on

**When the Moon Is in Virgo**      Now it's back to work, and back to reality. There's a sharp distinction between the Virgo moon mood and what precedes it, so you may shock yourself. Perhaps by deciding it's really time to get organized and then actually *doing* it. On the home front it's a great day to rearrange all those sloppy closets and cupboards. On the job, you couldn't pick a better time to wrestle with that nasty detail work you've been avoiding. However, all is not good news under Virgo moon. For one thing, by contrast to Leo moon's generosity, people will be positively stingy today—both with their money and their love. Even the best of situations could deteriorate today when one or the other of the involved parties decides to point out the other's flaws. Your best course under the Virgo moon is to check that impulse to criticize. People can become highly self-critical during this transit, too. One extreme example of the going-over some people can give themselves during a Virgo moon is to develop mysterious maladies or to discover aches and pains they never felt before. Not to worry; they'll be all better by the time the moon moves into the next sign. Virgo moon is also inspection time, so the boss may be particularly sensitive to messy desks today and sloppiness in general. Keep things buttoned up and tidy for best results.

It's a good time to:

Start a diet                   Start a new job
Get a physical                 Sew or mend something
Bake bread                     Read a good book
Quit smoking                   Get a complete makeover
Buy a pet                      Call your maiden aunt
Try to do without something Feel like a martyr
Buy health food                Do a puzzle

**When the Moon Is in Libra**      Now it's time to kiss and make up. Any relationships that suffered from the ragged nerves of Virgo moon time can be nicely patched up today. Pleasantries should be easy for one and all. In fact, even people who are normally rather gruff should smile a bit more today. Libra moon is one of the most social of moon periods; meeting and greeting should be prevalent activities. Most people will want to put their best foot forward, too, so the impulse to dress up and look your best may come upon you. You may feel rather self-indulgent as well; hard work is not as compatible with the Libra moon period as rest and relaxation are. It's definitely a time of togetherness, so even habitual loners may be looking for company. Most people will feel they need people—possibly one special person. Romance blossoms under the Libra moon in its purest form. It's not so much sex people want now as romantic love and companionship. No one's actually made a count, but it's a fair bet that more flowers get sent under the Libra moon than at any other time. Physical beauty is also highly important, so Libra moon is a great one under which to get yourself a whole new look or to redo anything that needs it. Something that's off-balance will bother you more at this time.

It's a good day to:

| | |
|---|---|
| Be tactful | Forgive and forget |
| Redecorate | Add color to your life |
| Give a party | Luxuriate |
| Fall in love | Sign up for a dance class |
| Join a singing group | Buy a stereo |
| Buy something beautiful | Buy a down comforter |
| Try a new makeup | Learn about wine |

**When the Moon Is in Scorpio**   Things could easily get heavy today, and the tendency will be to go to extremes. Haters will hate more; lovers will love more passionately and physically. The sex drive is stimulated in many people during this transit of the moon. With all those intense emotions flying around, it's not surprising that people easily get hot under the collar—and/or imagine that somebody is out to get them. However, there is an up side to the Scorpio moon, and that is the extra jot of will power it gives the most weak-willed people. If you've got to dig in your heels and clench your teeth to get something done, today's the day you will be able to do it. People *endure* a lot under the Scorpio moon. The only problem is that they may develop some resentment toward those they believe should be enduring with them. However, the tendency is to keep silent. In spite of the intense emotionalism of the Scorpio moon, there isn't a lot of outright complaining. People will let the pressure build up inside of them and then burst out into violent rages. If your temper isn't good under the best of circumstances, control it during the Scorpio moon, by all means. It's also a time when people tend to feel a bit claustrophobic; a good walk in the fresh air can work wonders at this time.

It's a good day to:

| | |
|---|---|
| See a psychiatrist | Have good sex |
| Buy a house | Face up to a crisis |
| Open a secret bank account | Read a good mystery |
| Make a firm decision | Take body-building |
| Do your taxes | Get a prescription filled |
| Throw away what you don't need | Buy life insurance |
| | Change your life |
| Do some strenuous exercise | |

**When the Moon Is in Sagittarius**     Things definitely lighten up when the moon moves into Sagittarius—and people loosen up, too. In fact, one danger under this moon is getting too relaxed—with your diet, your money, or your generous spirits. Moderation is not the mood of the day, so you may have to force it on yourself. It is not a good time to try to stop smoking—or to stop doing anything self-indulgent. There's definitely a "live and let live" attitude in the air when the moon is in Sagittarius, so bad relations should be easily improved. A spirit of good will is pervasive, as well as a light-hearted attitude. One thing that means is that even normally conservative people will be willing to take chances; those for whom a more liberal outlook is a natural state of affairs could really go too far out on a limb. If you gamble, bet *only* what you can afford to lose today. The place everyone will want to be today is outdoors. In fact, more than one person will simply disappear from the scene to do something either adventurous or relaxing. It's an excellent day to think big, but you may find the follow-through a bit difficult. The big picture is what's easiest to see right now; leave the fine brush strokes for another time. Enjoy the spirit of fun and generosity that should be in the air.

It's a good day to:

| | |
|---|---|
| Make a long-distance call | Go to church |
| Plan a trip | Enjoy a hobby |
| Buy a dog (or a horse) | Learn a new language |
| Contribute to a wildlife- | Do something charitable |
| foundation | Borrow money |
| Try a new approach | Run away from it all |
| Sell anything to anybody | Get a bigger place |
| Try your luck/feel lucky | |

**When the Moon Is in Capricorn**    In sharp contrast to the "easy come, easy go" feeling of the Sagittarius moon, the moon in Capricorn brings on a much more serious mood. You could call it the "workaholic's moon," and even those whose work style is less intense will find themselves wanting to get a lot done. It's important to *accomplish something* when the moon is in Capricorn, if you are to feel comfortable. Most people want to tread only on solid ground at this time, so there could be a bit of distrust in the air. No one wants to waste time— and least of all on things or people from whom they are not likely to derive some kind of benefit. Another curious facet of the Capricorn moon mood is a tendency to feel older and more serious; some lighter types dislike the feeling so much they will go out of their way to look young. It's the kind of day that matronly secretary in the office is likely to appear in something rather frilly. People can really handle things under the Capricorn moon too; endurance is *very* Capricorn. That means those who exercise will work out harder and longer; those who normally do not push themselves will do at least a little self-prodding. A good image is paramount to many people when the moon is in this sign, and the tendency is for people to be quite status conscious. Self-control is the order of the day, in every respect.

It's a good day to:

| | |
|---|---|
| Start a new job | Make a list |
| Buy antiques | Keep your money |

Buy anything for investment
Wear anything with a
    good label on it
Bet on a favorite
Go to the chiropractor
Buy insurance

Go to the dentist
Start a diet
Work late
Ask for repayment of a
    debt
Clean house

**When the Moon Is in Aquarius**    When the moon moves into the sign of Aquarius from the sign of Capricorn, it's as if somebody took the cork out of the bottle. Suddenly, the rather repressed mood bursts into a desire for change—a *need* for change. This is one of those days when people tend to make rash moves like quit a dull job, call it quits with a clinging person, throw out everything in their closet and start all over again. Reaching this point is easy to do under the Aquarian moon. However, it's usually very positive. What's important at this time is to try something new, not just get rid of something old. Some people decide to experiment with a new recipe, a new lover, or a new hair style. It's the kind of day when a woman with long hair will decide to get a crew cut. On the relationship side, the mood now is one of brotherly love and friendship rather than highly charged sexual encounters. Wanting to be with friends and feeling like part of a group is what's important now. No one is a stranger under the Aquarian moon, and talking to people on the street is very common. The thing to be careful of under this moon is doing something irreparable—like finally telling the boss what you really think of him. He/she could easily decide that it's time for a change of personnel.

It's a good day to:

Do something kinky
Try a new food
Do something friendly
Start flying lessons
Do something impulsive
Join a club
Make a speculative
    investment

Buy/wear something crazy
Color your hair
Contribute to a charity
Move to a new place
Buy a television/stereo
Make a new friend
Be fair

**When the Moon Is in Pisces**    This is a time when people wear their hearts on their sleeves and feel *very* vulnerable. There's a lot of ultrasensitivity under the Pisces moon, and a lot of crying on shoulders—if you can find one that isn't already occupied. Mixed in with the emotionalism is a real feeling of empathy with others; now's the time people feel that everyone is in the same boat. However, it may be a bit difficult to keep things afloat today, because there isn't a lot of firm direction from anyone or anything. It's confusion time, and even the clearest of messages can get a little garbled. Indecisiveness will spread like the plague, so don't expect to get any clear-cut answers today. Creative people get more creative under the Pisces moon, and anyone could feel just a bit poetic. Romantic relationships are heavenly under the Pisces moon as long as they don't get out of control. Keeping certain other things under control—like drinking and other forms of escapism—is a wise precaution, too. The most satisfying and least dangerous escape is to hold hands with someone you love while you watch a real tearjerker movie. Lots of people call in sick under the Pisces moon, and there's a good reason: Most people don't like to cry in public.

It's a good day to:

| | |
|---|---|
| Put on weight | Write a poem |
| Fall in love | Take in a stray dog or cat |
| Develop ESP | Visit the sick |
| Find God | See a therapist |
| Buy flowers or perfume | Stay home and read |
| Swear off something | Pamper yourself |
| Get hooked on something | Buy a camera |

# 6

## Venus and Mars

### Love and Sex
### Peace and War
### Cooperating and Competing

Next to your sun sign, your moon sign, and your rising sign, the positions of Venus and Mars in your horoscope are probably the most important indicators of your personal psychology. This is because Venus shows your affectional nature and Mars shows your sexual nature. To put it another way, *Venus shows your wants and needs in romantic love while Mars shows your sexual style and your manner of expressing it.*

In a broader sense, Venus and Mars are the principles of peace and war. Venus wants to cooperate and relate to others, to share life experiences. Mars is totally concerned with self and getting what you want. Everybody's got a Venus and Mars in their horoscope because every human being has to both live with others and assert him-/herself. It's all a matter of degree. If you want to, you can think of Venus as the "higher" side of human relationships; Mars the "lower." However, you've got to keep in mind that—like all other opposites in the universe—both *cooperating* and competing are necessary if the world is to continue going round.

Because Venus has to do with the need to share, the sign in which it is placed will tell a lot about how you attract people you want to share with. It will also show what attracts you to others. Beyond the love arena, the position of Venus in your horoscope shows your attitudes toward money and personal possessions, creature comforts, and things of beauty. Venus is "feminine" in nature, and women tend to relate to their Venus sign more than men. But for *both* sexes, it is an available energy.

**The good side of Venus is:**
  *Sharing, beautifying, peacemaking*
**The bad side is:**
  *acquisitiveness, self-indulgence, laziness*

Because the position of Mars shows how you go about getting what you want, it will tell a lot about your personal drive—how *much* you want what you want. It is the desire principle, and will indicate just how passionate your passions are. Ambition, assertiveness, and anger are just a few steps away from each other, so Mars will also reveal what makes you angry or what gets you going. The planet Mars is "masculine" in nature—highly so—and men will find it easier to get in touch with their Mars energy. However, every woman's got a Mars too, and sooner or later a woman's Mars energy will present itself.

**The "good" side of Mars is:**
  *Dynamic energy, courage, sexual drive*
**The "bad" side is:**
  *manipulation, cowardice, sexual abuse*

No matter what area of life you are relating these planets to, it is useful to think of them in sexual terms, and of our human sexual organs. Venus is open and receptive; Mars thrusts forward and penetrates. Because we normally attract someone or are attracted to someone before we get sexually involved, Venus energy precedes Mars energy. In other words, Venus shows how *receptive* you are; Mars shows how *active* you are. Venus also has a lot to do with our ideas and images of romance, our romantic fantasies, while Mars is an indicator of sexual fantasies—which may or may not be acted out, depending on the individual's degree of inhibition.

Just as some combinations of people can coexist in constant harmony while others are in constant conflict,

Venus and Mars in an individual person can work well together, or at cross-purposes. When your Venus doesn't get along well with your Mars, you've got a problem. Sometimes a sexual problem, but always an inner conflict. How can you tell if your Venus and Mars are "friends" or "foes"? First, by looking up the positions of your personal Mars and Venus in the charts provided at the end of this chapter, reading the descriptions of those planets in the signs they fall in for you. But, just to make things a bit clearer, here's a rundown of easy Mars/Venus relationships and difficult ones. (By the way, you can also apply this principle in comparing your Venus/Mars positions to those of someone else, as well.)

Venus and Mars are "at war" when:

• One is in a fire sign, and one is in an earth sign. Here you've got a conflict between the practical and the experimental sides of yourself.
• One is in a fire sign and one is in a water sign. One part of you says "let's do it"; the other side says, "I might get hurt," so you might be stalled.
• One is in an earth sign and one is in an air sign. Air likes to think about things a little; earth needs to know it will work. Once again, it may hold you back.
• One is in an air sign and one is in a water sign. Yours is a conflict between the mental relationship and the emotional one; you may find it hard to decide what you want.

Venus and Mars are on good terms when:

• One is in a fire sign, one is in an air sign.
• One is in an earth sign and one is in a water sign.
• Both are in the same element.

## Venus and Mars in The Signs

### Venus in Aries (fire element)

While this position of Venus in a man or a woman indicates the kind of person who falls in love impulsively, both sexes want to be conquered, when they have Venus in Aries. They may be outrageously flirtatious, but can lead others on a merry chase before they give in. There is a tendency to look for trouble when Venus is in ths position; actually, it is excitement Venus in Aries people crave. Their personal likes and dislikes will be quite clearly defined, and they will be vocal about them. In matters of taste, there is less refinement than when Venus is in a softer sign. Both the males and the females may play up their sexuality in the way they dress; they like very loud things like rock music and bright colors. There is also an impish charm in these people and a tendency to play love games. The *real* goal is to be swept away by a romantic lover who lives up to a mediaeval code of chivalry and/or chastity.

### Mars in Aries (fire element)

This is a highly competitive position for Mars; people with Mars in Aries leave no doubt about the fact that they want it, and they want it *now*—whatever "it" is. Mars in Aries can cut through a lot of life's red tape. When it comes to courtship, Mars in Aries people are equally able to disregard the small talk and get right down to business. However, this position of Mars often makes for a rather selfish lover—one who is so concerned with getting that he/she doesn't do an awful lot of giving. Mars in Aries people are likely to turn off as quickly as they turn on. Passion burns brightly, but is often short-lived. They are highly independent and likely to leave if a romantic partner gets too possessive or demanding. Mars in Aries is also always ready for a fight, so relationships are a bit stormy.

### Venus in Taurus (earth element)

This is a highly sensual position for Venus to be in. People with Venus in Taurus are turned on by sweet words and soft music—and any form of touching. They like all kinds of nice and beautiful things, and will be attracted by someone who dresses well and has expensive taste. Venus in Taurus people can be a little self-indulgent, but in the main their desire is to make the object of their affection comfortable. And they will do it in very tangible ways; Venus in Taurus people of both sexes like to do things for others. When someone with Venus in Taurus is attracted, he/she is loyal. Love does not come in a flash, as it does with Venus in Aries people, but when it comes, it usually stays. At least as far as the person with Venus in Taurus is concerned. These people are generally so devoted that a breakup is extremely unsettling. You can always make a Venus in Taurus person happy with candy or flowers. The best kind of love feels good, tastes good, looks good, and smells good.

### Mars in Taurus (earth element)

This Mars can express itself as ambition with a definite direction—or as controlled sexuality. Mars in Taurus people of both sexes can appear rather lazy, but actually their slow movements are usually on a deliberate course. Some people with Mars in Taurus are really looking for a safe position in a job or with a partner. Their manner of sexuality is highly sensual though they may be slow to get aroused. When a Mars in Taurus person enters into an affair, however, there is usually the intention to make it a long and serious one. These people are certainly capable of quick affairs, but they generally prefer a comfortable relationship where they do not constantly have to keep proving their love. There is a certain giving quality to Mars in Taurus, and the men are exceptionally considerate lovers. The women are fairly passive, but passionate and giving when they get going.

### Venus in Gemini

Venus in Gemini people of both sexes tend to be turned on more by *talk* than by physical stimulation. Relationships have to have a mental dimension in order for them to get involved. In fact, Venus in Gemini people are likely to make better friends than lovers. When their affections *are* engaged, the connection is likely to be a little tenuous, and the Venus in Gemini's feelings may not run as deep as his/her partner's. Fickleness is a reality with these people— they like a lot of changes, and that goes for people as well as environments. Job-hopping is a trait of Venus in Gemini, and so is a constant changing of the guard in their romantic lives. However, Venus in Gemini people make wonderful romantic partners, because they are really *interested* in the people they get involved with. Never tell a Venus in Gemini person to "shut up and make love"; he/she will be very likely to shut the door on the relationship.

### Mars in Gemini

Mars in Gemini people assert themselves rather erratically; there isn't a lot of staying power, in jobs or in relationships. The "alternating current" of Mars in Gemini energy makes for a rather on again, off again sexual life. People with Mars in this position are capable of having a number of purely mental relationships in between their sexual ones. These are the kind of people who talk their way into things, including a job and someone's bed. Their approach is a bit on the delicate side, and one may wonder when the Mars in Gemini person is really going to get started. However, once their passion is aroused, Mars in Gemini people like a lot of variety; sex can get quite original with these people. The tendency to bore easily goes both for their attitudes toward their sexual partners and the manner in which they have sex. Both sexes are real charmers, however, and sometimes get their way in a rather devious manner.

### Venus in Cancer (water element)

The overriding thing that people with Venus in Cancer want is *security*, really the emotional kind, but since a secure home base goes along with their needs, the material kind is important too. Venus in Cancer people can be highly traditional in their romantic values— home, mother, and apple pie are symbols of the things that turn these people on. If you want to engage the emotions of a Venus in Cancer person, all you have to do is look as if you *need* somebody— preferably a mother. Venus in Cancer people need to be needed, but sometimes can go overboard by totally taking over the other person's life. With Venus in this sign, people respond strongly to all kinds of romantic things, from the card that says "I love you" to a little token of affection for no special occasion. However, Venus in Cancer people are highly self-protective, so you first have to break down their natural reserve and fear of getting hurt. Once you do, you won't find a more faithful lover. Except perhaps Taurus.

### *Mars in Cancer (water element)*

Mars in Cancer people can sneak up on you when they've decided they want you; their approach is a bit sideways, like the locomotion of the crab that is the Cancer symbol. They are soft and subtle lovers and said by some to be among the best sexual partners in the zodiac. However, as sensitive and understanding as they tend to be in the sexual area, they can be overly possessive with people they love, and even turn rather cruel when they are rejected. Cancer is a water sign, and it is as if that water starts boiling—invisibly—then the lid totally pops off when the explosion comes. Mars in Cancer people tend to be a little blind to their sexual/ambition drive and can even pretend to themselves that it doesn't exist. For this reason, they make formidable enemies, because while they look as if they are asking for peace they are really preparing for battle.

### *Venus in Leo (fire element)*

There's a pretty simple way to get a Venus in Leo person to like you. Give him/her a lot of attention—*positive* attention. Venus in Leo people do want love, but they want admiration and adulation to come along with it. A bit like Venus in Aries, Venus in Leo wants a *courtly* lover—someone who will swear absolute loyalty. When it's a Leo sun sign person who also has Venus in Leo, you've got the absolute monarch of them all. Venus in Leo also goes only for the best, and is attracted to what looks expensive or rewarding—in both jobs and people. Venus in Leo expects you to dress and look your best, no matter what the circumstances. It is not a "casual" Venus. Demonstrations of love are very important, too. Words are great, of course, and so is a lot of hugging and the rest of the physical love spectrum. However, candy—or some other tangible token of affection—is expected. Venus in Leo has fierce pride, so if you even slip once and appear not to *respect* this person, he/she is likely to brush you off—with a very grand gesture of course.

### *Mars in Leo (fire element)*

Speaking of grand gestures, Mars in Leo wrote the book. This kind of person is the one who will lavish the object of his/her affection with all kinds of luxurious things. Mars in Leo is a real showy person and expects to be appreciated for it. Both the males and the females are aggressive about going after what they want, and once they are happily ensconced—with a lover or a job—they are loyal and steady. However, the down side of the Mars in Leo position is a violent temper: a *really* violent temper. Both sexes can get quite physical in expressing anger. This is the position of the female who throws plates and the man who slaps his faithless lover on the cheek. Mars in Leo is unrelentingly honest— and will expect you to be too. One devious move, and it's over

### Venus in Virgo (earth element)

Venus in Virgo wants a love that *works*. Pure sex or romance may appeal to Virgo's desire for the unadulterated, but there's got to be an element of the practical in it too. People with Venus in Virgo often actually fall in love with their jobs faster than they do with people. When Venus is in the sign, you often find the dedicated, loyal, "number two" person who spends a lifetime catering to the needs of a powerful boss. He/she is likely to be just a little bit in love with that boss too. As for sex, the Venus in Virgo person has a very healthy attitude toward it—possibly too healthy in the sense that it is sometimes regarded as an excellent form of exercise. Venus in Virgo people are not really cold—in fact, when they love someone they can't do enough for them, particularly in attending to their physical comfort. The problem is that this position of Venus makes a person overly analytical in determining what he/she wants. If the Venus in Virgo person keeps his/her mouth shut, and doesn't openly criticize, there is a much better possibility that he/she will make good, solid relationships.

### Mars in Virgo (earth element)

Virgo's inventive sexuality is one of the best-kept secrets in the zodiac; Mars in Virgo turns out some of the most experimental and skillful lovers of all. That is, if you can attract one of these people in the first place. Mars in Virgo people are far from promiscuous; in fact, their standards are likely to be a bit too high. They are constantly questioning their *own* desires and drives, picking them apart instead of acting upon them. Mars in Virgo is ideal for success in just about any job or profession. With any sun sign, it adds to the ability to cooly analyze problems and solve them with a reasonable amount of dispatch. When it comes to romantic involvement, this is not one of the more "romantic" Mars positions (unless the sun sign is Libra). You may feel as if your Mars in Virgo lover is checking you over first for anything that might turn him/her off. This is the sign that usually says "let's shower together" before he/she says "let's go to bed."

### Venus in Libra (air element)

First off, remember that when the planet Venus is in Libra, it's in its "home sign." When it comes to beauty, harmony, and balance, Venus in Libra people want it all. When Venus is in Libra, the most attractive things in life are the *nicest*—people, places, jobs, clothes, you name it. Venus in Libra people want it nice, but they also want it *easy*. In fact, this sometimes "cold" position of Venus can make for a person who marries for status or money. If you look comfortable in every sense of the word, you've got a shot at attracting that Venus in Libra person who catches your eye. And he/she will, because this position of Venus usually confers a great-looking body. Even if the Venus in Libra person loves or marries for convenience, he/she gives an awful lot in return. Once you've engaged his/her love the Venus in Libra person considers you the best, the most beautiful/handsome, and the brightest person in the universe and will treat you accordingly.

### Mars in Libra (air element)

This position of Mars often makes for a passive/aggressive type of individual—a specific psychological pattern. The Mars in Libra person rarely goes directly after what he/she wants, but more or less lingers in front of it, waiting for the other person to make the right move. Mars in Libra people don't get hired as quickly as other types because they don't seem to *care* enough about whether or not they get the job. When it comes to love, Mars in Libra can be quite frustrating. You really don't know what's going on here—does or doesn't he/she want to get involved? This is also a rather "refined" position for brash Mars. Mars in Libra people usually have excellent manners, and never appear to get ruffled. They will just sit and smile while you rant and rave. Suddenly, however, they can turn on their heel and walk out the door. The technique Mars in Libra people use to go about making their subtle conquests is *talk*—but it can easily fool you because it seems so casual.

### Venus in Scorpio (water element)

A lot of people with sun sign Scorpio have Venus in Scorpio too; (one's Venus sign is often one's sun sign because Venus is so close to the sun in the solar system). These double-whammy Scorpios are extraordinarily intense in all their emotional needs, but anyone with Venus in Scorpio is going to be touched by the madness of this intense sign. The curious paradox is that Venus in Scorpio people are either totally *turned on* by someone or something—or totally *turned off*. There are very few halfway deals in their lives. Venus in Scorpio can also be highly manipulative, adjusting his/her emotions to suit other needs—like money. When Venus is in Scorpio, people are attracted to what seems mysterious, dangerous, or hard-to-get. They love puzzles, and can be a bit of a puzzle themselves to prospective romantic partners. When they do get involved, however, they have a great deal of staying power—emotionally at least. They can fairly easily separate their physical *actions* from their mental states, however.

### Mars in Scorpio (water element)

People with Mars in Scorpio have a very strong "energy field" surrounding them; you can almost see it and feel it. What they want, they want passionately—and will seek in no uncertain terms. They are equally positive about what they *don't* want—so you will know whether you've got a shot with them right away. No waiting with *this* aggressive sign. The legendary supersexuality of Scorpio is real with Mars in Scorpio people. However, they may use their sexual power to control other people and situations. And, if they are rejected against their will (which doesn't happen too often) they are capable of the worst kind of venomous reactions. Jealous lovers who are violent to their former partners are a parody of the Mars in Scorpio type of intensity. One way Mars in Scorpio people can hurt or simply tease others is by withholding their love—and their physical passion. They have great powers of self-control.

### Venus in Sagittarius (fire element)

People with Venus in the restless, mobile sign of the Centaur often get the reputation for being fickle, and there is more than a grain of truth in that label. But the reason a Venus in Sagittarius person may move around or not become committed is that he/she is so vulnerable to deceit and dishonesty. As the saying goes, "once burned, twice shy," and openhearted, friendly Sagittarius is likely to get burned very early in life. When Venus in Sagittarius people do get involved, they are absolutely delightful to love. Broadminded, unpossessive, full of fun, they really want to enjoy romance. Sagittarius is also a very intellectual sign, so in order to get Venus in Sagittarius people to stick with you for a while, you've got to keep them interested. Sex is great, but sex with talk is even greater for these people. Venus in Sagittarius is also highly idealistic, so you've got to be a higher type to appeal to someone with Venus in this sign. Love is gallantry and honor and all those things that are so hard to find in life.

### Mars in Sagittarius (fire element)

Sagittarius is a sign that thinks in global terms, so when Mars is in the sign of Sagittarius, you find a person who wants it all—and often has to be satisfied with nothing. People with Mars in Sagittarius assert themselves bluntly and get right to the point. However, they tend to be so optimistic in their expectations that they may just as quickly decide they have made a mistake. Better luck next love. Mars in Sagittarius doesn't deliberately hurt people; this sign is kind to all—both animals and humans. Their sexual nature can also be rather "animalistic" because this is a lusty sign, and so fond of all outdoor sports that they often want to do it

65

anywhere, anytime. One way Mars in Sagittarius people get to your heart is through your sense of humor; they really know how to make people laugh. It is a powerful weapon in their professional lives too; it's hard to fire someone who is such a delight to have around—even if he/she isn't around that much. The big problem with Mars in Sagittarius people is that they sometimes don't want to take responsibility for their own actions, and lay things on other people. Even if Mars in Sagittarius is the one to break things up, he/she will somehow or other get you to believe that it's *your* fault.

### Venus in Capricorn (earth element)

Appearances count a lot to Venus in Capricorn people—in every sense of the word. In order to appeal to them, you've got to look solid and substantial—and fairly rich as well. Because there is a natural reserve to Capricorn, people with Venus in this sign will dislike public displays of affection; the cooler you are in your approach, the better. Their public image and their private one are not too far apart, either. Not that Venus in Capricorn isn't normal; he/she can be quite passionate in bed. But very, very *serious*, too. If you mistake this sign's sober approach to life for coldness, you will not be the first person who has. Once again, like those with Venus in Virgo, Venus in Capricorn is attracted to *practical* people—people who can really work for them in one way or another. While some do actually consciously go after a financially comfortable marital situation, what the vast majority will settle for is someone who is willing to help handle a lot of the more serious aspects of life. Male or female, Venus in Capricorn people want you to be *useful*. Unfortunately, some people with Venus in this sign have such a low sense of self-worth, that they will try to buy love—or sell it—because they don't feel anyone will accept them for what they are.

### Mars in Capricorn (earth element)

Mars in Capricorn people always want to know the rules before they enter the game; they assert themselves with extreme caution. However, when they *know* what they want, they have incredible powers to help them get it. One is patience; Mars in Capricorn can wait very well. Another thing they have going for them is self-control; their timing is excellent because they can hold themselves back when they want to. All this makes for a rather sexually confusing type, and sometimes one who is sexually confused. Mars in Capricorn people can go without sex for amazing lengths of time if nothing seems worth the effort. When they do go for it, their approach can be extremely lusty and earthy, as befits the earth element of Capricorn. Even more than someone with Mars in Scorpio, the person with Mars in Capricorn can be a user. In love or business, he/she can easily fake it to get the carrot on the end of the stick. Then, before you know it, the person who seemed so hot for you has now turned stone cold. Sad, but true.

### Venus in Aquarius (air element)

The best way to attract someone with Venus in Aquarius is to be a bit unconventional; these people love anyone or anything that is off-beat. However, you may find that you are considered a specimen rather than a romantic partner—or at least that's how it's likely to feel. People with Venus in Aquarius seem to have a real problem with deep involvement; often they really *want* it, but somehow or other their deepest wells of emotion are very difficult to tap.

Their habitual reaction to love is often "easy come, easy go." Are they cruel people? Generally not, and often Venus in Aquarius people suffer a lot from their difficulty with feeling. They will rarely tell you, however, because there is a real need for distance there. And distance is what they seek in one-on-one relationships. If you become possessive with, or jealous of a person with Venus in Aquarius, you will lose him/her very quickly. As with some of the other mental signs like Gemini and Libra, you have got to keep the affair or the marriage *interesting* in one way or another. This is a Venus position that often likes kinky sex, porno movies, and other forms of artificial stimulation. However, they usually don't care enough about sex-for-the-sake-of-sex to be unfaithful.

### Mars in Aquarius (air element)

When Mars is in this erratic sign, people tend to go through periods of feast and famine, largely because they can fluctuate between being extremely assertive and sure about what they want or totally inactive. During the latter periods you could actually call the Mars in Aquarius person lazy. In love, the Mars in Aquarius person tends to go after the unusual or difficult; involvements with people who are already attached are quite common. In many cases it is because the Mars in Aquarius person really is terribly afraid of deep involvement. There is a detachment about Mars in Aquarius people that sometimes works against permanent attachment to people or professional situations. Mars in Aquarius really prefers to go it alone. Perhaps the reason is that they always want to be free to experiment with the new. In sex, the Mars in Aquarius person is hung up on technique; he/she likes intelligent sex, and sometimes wants to prove how clever he/she is via this rather bizarre route.

### Venus in Pisces (water element)

For people with Venus in Pisces, what's attractive is often bound up with some kind of sacrifice. This is the position of Venus that leads to martyrdom of all kinds. Some Venus in Pisces people find it impossible to get involved with anything or anyone normal and healthy; their instinctive need is to care for the lame and needy. Therefore, many Venus in Pisces people are rather easily taken advantage of by unscrupulous types who use them or take them for all they're worth. By the same token, Venus in Pisces people can put a real *drain* on the object of their affections—demanding more and more proofs of undying love, soulful demonstrations, sometimes even more tangible support. However, in the broadest, most universal sense of the word, Pisces is the "best" position for Venus as it represents the principle of *true love*. True love is totally unselfish, totally self-sacrificing. Though few normal mortals are capable of such "divine" love, Venus in Pisces people come closest to being able to make it. On the more mundane side, people wth Venus in Pisces are attracted by all kinds of sentimental and often impractical things. They will love you most if you spend your last penny on a bouquet of violets rather than bread for the table. So what? You'll just live on love.

### Mars in Pisces (water element)

Mars in Pisces people can easily lose their way; the sign of Pisces is not stable enough for the aggressive energy of Mars, so Mars in Pisces people tend to scatter their energies in too many places. On the other hand, they are the most subtle and devious people in the zodiac when it comes to going after what they really *do* want. Their come-on is usually to be rather weak and helpless. Both the males and the females snare you by making you think they really *need* you. There's a lot of poetry to Mars in Pisces people, so the start of an affair is likely to be all moonlight and roses. However, you may find that once you are entangled, you can't get yourself out when you want out. Mars in Pisces people have a way of snarling you up in their webs of erratic energy. Just when they've agreed that you should go, they'll become helpless again and make you feel you have to stay. However, Mars in Pisces people do offer a very wonderful kind of love—soft, sensitive, and caring. The object of their desires is often someone similar or someone involved with art or music in some way. However, Pisces types are best off hooking up with a strong partner—someone who can keep their Mars energy on a straight and even course. The best part of Mars in Pisces people is that they are rarely, if ever, cold.

| | Aries | Taurus | Gemini | Cancer | Leo | Virgo |
|------|---------|---------|---------|---------|---------|---------|
| **1910** | 5/7-6/3 | 6/4-6/29 | 6/30-7/24 | 7/25-8/18 | 8/19-9/12 | 9/13-10/6 |
| **1911** | 2/28-3/23 | 3/24-4/17 | 4/18-5/12 | 5/13-6/8 | 6/9-7/7 | 7/8-11/8 |
| **1912** | 4/13-5/6 | 5/7-5/31 | 6/1-6/24 | 6/24-7/18 | 7/19-8/12 | 8/13-9/5 |
| **1913** | 2/3-3/6 | 3/7-5/1 | 7/8-8/5 | 8/6-8/31 | 9/1-9/26 | 9/27-10/20 |
| | 5/2-5/30 | 5/31-7/7 | | | | |
| **1914** | 3/14-4/6 | 4/7-5/1 | 5/2-5/25 | 5/26-6/19 | 6/20-7/15 | 7/16-8/10 |
| **1915** | 4/27-5/21 | 5/22-6/15 | 6/16-7/10 | 7/11-8/3 | 8/4-8/28 | 8/29-9/21 |
| **1916** | 2/14-3/9 | 3/10-4/5 | 4/6-5/5 | 5/6-9/8 | 9/9-10/7 | 10/8-11/2 |
| **1917** | 3/29-4/21 | 4/22-5/15 | 5/16-6/9 | 6/10-7/3 | 7/4-7/28 | 7/29-8/21 |
| **1918** | 5/7-6/2 | 6/3-6/28 | 6/29-7/24 | 7/25-8/18 | 8/19-9/11 | 9/12-10/5 |
| **1919** | 2/27-3/22 | 3/23-4/16 | 4/17-5/12 | 5/13-6/7 | 6/8-7/7 | 7/8-11/8 |
| **1920** | 4/12-5/6 | 5/7-5/30 | 5/31-6/23 | 6/24-7/18 | 7/19-8/11 | 8/12-9/4 |
| **1921** | 2/3-3/6 | 3/7-4/25 | 7/8-8/5 | 8/6-8/31 | 9/1-9/25 | 9/26-10/20 |
| | 4/26-6/1 | 6/2-7/7 | | | | |
| **1922** | 3/13-4/6 | 4/7-4/30 | 5/1-5/25 | 5/26-6/19 | 6/20-7/14 | 7/15-8/9 |
| **1923** | 4/27-5/21 | 5/22-6/14 | 6/15-7/9 | 7/10-8/3 | 8/4-8/27 | 8/28-9/20 |
| **1924** | 2/13-3/8 | 3/9-4/4 | 4/5-5/5 | 5/6-9/8 | 9/9-10/7 | 10/8-11/12 |
| **1925** | 3/28-4/20 | 4/21-5/15 | 5/16-6/8 | 6/9-7/3 | 7/4-7/27 | 7/28-8/21 |
| **1926** | 5/7-6/2 | 6/3-6/28 | 6/29-7/23 | 7/24-8/17 | 8/18-9/11 | 9/12-10/5 |
| **1927** | 2/27-3/22 | 3/23-4/16 | 4/17-5/11 | 5/12-6/7 | 6/8-7/7 | 7/8-11/9 |
| **1928** | 4/12-5/5 | 5/6-5/29 | 5/30-6/23 | 6/24-7/17 | 7/18-8/11 | 8/12-9/4 |
| **1929** | 2/3-3/7 | 3/8-4/19 | 7/8-8/4 | 8/5-8/30 | 8/31-9/25 | 9/26-10/19 |
| | 4/20-6/2 | 6/3-7/7 | | | | |
| **1930** | 3/13-4/5 | 4/6-4/30 | 5/1-5/24 | 5/25-6/18 | 6/19-7/14 | 7/15-8/9 |
| **1931** | 4/26-5/20 | 5/21-6/13 | 6/14-7/8 | 7/9-8/2 | 8/3-8/26 | 8/27-9/19 |

## VENUS SIGN 1910–1975

| Libra | Scorpio | Sagittarius | Capricorn | Aquarius | Pisces |
|---|---|---|---|---|---|
| 10/7-10/30 | 10/31-11/23 | 11/24-12/17 | 12/18-12/31 | 1/1-1/15 | 1/16-1/28 |
|  |  |  |  | 1/29-4/4 | 4/5-5/6 |
| 11/19-12/8 | 12/9-12/31 |  | 1/1-1/10 | 1/11-2/2 | 2/3-2/27 |
| 9/6-9/30 | 1/1-1/4 | 1/5-1/29 | 1/30-2/23 | 2/24-3/18 | 3/19-4/12 |
|  | 10/1-10/24 | 10/25-11/17 | 11/18-12/12 | 12/13-12/31 |  |
| 10/21-11/13 | 11/14-12/7 | 12/8-12/31 |  | 1/1-1/6 | 1/7-2/2 |
|  |  |  |  |  |  |
| 8/11-9/6 | 9/7-10/9 | 10/10-12/5 | 1/1-1/24 | 1/25-2/17 | 2/18-3/13 |
|  | 12-6/12-30 | 12/31 |  |  |  |
| 9/22-10/15 | 10/16-11/8 | 1/1-2/6 | 2/7-3/6 | 3/7-4/1 | 4/2-4/26 |
|  |  | 11/9-12/2 | 12/3-12/26 | 12/27-12/31 |  |
| 11/3-11/27 | 11/28-12/21 | 12/22-12/31 |  | 1/1-1/19 | 1/20-2/13 |
| 8/22-9/16 | 9/17-10/11 | 1/1-1/14 | 1/15-2/7 | 2/8-3/4 | 3/5-3/28 |
|  |  | 10/12-11/6 | 11/7-12/5 | 12/6-12/31 |  |
| 10/6-10/29 | 10/30-11/22 | 11/23-12/16 | 12/17-12/31 | 1/1-4/5 | 4/6-5/6 |
| 11/9-12/8 | 12/9-12/31 |  | 1/1-1/9 | 1/10-2/2 | 2/3-2/26 |
| 9/5-9/30 | 1/1-1/3 | 1/4-1/28 | 1/29-2/22 | 2/23-3/18 | 3/19-4/11 |
|  | 9/31-10/23 | 10/24-11/17 | 11/18-12/11 | 12/12-12/31 |  |
| 10/21-11/13 | 11/14-12/7 | 12/8-12/31 |  | 1/1-1/6 | 1/7-2/2 |
| 8/10-9/6 | 9/7-10/10 | 10/11-11/28 | 1/1-1/24 | 1/25-2/16 | 2/17-3/12 |
|  | 11/29-12/31 |  |  |  |  |
| 9/21-10/14 | 1/1 | 1/2-2/6 | 2/7-3/5 | 3/6-3/31 | 4/1-4/26 |
|  | 10/15-11/7 | 11/8-12/1 | 12/2-12/25 | 12/26-12/31 |  |
| 11/3-11/26 | 11/27-12/21 | 12/22-12/31 |  | 1/1-1/19 | 1/20-2/12 |
| 8/22-9/15 | 9/16-10/11 | 1/1-1/14 | 1/15-2/7 | 2/8-3/3 | 3/4-3/27 |
|  |  | 10-12/11-6 | 11/7-12/5 | 12/6-12/31 |  |
| 10/6-10/29 | 10/30-11/22 | 11/23-12/16 | 12/17-12/31 | 1/1-4/5 | 4/6-5/6 |
| 11/10-12/8 | 12/9-12/31 | 1/1-1/7 | 1/8 | 1/9-2/1 | 2/2-2/26 |
| 9/5-9/28 | 1/1-1/3 | 1/4-1/28 | 1/29-2/22 | 2/23-3/17 | 3/18-4/11 |
|  | 9/29-10/23 | 10/24-11/16 | 11/17-12/11 | 12/12-12/31 |  |
| 10/20-11/12 | 11/13-12/6 | 12/7-12/30 | 12/31 | 1/1-1/5 | 1/6-2/2 |
|  |  |  |  |  |  |
| 8/10-9/6 | 9/7-10/11 | 10/12-11/21 | 1/1-1/23 | 1/24-2/16 | 2/17-3/12 |
|  | 11/22-12/31 |  |  |  |  |
| 9/20-10/13 | 1/1-1/3 | 1/4-2/6 | 2/7-3/4 | 3/5-3/31 | 4/1-4/25 |
|  | 10/14-11/6 | 11/7-11/30 | 12/1-12/24 | 12/25-12/31 |  |

| | Aries | Taurus | Gemini | Cancer | Leo | Virgo |
|---|---|---|---|---|---|---|
| **1932** | 2/12-3/8 | 3/9-4/3 | 4/4-5/5<br>7/13-7/27 | 5/6-7/12<br>7/28-9/8 | 9/9-10/6 | 10/7-11/1 |
| **1933** | 3/27-4/19 | 4/20-5/28 | 5/29-6/8 | 6/9-7/2 | 7/3-7/26 | 7/27-8/20 |
| **1934** | 5/6-6/1 | 6/2-6/27 | 6/28-7/22 | 7/23-8/16 | 8/17-9/10 | 9/11-10/4 |
| **1935** | 2/26-3/21 | 3/22-4/15 | 4/16-5/10 | 5/11-6/6 | 6/7-7/6 | 7/7-11/8 |
| **1936** | 4/11-5/4 | 5/5-5/28 | 5/29-6/22 | 6/23-7/16 | 7/17-8/10 | 8/11-9/4 |
| **1937** | 2/2-3/8<br>4/14-6/3 | 3/9-4/17<br>6/4-7/6 | 7/7-8/3 | 8/4-8/29 | 8/30-9/24 | 9/25-10/18 |
| **1938** | 3/12-4/4 | 4/5-4/28 | 4/29-5/23 | 5/24-6/18 | 6/19-7/13 | 7/14-8/8 |
| **1939** | 4-25/5/19 | 5/20-6/13 | 6/14-7/8 | 7/9-8/1 | 8/2-8/25 | 8/26-9/19 |
| **1940** | 2/12-3/7 | 3/8-4/3 | 4/4-5/5<br>7/5-7/31 | 5/6-7/4<br>8/1-9/8 | 9/9-10/5 | 10/6-10/31 |
| **1941** | 3/27-4/19 | 4/20-5/13 | 5/14-6/6 | 6/7-6/1 | 7/2-7/26 | 7/27-8/20 |
| **1942** | 5/6-6/1 | 6/2-6/26 | 6/27-7/22 | 7/23-8/16 | 8/17-9/9 | 9/10-10/3 |
| **1943** | 2/25-3/20 | 3/21-4/14 | 4/15-5/10 | 5/11-6/6 | 6/7-7/6 | 7/7-11/8 |
| **1944** | 4-10/5-3 | 5/4-5/28 | 5/29-6/21 | 6/22-7/16 | 7/17-8/9 | 8/10-9/2 |
| **1945** | 2/2-3/10<br>4/7-6/3 | 3/11-4/6<br>6/4-7/6 | 7/7-8/3 | 8/4-8/29 | 8/30-9/23 | 9/24-10/18 |
| **1946** | 3/11-4/4 | 4/5-4/28 | 4/29-5/23 | 5/24-6/17 | 6/18-7/12 | 7/13-8/8 |
| **1947** | 4/25-5/19 | 5/20-6/12 | 6/13-7/7 | 7/8-8/1 | 8/2-8/25 | 8/26-9/18 |
| **1948** | 2/11-3/7 | 3/8-4/3 | 4/4-5/6<br>6/29-8/2 | 5/7-6/28<br>8/3-9/7 | 9/8-10/5 | 10/6-10/31 |
| **1949** | 3/26-4/19 | 4/20-5/13 | 5/14-6/6 | 6/7-6/30 | 7/1-7/25 | 7/26-8/19 |
| **1950** | 5/5-5/31 | 6/1-6/26 | 6/27-7/21 | 7/22-8/15 | 8/16-9/9 | 9/10-10/3 |
| **1951** | 2/25-3/21 | 3/22-4/15 | 4/16-5/10 | 5/11-6/6 | 6/7-7/7 | 7/8-11/9 |
| **1952** | 4/10-5/4 | 5/5-5/28 | 5/29-6/21 | 6/22-7/16 | 7/17-8/9 | 8/10-9/3 |
| **1953** | 2/2-3/13<br>4/1-6/5 | 3/4-3/31<br>6/6-7/7 | 7/8-8/3 | 8/4-8/29 | 8/30-9/24 | 9/25-10/18 |

| Libra | Scorpio | Sagittarius | Capricorn | Aquarius | Pisces |
|---|---|---|---|---|---|
| 11/2-11/25 | 11/26-12/20 | 12/21-12/31 | | 1/1-1/18 | 1/19-2/11 |
| | | | | | |
| 8/21-9/14 | 9/15-10/10 | 1/1-1/13 | 1/14-2/6 | 2/7-3/2 | 3/3-3/26 |
| | | 10/11-11/5 | 11/6-12/4 | 12/5-12/31 | |
| 10/5-10/28 | 10/29-11/21 | 11/22-12/15 | 12/16-12/31 | 1/1-4/5 | 4/6-5/5 |
| 11/9-12/7 | 12/8-12/31 | | 1/1-1/7 | 1/8-1/31 | 2/1-2/25 |
| 9/5-9/27 | 1/1-1/2 | 1/3-1/27 | 1/28-2/21 | 2/22-3/16 | 3/17-4/10 |
| | 9/28-10/22 | 10/23-11/15 | 11/16-12/10 | 12/11-12/31 | |
| 10/19-11/11 | 11/12-12/5 | 12/6-12/29 | 12/30-12/31 | 1/1-1/5 | 1/6-2/1 |
| | | | | | |
| 8/9-9/6 | 9/7-10/13 | 10/14-11/14 | 1/1-1/22 | 1/23-2/15 | 2/16-3/11 |
| | 11/15-12/31 | | | | |
| 9/20-10/13 | 1/1-1/3 | 1/4-2/5 | 2/6-3/4 | 3/5-3/30 | 3/31-4/24 |
| | 10/14-11/6 | 11/7-11/30 | 12/1-12/24 | 12/25-12/31 | |
| 11/1-11/25 | 11/26-12/19 | 12/20-12/31 | | 1/1-1/18 | 1/19-2/11 |
| | | | | | |
| 8/21-9/14 | 9/15-10/9 | 1/1-1/12 | 1/13-2/5 | 2/6-3/1 | 3/2-3/26 |
| | | 10/10-11/5 | 11/6-12/4 | 12/5-12/31 | |
| 10/4-10/27 | 10/28-11/20 | 11/21-12/14 | 12/15-12/31 | 1/1-4/4 | 4/6-5/5 |
| 11/9-12/7 | 12/8-12/31 | | 1/1-1/7 | 1/8-1/31 | 2/1-2/24 |
| 9/3-9/27 | 1/1-1/2 | 1/3-1/27 | 1/28-2/20 | 2/21-3/16 | 3/17-4/9 |
| | 9/28-10/21 | 10/22-11/15 | 11/16-12/10 | 12/11-12/31 | |
| 10/19-11/11 | 11/12-12/5 | 12/6-12/29 | 12/30-12/31 | 1/1-1/4 | 1/5-2/1 |
| | | | | | |
| 8/9-9/6 | 9/7-10/15 | 10/16-11/7 | 1/1-1/21 | 1/22-2/14 | 2/15-3/10 |
| | 11/8-12/31 | | | | |
| 9/19-10/12 | 1/1-1/4 | 1/5-2/5 | 2/6-3/4 | 3/5-3/29 | 3/30-4/24 |
| | 10/13-11/5 | 11/6-11/29 | 11/30-12/23 | 12/24-12/31 | |
| 11/1-1/25 | 11/26-12/19 | 12/20-12/31 | | 1/1-1/17 | 1/18-2/10 |
| | | | | | |
| 8/20-9/14 | 9/15-10/9 | 1/1-1/12 | 1/13-2/5 | 2/6-3/1 | 3/2-3/25 |
| | | 10/10-11/5 | 11/6-12/5 | 12/6-12/31 | |
| 10/4-10/27 | 10/28-11/20 | 11/21-12/13 | 12/14-12/31 | 1/1-4/5 | 4/6-5/4 |
| 11/10-12/7 | 12/8-12/31 | | 1/1-1/7 | 1/8-1/31 | 2/1-2/24 |
| 9/4-9/27 | 1/1-1/2 | 1/3-1/27 | 1/28-2/20 | 2/21-3/16 | 3/17-4/9 |
| | 9/28-10/21 | 10/22-11/15 | 11/16-12/10 | 12/11-12/31 | |
| 10/19-11/11 | 11/12-12/5 | 12/6-12/29 | 12/30-12/31 | 1/1-1/5 | 1/6-2/1 |

| | Aries | Taurus | Gemini | Cancer | Leo | Virgo |
|---|---|---|---|---|---|---|
| 1954 | 3/12-4/4 | 4/5-4/28 | 4/29-5/23 | 5/24-6/17 | 6/18-7/13 | 7/14-8/8 |
| 1955 | 4/25-5/19 | 5/20-6/13 | 6/14-7/7 | 7/8-8/1 | 8/2-8/25 | 8/26-9/18 |
| 1956 | 2/12-3/7 | 3/8-4/4 | 4/5-5/7 6:24-8/4 | 5/8-6/23 8/5-9/8 | 9/9-10/5 | 10/6-10/31 |
| 1957 | 3-26/4-19 | 4/20-5/13 | 5/14-6/6 | 6/7-7/1 | 7/2-7/26 | 7/27-8/19 |
| 1958 | 5-6/5-31 | 6/1-6/26 | 6/27-7/22 | 7/23-8/15 | 8/16-9/9 | 9/10-10/3 |
| 1959 | 2-25/3-20 | 3/21-4/14 | 4/15-5/10 | 5/11-6/6 | 6/7-7/8 9/21-9/24 | 7/9-9/20 9/25-11/9 |
| 1960 | 4-10/5-3 | 5/4-5/28 | 5/29-6/21 | 6/22-7/15 | 7/16-8/9 | 8/10-9/2 |
| 1961 | 2-3/6-5 | 6/6-7/7 | 7/8-8/3 | 8/4-8/29 | 8/30-9/23 | 9/24-10/17 |
| 1962 | 3/11-4/3 | 4/4-4/28 | 4/29-5/22 | 5/23-6/17 | 6/18-7/12 | 7/13-8/8 |
| 1963 | 4/24-5/18 | 5/19-6/12 | 6/13-7/7 | 7/8-7/31 | 8/1-8/25 | 8/26-9/18 |
| 1964 | 2/11-3/7 | 3/8-4/4 | 4/5-5/9 6/18-8/5 | 5/10-6/17 8/6-9/8 | 9/9-10/5 | 10/6-10/31 |
| 1965 | 3/26-4/18 | 4/19-5/12 | 5/13-6/6 | 6/7-6/30 | 7/1-7/25 | 7/26-8/19 |
| 1966 | 5/6-6/31 | 6/1-6/26 | 6/27-7/21 | 7/22-8/15 | 8/16-9/8 | 9/9-10/2 |
| 1967 | 2/24-3/20 | 3/21-4/14 | 4/15-5/10 | 5/11-6/6 | 6/7-7/8 9/10-10/1 | 7/9-9/9 10/2-11/9 |
| 1968 | 4/9-5/3 | 5/4-5/27 | 5/28-6/20 | 6/21-7/15 | 7/16-8/8 | 8/9-9/2 |
| 1969 | 2/3-6/6 | 6/7-7/6 | 7/7-8/3 | 8/4-8/28 | 8/29-9/22 | 9/23-10/17 |
| 1970 | 3/11-4/3 | 4/4-4/27 | 4/28-5/22 | 5/23-6/16 | 6/17-7/12 | 7/13-8/8 |
| 1971 | 4/24-5/18 | 5/19-6/12 | 6/13-7/6 | 7/7-7/31 | 8/1-8/24 | 8/25-9/17 |
| 1972 | 2/11-3/7 | 3/8-4/3 | 4/4-5/10 6/12-8/6 | 5/11-6/11 8/7-9/8 | 9/9-10/5 | 10/6-10/30 |
| 1973 | 3/25-4/18 | 4/18-5/12 | 5/13-6/5 | 6/6-6/29 | 7/1-7/25 | 7/26-8/19 |
| 1974 | | 5/5-5/31 | 6/1-6/25 | 6/26-7/21 | 7/22-8/14 | 8/15-9/8 | 9/9-10/2 |
| 1975 | 2/24-3/20 | 3/21-4/13 | 4/14-5/9 | 5/10-6/6 | 6/7-7/9 9/3-10/4 | 7/10-9/2 10/5-11/9 |

## VENUS SIGN 1910-1975

| Libra | Scorpio | Sagittarius | Capricorn | Aquarius | Pisces |
|---|---|---|---|---|---|
| 8/9-9/6 | 9/7-10/22 | 10/23-10/27 | 1/1-1/22 | 1/23-2/15 | 2/16-3/11 |
| | 10/28-12/31 | | | | |
| 9/19-10/13 | 1/1-1/6 | 1/7-2/5 | 2/6-3/4 | 3/5-3/30 | 3/31-4/24 |
| | 10/14-11/5 | 11/6-11/30 | 12/1-12/24 | 12/25-12/31 | |
| 11/1-11/25 | 11/26-12/19 | 12/20-12/31 | | 1/1-1/17 | 1/18-2/11 |
| | | | | | |
| 8/20-9/14 | 9/15-10/9 | 1/1-1/12 | 1/13-2/5 | 2/6-3/1 | 3/2-3/25 |
| | | 10/10-11/5 | 11/6-12/16 | 12/7-12/31 | |
| 10/4-10/27 | 10/28-11/20 | 11/21-12/14 | 12/15-12/31 | 1/1-4/6 | 4/7-5/5 |
| 11/10-12/7 | 12/8-12/31 | | 1/1-1/7 | 1/8-1/31 | 2/1-2/24 |
| | | | | | |
| 9/3-9/26 | 1/1-1/2 | 1/3-1/27 | 1/28-2/20 | 2/21-3/15 | 3/16-4/9 |
| | 9/27-10/21 | 10/22-11/15 | 11/16-12/10 | 12/11-12/31 | |
| 10/18-11/11 | 11/12-12/4 | 12/5-12/28 | 12/29-12/31 | 1/1-1/5 | 1/6-2/2 |
| 8/9-9/6 | 9/7-12/31 | | 1/1-1/21 | 1/22-2/14 | 2/15-3/10 |
| 9/19-10/12 | 1/1-1/6 | 1/7-2/5 | 2/6-3/4 | 3/5-3/29 | 3/30-4/23 |
| | 10/13-11/5 | 11/6-11/29 | 11/30-12/23 | 12/24-12/31 | |
| 11/1-11/24 | 11/25-12/19 | 12/20-12/31 | | 1/1-1/16 | 1/17-2/10 |
| | | | | | |
| 8/20-9/13 | 9/14-10/9 | 1/1-1/12 | 1/13-2/5 | 2/6-3/1 | 3/2-3/25 |
| | | 10/10-11/5 | 11/6-12/7 | 12/8-12/31 | |
| 10/3-10/26 | 10/27-11/19 | 11/20-12/13 | 2/7-2/25 | 1/1-2/6 | 4/7-5/5 |
| | | | 12/14-12/31 | 2/26-4/6 | |
| 11/10-12/7 | 12/8-12/23 | | 1/1-1/6 | 1/7-1/30 | 1/31-2/23 |
| | | | | | |
| 9/3-9/26 | 1/1 | 1/2-1/26 | 1/27-2/20 | 2/21-3/15 | 3/16-4/8 |
| | 9/27-10/21 | 10/22-11/14 | 11/15-12/9 | 12/10-12/31 | |
| 10/18-11/10 | 11/11-12/4 | 12/5-12/28 | 12/29-12/31 | 1/1-1/4 | 1/5-2/2 |
| 8/9-9/7 | 9/8-12/31 | | 1/1-1/21 | 1/22-2/14 | 2/15-3/10 |
| 9/18-10/11 | 1/1-1/7 | 1/8-2/5 | 2/6-3/4 | 3/5-3/29 | 3/30-4/23 |
| | 10/12-11/5 | 11/6-11/29 | 11/30-12/23 | 12/24-12/31 | |
| | 11/25-12/18 | 12/19-12/31 | | 1/1-1/16 | 1/17-2/10 |
| 10/31-11/24 | | | | | |
| 8/20-9/13 | | 1/1-1/12 | 1/13-2/4 | 2/5-2/28 | 3/1-3/24 |
| | | 10/9-11/5 | 11/6-12/7 | 12/8-12/31 | |
| | | | 1/30-2/28 | 1/1-1/29 | |
| 10/3-10/26 | 10/27-11/19 | 11/20-12/13 | 12/14-12/31 | 3/1-4/6 | 4/7-5/4 |
| | | | 1/1-1/6 | 1/7-1/30 | 1/31-2/23 |
| 11/10-12/7 | 12/8-12/31 | | | | |

## MARS SIGN 1910-1975

| | Jan. | Feb. | Mar. | Apr. | May | June | July | Aug. | Sept. | Oct. | Nov. | Dec. |
|---|---|---|---|---|---|---|---|---|---|---|---|---|
| 1910 | AR | TA | GE | GE | CA | CA | LE | VI | VI | LI | SC | SC |
| 1911 | SA | CP | AQ | AQ | PI | AR | TA | TA | GE | GE | GE | TA |
| 1912 | TA | GE | GE | CA | CA | LE | LE | VI | LI | LI | SC | SA |
| 1913 | CP | CP | AQ | PI | AR | AR | TA | GE | CA | CA | CA | CA |
| 1914 | CA | CA | CA | CA | LE | LE | VI | LI | LI | SC | SA | SA |
| 1915 | CP | AQ | PI | PI | LE | TA | GE | GE | CA | LE | LE | LE |
| 1916 | LE | LE | LE | LE | LE | VI | VI | LI | SC | SC | SA | CP |
| 1917 | AQ | AQ | PI | AR | TA | GE | GE | CA | LE | LE | VI | VI |
| 1918 | LI | LI | VI | VI | VI | VI | LI | LI | SC | SA | CP | CP |
| 1919 | AQ | PI | AR | TA | GE | CA | CA | LE | VI | VI | VI | LI |
| 1920 | LI | SC | SC | SC | LI | LI | SC | SC | SA | SA | CP | AQ |
| 1921 | PI | AR | AR | TA | GE | GE | CA | LE | LE | VI | LI | LI |
| 1922 | SC | SC | SA | SA | SA | SA | SA | SA | CP | CP | AQ | AQ |
| 1923 | PI | AR | TA | TA | GE | CA | CA | LE | VI | VI | LI | SC |
| 1924 | SC | SA | CP | CP | AQ | AQ | PI | PI | AQ | AQ | PI | PI |
| 1925 | AR | TA | TA | GE | CA | CA | LE | VI | VI | LI | SC | SC |
| 1926 | SA | CP | CP | AQ | PI | AR | AR | TA | TA | TA | TA | TA |
| 1927 | TA | TA | GE | GE | CA | LE | LE | VI | TA | LI | SC | SA |
| 1928 | SA | SA | AQ | PI | PI | AR | TA | GE | GE | CA | CA | CA |

76

**MARS SIGN 1910–1975**

| | Jan. | Feb. | Mar. | Apr. | May | June | July | Aug. | Sept. | Oct. | Nov. | Dec. |
|---|---|---|---|---|---|---|---|---|---|---|---|---|
| 1929 | GE | GE | CA | CA | LE | LE | VI | VI | LI | SC | SC | SA |
| 1930 | CP | AQ | AQ | PI | AR | TA | GE | GE | CA | CA | LE | LE |
| 1931 | LE | LE | CA | LE | LE | VI | VI | LI | LI | SC | SA | CP |
| 1932 | CP | AQ | PI | AR | TA | TA | GE | CA | CA | LE | VI | VI |
| 1933 | VI | VI | VI | VI | VI | VI | LI | LI | SC | SA | SA | CP |
| 1934 | AQ | PI | AR | AR | TA | GE | GE | CA | LE | LE | VI | LI |
| 1935 | LI | LI | LI | LI | LI | LI | LI | SC | SC | SA | VI | AQ |
| 1936 | PI | PI | AR | TA | GE | GE | CA | LE | LE | VI | CP | LI |
| 1937 | SC | SC | SA | SA | SC | SC | SC | SA | SA | CP | LI | AQ |
| 1938 | PI | AR | TA | TA | GE | CA | CA | LE | VI | VI | AQ | SC |
| 1939 | SC | SA | SA | CP | CP | AQ | AQ | CP | CP | AQ | LI | PI |
| 1940 | AR | AR | TA | GE | GE | CA | LE | LE | VI | VI | AQ | SC |
| 1941 | SA | SA | CP | AQ | AQ | PI | AR | AR | AR | AR | LI | AR |
| 1942 | TA | TA | GE | GE | CA | LE | LE | VI | VI | LI | AR | SC |
| 1943 | SA | CP | AQ | AQ | PI | AR | TA | TA | GE | GE | SC | GE |
| 1944 | GE | GE | GE | CA | CA | LE | TA | VI | LI | SC | GE | SA |
| 1945 | CP | AQ | AQ | PI | AR | TA | VI | GE | CA | CA | SC | LE |
| 1946 | CA | CA | CA | CA | LE | LE | VI | LI | LI | SC | SA | SA |
| 1947 | CP | AQ | PI | AR | AR | TA | GE | CA | CA | LE | LE | VI |

**MARS SIGN 1910–1975**

| | Jan. | Feb. | Mar. | Apr. | May | June | July | Aug. | Sept. | Oct. | Nov. | Dec. |
|---|---|---|---|---|---|---|---|---|---|---|---|---|
| 1948 | VI | LE | LE | LE | LE | VI | VI | LI | SC | SC | SA | CP |
| 1949 | AQ | PI | PI | AR | TA | GE | GE | CA | LE | LE | VI | VI |
| 1950 | LI | LI | LI | VI | VI | LI | LI | SC | SC | SA | CP | CP |
| 1951 | AQ | PI | AR | TA | TA | GE | CA | CA | LE | VI | VI | LI |
| 1952 | LI | SC | SC | SC | SC | SC | SC | SC | SA | CP | CP | AQ |
| 1953 | AR | AR | AR | TA | GE | GE | CA | CA | VI | VI | LI | LI |
| 1954 | SC | SA | SA | CP | CP | CP | SA | SA | CP | CP | AQ | PI |
| 1955 | PI | AR | TA | GE | GE | CA | LE | LE | VI | LI | LI | SC |
| 1956 | SA | SA | CP | AQ | AQ | PI | PI | PI | PI | PI | PI | AR |
| 1957 | AR | TA | TA | GE | CA | CA | LE | VI | VI | LI | SC | SC |
| 1958 | SA | CP | CP | AQ | PI | AR | AR | VI | TA | GE | TA | TA |
| 1959 | TA | GE | GE | CA | CA | LE | TA | TA | LI | LI | SC | SA |
| 1960 | CP | CP | AQ | PI | AR | AR | VI | VI | GE | CA | CA | CA |
| 1961 | CA | CA | CA | CA | LE | LE | GE | GE | LI | SC | SA | SA |
| 1962 | CP | AQ | PI | PI | AR | TA | VI | GE | CA | LE | CA | SA |
| 1963 | LE | LE | LE | LE | LE | VI | GE | LI | SC | SC | LE | LE |
| 1964 | AQ | AQ | PI | AR | TA | TA | GE | CA | LE | LE | SA | CP |
| 1965 | VI | VI | VI | VI | VI | VI | LI | LI | SC | SA | VI | VI |
| 1966 | AQ | PI | AR | AR | TA | GE | CA | CA | LE | VI | CP | CP |

**MARS SIGN 1910-1975**

| | Jan. | Feb. | Mar. | Apr. | May | June | July | Aug. | Sept. | Oct. | Nov. | Dec. |
|---|---|---|---|---|---|---|---|---|---|---|---|---|
| 1967 | LI | SC | SC | LI | LI | LI | LI | SC | SA | SA | CP | AQ |
| 1968 | PI | PI | AR | TA | GE | GE | CA | LE | LE | VI | LI | LI |
| 1969 | SC | SC | SA | SA | SA | SA | SA | SA | SA | CP | AQ | PI |
| 1970 | PI | AR | TA | TA | GE | CA | CA | LE | VI | AQ | LI | SC |
| 1971 | SC | SA | CP | CP | AQ | AQ | AQ | AQ | AQ | AQ | PI | PI |
| 1972 | AR | TA | TA | GE | CA | CA | LE | LE | VI | LI | SC | SC |
| 1973 | SA | CP | CP | AQ | PI | PI | AR | LE | TA | TA | AR | AR |
| 1974 | TA | TA | GE | GE | CA | LE | LE | VI | LI | LI | SC | SA |
| 1975 | SA | CP | AQ | PI | PI | AR | TA | GE | GE | GE | CA | GE |

AR—Aries    LE—Leo    SA—Sagittarius
TA—Taurus    VI—Virgo    CP—Capricorn
GE—Gemini    LI—Libra    AQ—Aquarius
CA—Cancer    SC—Scorpio    PI—Pisces

# 9

## The Planets As "Stars"

### The Astrological Cast of Characters in Order of Their Appearance

As you learned in the chapter "Defining Terms," the planets are the *sine qua non* of astrology—the factor without which there would be no such study. It is the placement of the planets in the signs of the zodiac that give those signs meaning in human terms, and the placement of the planets in an individual horoscope that "spell out" that individual's character/personality. As for forecasting, it is the movement (transits) of the planets throughout our lifetime that activate one part of our chart or another and bring out certain life conditions.

Those planets are moving bodies and not "stars" in the astrological sense, though they are sometimes referred to with that word. In Shakespeare's play, *Julius Caesar*, Cassius, one of the conspirators, states, "The fault, dear Brutus, is not in our stars but in ourselves that we are underlings." Shakespeare (Cassius) actually knew what he was talking about because astrology was part and parcel of daily life in Elizabethan times when the play was written, as well as in Caesar's ancient Rome. However, Shakespeare seems to have preferred "stars" as a more poetic word than "planets." He also was right about another thing: The "stars" (planets) don't push people around unless you let them. The key is to understand the role each planet plays in your basic astrological makeup through your natal chart and to get to know yourself via this ancient and pragmatic science. Then you will better understand how the transits of the different planets are most likely to affect you.

Though the planets are not stars by astronomical definition (except for the sun), they do play the starring roles in the great cosmic drama that is acted out every day of our lives, and has been since the beginning of life on earth. There are other heavenly bodies—like the asteroids—that play supporting roles, but most astrologers take the Big Ten into consideration when they do a chart or a personal forecast: the sun, the moon, Mercury, Venus, Mars, Jupiter, Saturn, Uranus, Neptune, and Pluto. (Some of these planets, like the Moon, Venus, and Mars, are touched on in other parts of this book, and you may want to read those sections to get a better understanding of their characteristics.)

Each planet rules one or more signs of the zodiac—i.e., is very closely associated with that sign or signs. The one that rules your sun sign is your own personal planet, so to speak, and its description will fill in more of the background of your sign.

The following is a rundown of the planetary cast of characters, presented in their order of appearance, their actual position in our solar system As you know, the sun is the center of our solar system, and the orbits of the planets form rings around it. Looking at the planets this way underscores the fact that the *closer* planets influence us much more strongly as individuals. Planets farther out in the solar system are not only farther away, they also move much more slowly. While a transit of the moon lasts two days, for instance, a transit of Uranus (which takes eighty-four years to circle the zodiac) may influence your life for many months. However, even with these distant planets, their position in a specific *house* of your own horoscope will greatly influence your astrological makeup.

## The Sun

*Vital Statistics*: 864,000 miles in diameter; average distance from earth, 93 million miles; gaseous nature. Appears to circle the zodiac in 365 days.

*Rules*:    The sign of Leo
            Fourth period of life: ages 23 to 41
*Role*:     The true "star" . . . the male lead . . . the
            doer . . . the activator.
*Facts and Foibles*:    The position of the sun in anyone's
horoscope is the central fact about that person, astrologically speaking. Your sun sign is your core—your
individuality. It is your ego in the best sense of the
word, the part of you that moves you in a certain life
direction. No matter what your sun sign is, true self-
development means developing the highest potential of
that sign. People really grow into their sun signs as they
mature, and the sun symbolically governs that stage of
life (23 to 41) at which we are (or should be) mature
individuals who are concerned with creating something
in our own right. The sun is considered a masculine
planet, because it is the fiery, animating force of life.
We are meant to *express* our sun sign; those who do not
can literally have a lifeless quality about them.

Those born under the sign of Leo have been said to
be favored because of their rulership by the most important "planet" of them all. In ancient times, the sun
was often the chief deity and was worshipped for its
extraordinary power. It was recognized that without
the sun, life on earth could not exist, and the dimming
of its light via an eclipse was a terrifying experience for
early civilizations that recognized their dependence upon
its warmth and vitalizing nature. Whether or not Leo is
a special sign is debatable, but there is no doubt that
there is a tendency in some Leo sun sign people to
become overly self-centered. Perhaps even unconsciously,
they sense that it is a heady destiny to be ruled by the
sun, but they are unable to handle its tremendous energies properly.

## The Moon

*Vital Statistics*:    238,857 miles from the earth; 2,160
miles in diameter (one-fourth earth's size). Revolves
around the earth (circles the zodiac) in about 27 ½ days
*Rules*:    The sign of cancer
            The first four years of human life

*Role*:    The leading lady . . . the "feeler" . . . the mother
           . . . the reactor.

*Facts and Foibles*:    The moon is not exactly a planet, either;
it is a satellite of our own planet, earth. However, it is the
largest satellite with respect to its parent planet anywhere
in the solar system that we know of. It has a tremendous
gravitational pull, which is demonstrated on earth by the
changing of the tides and other natural phenomena.

The moon has no light of its own, and we can see it
shining only because it reflects the sun. Therefore, the
moon is considered a *receptive* or "feminine" planet,
rather than an active one like the sun. The moon in
mythology has always been a woman—often the "Great
Mother" to ancient peoples who saw the sun as the
"Great Father." Accordingly, the moon rules the first
four years of human life, when we are totally dependent on our mothers, and the motherly sign of Cancer,
which is closely associated with nurturing and growth.
In an individual horoscope, the position of the moon
indicates our ability to feel and to respond emotionally.
It is our impressionability and sensitivity, i.e., our subjective rather than our objective sign. The moon reacts
to experience and remembers it. All our memories are
stored in our subconscious, which is the part of the
human psyche the moon signifies. In a sense, as the
moon rules the night, it rules our dark or hidden side.
As it takes some time for us to develop or grow into
our sun sign, the moon sign manifests itself much more
strongly in young children than the sun sign does. The
moon represents the instinctual nature connected with
infantile responses; our moon sign acts from habit,
often without thinking.

# Mercury

*Vital Statistics*:    36 million miles away from the sun;
2,900 miles in diameter; orbits sun at 108,000 miles per
hour; goes through zodiac in 88 days.

*Rules*:    The signs of Gemini and Virgo
          Age of curiosity: 4 through 14

*Role*:    The young male lead . . . the observer . . . the
          messenger . . . the communicator.

*Facts and Foibles:* Mercury is the hottest, quickest, and smallest of the planets, and is closest to the sun. It is so closely associated with the sun in an astronomical sense, that Mercury is very often in the same sign as the sun in a natal chart. In any horoscope, it is never more than two signs away from your sun sign.

In ancient times Mercury was regarded as the sun's messenger, and the gods with whom it was associated always had some kind of communicating function. In Egypt, Mercury was Thoth—scribe to the gods, keeper of the divine books. The Greeks called him Hermes, the messenger; the Romans renamed him Mercury, but assigned similar functions. Hermes/Mercury always had a golden tongue, and was regarded as the great persuader. Quickness and deftness also associate Mercury with all kinds of human skills requiring manual and mental dexterity.

Mercury has a double role to play as ruler of the signs of Gemini and Virgo. In a sense, Mercury is two-faced; the communicative side in Gemini, his precise specialist side in Virgo. No matter what your sun sign is, in your horoscope Mercury symbolizes your style of thinking and communicating—not so much how intelligent you are as how you tend to put things together mentally.

Mercury is a very human planet, and has a very human foible; occasionally he gets things all mixed up and causes a lot of trouble. About three times a year, for about three weeks at a time, Mercury seems to be going *backwards*. (That appearance is caused by the varying rates of speed of various planets—like two trains traveling in the same direction that can seem as if they are traveling in two different directions.) During these periods Mercury is said to be *retrograde*, it is known to cause problems in all kinds of human interactions. People get the wrong message, or don't get it at all. People who are supposed to meet on a street corner never find each other. Trains and planes are missed, luggage is lost, orders simply never get transmitted or seem to vanish in thin air. There has been quite a bit of research on Mercury retrograde, and it all proves out. Even if people don't know *why* retrograde Mercury makes things go wrong, they sure know it does. In 1986 Mercury will be retrograde during these periods:

March 7 through March 30.

July 9 through August 3.

November 2 through November 22.

## Venus

*Vital Statistics*: 67.2 million miles from the sun; 26 million to 160 million miles from earth; approximately the same size and volume as earth. Goes through all twelve signs of the zodiac in about 225 days.

*Rules*: The signs of Taurus and Libra

Period of developing sexuality: ages 14 to 21

*Role*: The young, nubile female lead . . . the love interest . . . the artist.

*Facts and Foibles*: Like Mercury, Venus follows the sun very closely, so in anyone's horoscope it is never very far away from your sun sign. Symbolically, Venus represents your capacity to love and relate, and the capacity to appreciate beauty. In ancient myth, Venus was seen as the daughter of the moon, a feminine planet associated with many of the earthly things traditionally associated with women: the providing of food and shelter, the beautifying of the home, the harmonizing of opposites and settler of strife. Venus is a peaceful planet in every sense of the word. Aphrodite to the Greeks, Venus to the Romans, this goddess/planet was seen as the bounteous giver of life's gifts and pleasures—the personification of beauty. She is supposed to inspire us with the desire for both material and spiritual growth.

Like Mercury, Venus has two faces, but, strangely, one rules a feminine sign, Taurus, and one rules a masculine sign, Libra. In Taurus, Venus shows her earthier side, more concerned with creature comforts, sex, and material prosperity. In Libra, a more refined Venus shines forth as the graceful "hostess," the one who beautifies things and relates to others.

Though most Libra males are quite virile, their rulership by the planet Venus often manifests itself in extremely good looks and a great appreciation of beauty. The virile male hairdresser or interior decorator is the personification of this side of Venus. Because Venus seeks peace rather than war, harmony rather than discord, she rules lawyers, mediators, and arbitrators.

Since Venus rules one feminine earth sign and one masculine air sign, she is sometimes seen as a symbol for the fact that all things in the universe can be made to work in harmony—even the incompatible elements of air (Libra) and earth (Taurus) and the often antagonistic principles of male and female—in real life as in astrology. Divorce courts come under the rulership of Venus.

## Mars

*Vital Statistics*:   14 million miles from the sun; 35 million miles from earth; 10 percent of earth's size; circles the zodiac in about 687 days.

*Rules:*   The sign of Aries
        Ages 42 to 56

*Role*:   The virile male antagonist . . . the lover . . . the warrior.

*Facts and foibles*:   Mars is a rather small planet and has sometimes been called "Earth's little brother." However, since ancient times Mars has been attributed with great powers—possibly because of its fiery red color. Even the earliest peoples associated Mars with strife and sex and a warriorlike attitude. In fact, Mars has had a rather bad reputation in astrology and was sometimes known as the "lesser malefic." But some groups assigned Mars another role and gave him a different dimension. The Egyptians called Mars Artes, and connected him with personal creative expression; to the Hebrews he played a similar role. When you think about it, sex, strife, and creative expression are only a few steps away from each other. Certainly, the act of procreation is a creative one, as it gives new life. War and strife are divisive, but often a new order comes out of them as well.

Mars is pure masculine energy—sometimes a bit rough, but always determined. In a personal horoscope, the sign position of Mars tells how you tend to assert yourself, how aggressive you are likely to be when going after what you want, even how much you will want it. Mars is our desire nature. (See the chapter on Venus and Mars to find out more about Mars in your own horoscope.) As the god of war, Mars is associated with courage and bravery, traits that are available to the Aries sun sign person if he/she cares to develop them. Mars is moral courage too, and the Mars-ruled Aries sun sign person at his/her best will never desert a cause or a person—no matter how rough the going gets.

About once every two years Mars returns to the same place it occupied on the day of your birth; to astrologers this is known as the "Mars return." It is a period of time during which one can make great strides, because Mars is stimulating that area of the natal chart connected with taking on the world. People often feel a great surge of energy during their Mars return, but if that energy is not directed in a productive channel, it can cause a lot of problems in relationships. You are far better taking out your Mars return aggressiveness on another job or another creative project rather than another person.

## Jupiter

*Vital Statistics*: Largest planet in the solar system, 318 times larger than earth; 365 million to 600 million miles from earth; gaseous nature; circles the zodiac in about 12 years.

*Rules*: The sign of Sagittarius
        Ages 57 to 68

*Role*: The hero ... the "father confessor" ... the one who saves the day.

*Facts and Foibles:* From earliest times, Jupiter was assigned a role in the "cosmic drama" almost as important as that of the sun. Huge and luminous, Jupiter was easily visible to the naked eye eons before the age of the telescope. The sun may have been god in the all-encompassing sense, but Jupiter was *the* god who could make things happen, even interfere in human affairs if he was needed. And he has always been a "good guy." The Hindus, whose roots lie in antiquity, call him Vishnu, the preserver. To the Greeks, he was Zeus, the god who reigned supreme on Mount Olympus; he became Jupiter under the Romans. The important thing about this masculine god-planet is that it has always been very godly but very human at the same time. Zeus frequently came down from Mount Olympus to bestow his favors on people—particularly women who caught his fancy (causing his wife Hera to become jealous). Jupiter-Zeus is the god who keeps one foot in heaven and one foot firmly planted on the earth. Since the planet itself is large and impressive-looking, it has always been associated with benevolence and expansiveness. Our English word "jovial" has its roots in the name Jove, by which name Jupiter was sometimes called.

Joviality is one of the characteristics that is available to people born under the sign of Sagittarius, which Jupiter rules. Some Sagittarians are jovial, they spend all their money and all their energy on making life one long party.

But Jupiter has a serious side, too. Jupiter is associated with the divine law, and the ability to make that law known to men on earth. The higher Sagittarian, ruled by Jupiter, has a sense of this mission, and often takes the real-life role of priest-missionary or teacher of higher studies. While Venus and Libra, the sign Venus rules, are associated with the *practice* of law, Jupiter and Sagittarius are connected with the *making* and *interpretation* of laws.

## Saturn

*Vital Statistics*:   75,000 miles in diameter, 95 times as big as earth; 886 million miles from the sun; takes 29 years to circle the zodiac.

*Rules*:   The sign of Capricorn
Ages 68 on

*Role*:   The "older man" . . . the taskmaster . . . the disciplining father.

*Facts and Foibles*:   Like Jupiter, Saturn is so large it can be seen with the naked eye from earth and was watched carefully by early peoples. It was quickly observed that certain transits of Saturn brought trials and troubles on earth and so the planet earned itself the name of the "greater malefic" by the time astrologers had begun to record their findings. Is Saturn really a "bad guy" as so many astrology books will tell you? There is no question that Saturn represents the principle of limitation; when you go too far out on a limb or get over expansive, Saturn is always there to teach you that there are rules and restrictions. However, as Saturn also represents the principle of contraction, this planet can and does bring periods of time in which we can consolidate our forces and make a secure place for ourselves in this world.

Saturn is also sometimes called the "lord of Karma." Translated into human terms, that means that Saturn represents our inevitable responsibilities, our "fated" duties in this world. Once again, there is a positive side. When Saturn is strongly placed in an individual's chart, that individual is exceptionally able to handle responsibility and achieve worldly success. As ruler of the sign of Capricorn, Saturn brings to that sign an extraordinary talent for working long and hard as well as reaping the material rewards that come with dedication to a task.

Kronos (or Chronos) was the ancient Greek god who is generally regarded as the prototype for Saturn's particular personality or role, and his story sheds a lot of light on the perceptions of this planet. Kronos was born to the very highest ancient god, Ouranos, and to the original earth mother, Ge. Kronos got a little carried away with this position and overthrew his father (castrating him) to take over the throne. When Kronos was told one of his own children would do the same to him, he swallowed them all—except Zeus, who was miraculously saved and became the "avenger." Later on, Zeus banished Kronos into exile. We know Kronos as Father Time—that shadowy old man who reminds us that it's later than we think. Kronos/Saturn also cautions against runaway ambitions, which is often punished by a downfall like his.

One of the most fascinating aspects of Saturn is that it is an uncannily accurate cosmic clock. Taking about 29 years to make a full circle of the zodiac, Saturn returns to the same place it occupied in your horoscope at your birth when you are about 29 years old. The "Saturn return" is regarded by astrologers as the true end of childhood (astrology is kind to us weak mortals by giving us more time to "grow up" than conventional earthly wisdom does). When Saturn begins to creep up on us in our late twenties, we generally begin to feel that it's time to settle down and do something big in the way of taking on earthly responsibility. Many people go through a "life crisis" at this time, because they feel the push that Saturn is giving them, but have trouble knowing what to do about it. Many, many people resolve the dilemma by getting married, buying a home, having a child, or getting divorced. The point is that it is time to *do something decisive* and to take responsibility for our own lives and actions. There are an incredible number of "Saturn return babies" because having a child is probably the most joyful as well as the biggest responsibility a person can assume.

On its second return—at about the human age of 58—people are generally ready to start relaxing their responsibilities and enjoying the fruits of their labors. It is a wise precaution to make ready for the second Saturn return, because just as Saturn tells us we have to *work*, he also tells us when it is time to *stop* working. But remain a productive human being, with real interests and the wherewithal to pursue them.

## Uranus

---

*Vital Statistics*:   1.7 billion miles from earth; 29,300 miles in diameter, 15 times larger than earth; takes 84 years to circle the zodiac; has an erratic orbit.
*Rules*:   The sign of Aquarius
           Teenagers
*Role*:   The rebel . . . the home-wrecker . . . the visionary.
*Facts and Foibles*:   Uranus is the first of the "modern" planets, i.e., those unknown to the ancients, and only discovered via the telescope. Uranus, the first planet to be discovered in this manner, was thus a shock to both astronomers and astrologers. Both groups believed the orbit of Saturn defined the limits of our solar system,

and both had to revise their thinking at this discovery. Astrologers took things in their stride by calling Uranus a "planet of the higher octave" and interpreting it as a breakthrough from the realm of purely earthly influences (with Saturn as the dividing line) to the "cosmic" or "higher" order of things. They decided that Uranus—an unconventional planet in many respects—must be the ruler of the quirky sign of Aquarius (which had been formerly ruled by Saturn). In a way it is uncanny that the sudden discovery of Uranus in 1781 heralded all the breakthrough discoveries of the 19th and 20th centuries. In a sense, Uranus ushered in the modern world; it also rules our current Age of Aquarius. As that age (approximately 2000 years long) will continue to shock us with discovery after discovery, it hopefully will also bring us the sense of brotherhood of humanity that is the hallmark of the sign of Aquarius.

As Uranus takes 84 years to circle the zodiac, it stays in each sign about seven years. (It is currently about two-thirds of the way through the sign of Sagittarius.) Whatever Uranus touches as it transits a person's natal chart gets a real jolt. Sometimes very suddenly. Uranus hates the status quo and almost always shakes it up. That means that a lot of changes take place when Uranus comes along, but for most people those changes are eventually positive ones. Uranus gets you out of whatever rut you happen to be in and does it quite forcefully. However, those who resist the changes Uranus "suggests" can cause themselves a lot of trouble. If you aren't willing to bend, Uranus can really "break you up."

Uranus is appropriately associated with the teen years, during which young people are often in a state of rebellion. However, here too, it is a *necessary* fact of life that people must eventually rebel against the strictures of childhood in order to become separate individual human beings. Uranus is associated not only with teenagers, but also with many of the things that represent their rebellion, like rock music, blaring radios, and all that goes with them. In essence, Uranus is the symbol of the electronic modern world.

*Vital Statistics*:   2.6 billion miles from earth; 2.7 billion miles from the sun; takes about 165 years to circle the zodiac.

*Rules*:   The sign of Pisces
No specific age.

*Role*:   The fascinating stranger . . . the poet . . . the one who confuses the issue. . . the dreamer of great dreams.

*Facts and Foibles*:   As it is difficult to get a handle on people heavily influenced by Neptune (like Pisceans), it took astronomers a while to figure out what Neptune really was. At first they observed nothing but some rather weird abberations in the orbit of Uranus as they began to plot that planet's orbit. In the early 1840s, some of them proved mathematically that there *must* be another planet out there, although it couldn't be seen. Finally, using all the data at hand, a German astronomer spotted Neptune in 1846.

There is a rather "sneaky" character to Neptune, but what this nebulous planet really symbolizes is the love that passes all understanding, the all-encompassing universal love that is virtually impossible for mortals to feel and give. Venus represents two-way love, the sharing kind. Neptune's love goes only in one direction. Neptune gives in a sense of self-sacrifice, and takes nothing in return.

There is evidence that even though no one really *saw* Neptune until 1846, the ancients knew all about its principles, and embodied them in the mythical figure of Poseidon (later called Neptune), the lord of the seas, master of the deep. When you think that more than three-quarters of the earth's surface is covered by water, you realize that Neptune was pretty important in the overall scheme of things. In fact, according to the Greeks, when the universe was created, it was divided among Zeus-Jupiter, who took the heavens, Hades-Pluto who took the underworld, and Poseidon-Neptune who took the oceans.

Just as water is difficult to contain, it is difficult for many people to get in touch with Neptune's higher qualities in their own charts. Water is soul and spirit, meta-physically speaking, so Neptune should make us aspire to much higher things. Not only universal love, but poetry, music and art in its purest forms. However, what Neptune touches in most people's natal charts often turns into an area of confusion rather than cre-ativity. Neptune rules liquid in all its forms and, un-fortunately, some people react to Neptune's confusing vibes by turning to alcohol or drugs. For many drug and alcohol abusers, however, the real goal of their vice is to attain a kind of "cosmic consciousness" which is the real realm of Neptune.

Since Neptune takes 165 years to circle the zodiac, it stays in one sign for 13 years or more. Therefore, it is the zodiacal *sign* Neptune makes to the "personal plan-ets" in your chart that really count. People positively influenced by Neptune make the true artists and poets of this world—as well as the visionaries who interpret its meaning in more philosophical and metaphysical terms.

## Pluto

*Vital Statistics*:  3,666 billion miles from the sun; takes about 242 years to circle the zodiac.
*Rules*:  The sign of Scorpio
      Prenatal
*Role*:  The "heavy" . . . the transformer . . . the tragic hero.
*Facts and Foibles:* As you will note, Pluto is a little light on vital statistics. That's because this immensely distant planet, only discovered in 1930, has yet to reveal some of its secrets to astronomers. Like Neptune, it was dis-covered only because of the erratic nature of the orbit of Uranus. But, even when Pluto was conclusively sighted in 1930, its small size relative to its extremely strong gravitational pull didn't make sense to astronomers. Either Pluto is much larger than we now think or it is so dense that it exerts a force much greater than its size should account for.

Either way, there's no doubt that Pluto represents *power*. In fact, many astrologers connect the discovery

93

of Pluto with the discovery by man of the extraordinary power in matter itself—the power of the atom. As with Neptune, Pluto's "realm" had been staked out in myth and astrology long before its actual discovery. Pluto is Hades, lord of the underworld—the place of darkness that all men fear. However, since most older religions regard life and death as a cycle, Pluto represents rebirth as well. We die only to be reborn. One of the symbols for Pluto is the Phoenix that rises triumphantly from its own ashes. Pluto—and the sign of Scorpio that it rules—hold onto their secrets, but have an incredible power to endure and triumph over life's circumstances. The extremes of life and death that Pluto/Scorpio is associated with connect neatly with the extremism of this astrological sign. "Plutonic" Scorpios often regard the world as totally black and white, with very few grays in between. They can also be the "best" of people, like reformers and religious leaders, or the "worst" of people, like criminals and those who manipulate others for their own purposes.

# 10

## Astrotrivia

### How Do You Rate in the Best Game in Town?

The ancient art of astrology is loaded with bits and pieces of miscellaneous information—all of it fascinating, and some of it more useful than you may think. For instance, did you know that every zodiac sign has a special day of the week and certain colors assigned to it? And, how good are you at guessing sun signs of celebrities—those larger-than-life models of sun signs in the flesh? The Astrotrivia that follows is partly in quiz form, partly in short-take astrological facts. In the first part, you can test your own astrological perceptivity; in the second, you can add a lot to your fund of astrological information—and maybe even learn a few things, you can use in your daily life.

### Astrotrivia Part I
### Sun Signs of the Rich and Famous

Try to answer the following questions yourself; if you're stumped you'll find the answers on page 103–104.

1. What famous stripper and the famous actress who played her mother in a Broadway show have the sign of Capricorn in common?

2. What two show biz buddies—who run in the same pack—are both Sagittarians?

3. What do these people have in common: Joseph Stalin, Richard Nixon, Herman Goering, Al Capone, and Mao Tse Tung?

4. What two handsome male movie stars, both known for their progressive ideas, have the same sun sign? And, what is it?

5. What highly Scorpionic actor had an on-again, off-again lifetime romance with a glamourous Pisces actress?

6. What two female tennis pros are both athletic Sagittarians?

7. What U.S. president had a "show-me-I'm-from-Missouri" personality, and what was his sun sign?

8. What two famous "lonely hearts" columnists get their soft Cancerian shoulders cried on all the time?

9. What two "greats" of American popular music were both thoroughly American, and both born on the Fourth of July?

10. Under what sign were these warrior peacemakers all born: Dwight D. Eisenhower, David Ben Gurion, Jimmy Carter, Mohandus Ghandi, and Eleanor Roosevelt?

11. What anti-American villainess of World War II was born on the Fourth of July?

12. What sun sign do these people have in common: Oscar Wilde, Truman Capote, and Gore Vidal?

13. What two famous rock stars—one early, one late—were born not only under the same sign, but on the same day?

14. Which of the following is/was not a Scorpio?

| | |
|---|---|
| Charles Manson | Robert Kennedy |
| Bo Derek | Pablo Picasso |
| Katherine Hepburn | Indira Ghandi |
| Princess Grace | Johnny Carson |
| Henry Kissinger | Billy Graham |

15. All of the following were born under the two most musical signs of the zodiac. What are they?

| | |
|---|---|
| Judy Collins | Michael Jackson |
| Barbra Steisand | George Gershwin |
| Stevie Wonder | Luciano Pavarotti |
| Fred Astaire | Paul Simon |
| Irving Berlin | Julie Andrews |
| Bing Crosby | Anthony Newly |
| Beverly Sills | John Lennon |
| Bobby Darin | Guiseppe Verdi |

16. All the following ladies of the stage and screen are masters of their craft. Which craftsman-like sun sign were they all born under?

| | |
|---|---|
| Lauren Bacall | Celeste Holm |
| Anne Bancroft | Greer Garson |
| Ingrid Bergman | Twiggy |
| Greta Garbo | Jo Ann Worley |
| Sophia Loren | Claudette Colbert |
| Lilly Tomlin | Raquel Welch |

17. What sun sign do the following famous rebels and rule-breakers have in common: Marlon Brando, Warren Beatty, Eddie Murphy, Charlie Chaplin, Hugh Hefner?

18. What sun sign do these medical and research geniuses have in common: Madame Curie, Jonas Salk, Christian Bernard?

19. What present-day famous Leo "princess" lived in Camelot with her Gemini "prince"?

20. What two great ballet stars were both born in the same country, and share the graceful sun sign, Pisces?

Answers on p. 103–104

## Astrotrivia Part II
## More Celebrity Sun Sign Lore

Just a handful of the many, many stage/screen-struck Leos:

| | |
|---|---|
| Robert DeNiro | Julia Child |
| Mike Jagger | Arlene Dahl |
| Lucille Ball | Alfred Hitchcock |
| Dustin Hoffman | Mae West |
| Cecil B. Demille | George Bernard Shaw |
| John Derek | Dino D. Laurentis |
| Mike Douglas | Robert Mitchum |
| Robert Redford | Peter O'Toole |
| Jason Robards Jr. | Roman Polanski |
| Esther Williams | Jill St. John |
| Stanley Kubrick | Robert Taylor |
| Shelly Winters | Keenan Wynn |

And here are some Leos who make/made the international scene their stage:

| | |
|---|---|
| Fidel Castro | Henry Ford |
| Jackie Onassis | Alex Haley |
| Coco Chanel | Lawrence of Arabia |
| Benito Mussolini | Mata Hari |
| Rasputin | Napoleon |
| Neil Armstrong | Andy Warhol |
| Mike Conners | |

Librans are often lovely, like Catherine Deneuve and Brigitte Bardot. Barbara Walters is the ultimate "cool" Libra.

Cancer is the second fame sign, because Cancer rules the public. Cancers who have made it somehow or other are:

| | |
|---|---|
| Bill Cosby | Ringo Starr |
| Jimmy Cagney | John Glenn |
| Ernest Hemingway | Arthur Ashe |
| Gerald Ford | The Mayo brothers (of the Mayo clinic) |

Some outspoken, inventive Aquarians whose opinions have not always been popular, but were always ahead of their time:

| | |
|---|---|
| Norman Mailer | Ralph Nader |
| Charles Darwin | Thomas Edison |
| Jules Verne | Betty Friedan |
| Ayn Rand | Vanessa Redgrave |
| Galileo | Franklin D. Roosevelt |

## Astrotrivia Part III
## Fascinating Facts About the Signs

Here are the colors that, by tradition, match each of the signs of the zodiac:

1. Aries: bright red, scarlet, magenta

2. Taurus: pastels in most shades, especially pink and turquoise

3. Gemini: beiges and light gray

4. Cancer: shimmery and irridescent shades of gray and silver; anything luminous

5. Leo: bright golds and yellows

6. Virgo: dark navy, brown, gray

7. Libra: cloudy pales, especially blue-green

8. Scorpio: murky colors, especially blood red and black

9. Sagittarius: rich blues, purples, greens

10. Capricorn: black, "no-color" colors

11. Aquarius: checks, stripes, patterns, electric blue

12. Pisces: deep lilac, mauve, sea green

Each Sign/Planet owns a day of the week:

Sunday = Sun/Leo

Monday = Moon/Cancer

Tuesday = Mars/Aries, Mars/Scorpio

Wednesday = Mercury/Gemini, Mercury/Virgo

Thursday = Jupiter/Sagittarius, Neptune/Pisces

Friday = Venus/Taurus, Venus/Libra

Saturday = Saturn/Capricorn, Saturn/Aquarius

(Since there are only seven days and twelve signs, some of the signs double up. Also, since the ancients only knew seven planets, there are only enough days to match seven of the ten planets we now recognize.)

## Astrotrivia Part IV
## Where Do You Belong?

Each sign is said to have certain places where it belongs. Long ago, the world was divided up according to astrological tradition, so there are certain countries, cities, and areas that have the vibrations of certain signs. Tradition divides up other kinds of spaces, too, as you will see.

- *Aries places:* In the world: Birmingham, Oldman, Leicester, and Blackburn, *England* . . . Florence, Naples, Verona and Padua *Italy* . . . Marseilles and Burgundy *France* . . . *Denmark, Germany, Palestine, Syria, Japan.*

  Anywhere: sheepfolds, forges, tool houses, fireplaces, on sandy soil, kilns, ceilings, fire houses, emergency rooms.

- *Taurus places:* In the world: Dublin, *Ireland* . . . Mantua, Parma, Palermo, *Italy* . . . St. Louis, *U.S.A.* . . . *The Greek Islands, Asia Minor,* the *Caucasus.*

  Anywhere: banks, dairies, pastures, shady places, corn fields, middle rooms of houses, altars, maypoles.

- *Gemini places:* In the world: San Francisco, *U.S.A.* . . . London and Plymouth, *England* . . . Bruges, *Belgium* . . . Versailles and Louvaine, *France* . . . Nurenburg, *Germany* . . . *Lower Egypt, Armenia, Wales.*

  Anywhere: buildings with pillars, bookcases, hills and mountains, upper back rooms, graineries.

- *Cancer places:* In the world; St. Andrews, *Scotland* . . . Amsterdam, *Holland* . . . New York City, *U.S.A.* . . . Stockholm, *Sweden* . . . Genoa, Venice, Milan, *Italy* . . . *Paraguay, North and West Africa.*

Anywhere: lakes and brooks, salt marshes, pubs, kitchens, cellars, corner houses facing north.

- *Sagittarius places:* In the world: Avignon, *France* . . . Stuttgart, Cologne, *Germany* . . . Nottingham, Sheffield, Bradford, *England* . . . Provence, *France* . . . *Hungary, Arabia, Tuscany.*

    Anywhere: highest place around, topmost room in house, stables for racing horses, obelisks, places near fire, where incense is burned.

- *Capricorn places:* In the world: Brussels, *Belgium* . . . Port Said, *Egypt* . . . *India, Afghanistan, Mexico, Lithuania, Orkney Islands, Macedonia.*

    Anywhere: vaults, convents, thick forests, gates and hinges, old trees, jails, cattle barns, door knockers, game preserves.

- *Aquarius places:* In the world: Brighton and Trent, *England* . . . Salszburg, *Austria* . . . Hamburg, *Germany* . . . the Piedmont, *Italy* . . . *Prussia, Red Russia, Westphalia.*

    Anywhere: buses, bridges, ladders, garages, airplanes, power transmitters, fountains, springs and streams, sleds, ice caps.

- *Pisces places:* In the world; Alexandria, *Egypt* . . . Seville, *Spain* . . . Southport, Lancaster, Bournemouth, Tiverton, *England* . . . *Portugal, Calabria, Normandy, Sahara.*

    Anywhere: fish ponds, oceans, oil fields, submarines, séances, flooded areas, bars, aquariums, boat yards, swimming pools, hospitals.

- *Leo Places:* In the world: Rome, Ravenna, *Italy* . . . Bath, Bristol, Portsmouth, Blackpool, *England* . . . Philadelphia, Chicago, *U.S.A.* . . . *Bohemia, Sicily, the Alps, Damascus.*

    Anywhere: wild animal preserves, deserts and forests, castles, furnaces, gold mines, porches, forts.

- *Virgo places:* In the world: Paris, Lyons, Toulouse, *France* . . . Boston, Los Angeles, *U.S.A.* . . . Heidelberg, *Germany* . . . *Turkey, West Indies, Brazil, Silesia, Switzerland.*

    Anywhere: pantries, restaurants, refrigerators, medicine cabinets, desks, malt houses.

- *Libra places:* In the world: Dover, Liverpool, New-castle, *England* . . . Messina, *Italy* . . . Halifax, *Nova Scotia* . . . *China, Norway, The Transvaal, the Barbary coast.*

  Anywhere: windmills, wood sheds, harbors, tops of mountains, garrets and lofts, guest rooms, tops of dressers, domed buildings.

- *Scorpio places:* In the world: Copenhagen, *Denmark* . . . Leeds, Nottingham, *England* . . . Johannesburg, *South Africa* . . . Burma, *India* . . . *Tibet, North China, Argentina.*

  Anywhere: junk yards, meat markets, laboratories, low gardens and streams, vineyards, deepest part of ocean.

## Astrotrivia Part V
## Which Animal Best Suits You?

Each sign is said to have an affinity with certain kinds of pets. Here's the rundown.

Aries:    No animal that needs a lot of taking care of; but if Aries has one pet, he/she will usually have two, so the animals can take care of each other.

Taurus:   Almost any kind of soft, warm creature. Taurus is a great nature lover, so even a skunk would be welcome.

Gemini:   Anything with fascinating habits, like bees or ants, or anything that talks, like a parrot or a minah bird.

Cancer:   Anything in need of a mother is welcome in Cancer's house, no matter how sloppy or in need of care.

Leo:      Cats, of course, preferably with good breeding. Peacocks or anything with bright colors or plumage are fine too.

Virgo:    Cats are preferable, because they are clean animals, but any animal in distress brings out Virgo's warmth.

| | |
|---|---|
| *Libra:* | This sign would just as soon do without, but if a pet is preferred, it's the perfectly groomed poodle or other refined breed of dog or cat. |
| *Scorpio:* | This sign goes for rather dangerous pets, such as snakes, or anything with a sting. Basically, animals are creatures to be observed, not coddled. |
| *Sagittarius:* | Horses—at home or at the race track. Any very large dog in the city, almost anything of immense size in the country. |
| *Capricorn:* | Capricorns *need* pets to help pull them out of their frequent depressions. The friendliest kind of animals are the best bet, like sheepdogs. |
| *Aquarius:* | This sign needs a very smart animal, so is picky about the breed of dog or cat. Actually, birds are preferable to this cool sign. |
| *Pisces:* | Many people born under this sign will take in any stray that strays into their path, no matter how scraggly or ugly. They often put animals before humans in their scheme of things. |

### Astrotrivia Part I answers

1. Gypsy Rose Lee and Ethel Merman (who played Gypsy's mother in *Gypsy*).
2. Frank Sinatra and Sammie Davis, Jr.
3. They were all born under the calculating sign of Capricorn.
4. Paul Newman and Alan Alda were both born under the sign of Aquarius.
5. Richard Burton was the Scorpio; Liz Taylor the Pisces.
6. Billie Jean King and Chris Evert.
7. Harry S. Truman, a Taurus.
8. Abigail Van Buren ("Dear Abby") and Ann Landers.

9. George M. Cohan ("Yankee Doodle Dandy") and Louis "Satchmo" Armstrong.
10. Libra.
11. Tokyo Rose.
12. Libra.
13. Elvis Presley and David Bowie (January 5—Capricorn).
14. Henry Kissinger. He's a wily Gemini, but he could easily fool you, because his moon sign is Scorpio.
15. The column on the left are Taureans; those on the right are Librans.
16. Virgo.
17. Aries.
18. Scorpio.
19. Jackie Kennedy Onassis is a Leo; John F. Kennedy was a Gemini.
20. Rudolph Nureyev and Vaslav Nijinsky.

# 11

# Sun Sign Changes. 1920–1975

If you were born "on the cusp" (very near the end or the beginning of a sign) you can find out what your sign really is by using the chart that follows. Many people do not realize that the sun does not "change signs" on the same day every year—or, for that matter, at the same time. For this reason the chart of sun sign changes is calculated to the minute.

## How to Use the Chart

Locate your year of birth, then the month in which you were born. Let's say you were born in April of 1942. In the box for that month and year you will see

20–Tau
12:30 P.M.

That means if you are born *after* 12:30 p.m. on April 20 in 1942, you are a Taurus. If you were born before that date and time, your sun sign is the preceding one, Aries.

In this chart (as well as in the rising-sign chart) the signs are abbreviated as follows:

Ar = Aries
Tau = Taurus
Gem = Gemini
Can = Cancer
Leo = Leo
Vir = Virgo
Lib = Libra
Sc = Scorpio

Sag = Sagittarius
Cap = Capricorn
Aq = Aquarius
Pis = Pisces

**NOTE:** All times given in the sun sign changes chart are Eastern Standard. You must correct for daylight savings time (subtract one hour) and for time zone. For Central Standard Time subtract one hour; for Mountain Standard Time subtract two hours; for Pacific Standard Time subtract three hours.

|        | 1920 | 1921 | 1922 | 1923 | 1924 | 1925 | 1926 | 1927 | 1928 | 1929 |
|--------|------|------|------|------|------|------|------|------|------|------|
| **Jan** | 21–Aq 4:05 pm | 20–Aq 8:55 am | 20–Aq 2:48 pm | 20–Aq 8:35 pm | 21–Aq 2:29 am | 20–Aq 8:20 am | 20–Aq 2:13 pm | 20–Aq 8:12 pm | 21–Aq 1:57 am | 20–Aq 7:42 am |
| **Feb** | 19–Pis 5:29 am | 18–Pis 11:21 pm | 19–Pis 5:16 pm | 19–Pis 11:00 am | 19–Pis 4:51 pm | 18–Pis 11:43 pm | 18–Pis 4:35 am | 19–Pis 10:35 am | 19–Pis 4:20 pm | 18–Pis 10:07 pm |
| **Mar** | 20–Ar 5:00 pm | 20–Ar 10:51 pm | 21–Ar 4:49 pm | 21–Ar 10:29 am | 20–Ar 4:20 pm | 20–Ar 11:13 am | 21–Ar 4:01 am | 21–Ar 11:59 am | 20–Ar 3:44 pm | 20–Ar 9:35 pm |
| **Apr** | 20–Tau 4:39 am | 20–Tau 10:32 am | 20–Tau 4:29 am | 20–Tau 10:06 pm | 20–Tau 3:59 am | 20–Tau 10:51 pm | 20–Tau 3:36 pm | 20–Tau 9:32 pm | 20–Tau 3:17 am | 20–Tau 9:11 am |
| **May** | 21–Gem 4:22 am | 21–Gem 10:17 am | 21–Gem 9:11 pm | 22–Gem 9:45 pm | 21–Gem 3:41 am | 21–Gem 10:33 pm | 21–Gem 3:15 pm | 21–Gem 9:08 pm | 21–Gem 2:53 am | 21–Gem 8:48 am |
| **June** | 21–Can 12:40pm | 21–Can 6:36 pm | 22–Can 12:27 am | 22–Can 6:03 am | 21–Can 12:noon | 21–Can 5:50 pm | 21–Can 11:45 pm | 22–Can 11:30 pm | 21–Can 11:07 am | 21–Can 5:01 pm |
| **July** | 22–Leo 11:40 pm | 23–Leo 5:31 am | 23–Leo 11:20 am | 23–Leo 5:01 pm | 22–Leo 11:58 pm | 23–Leo 4:45 am | 23–Leo 10:25 am | 23–Leo 4:17 pm | 22–Leo 11:02 pm | 23–Leo 3:54 am |
| **Aug** | 23–Vir 6:22 am | 23–Vir 12:15 pm | 23–Vir 6:04 pm | 23–Vir 11:52 pm | 23–Vir 5:48 am | 23–Vir 11:33 am | 23–Vir 5:14 pm | 23–Vir 11:06 pm | 23–Vir 4:53 am | 23–Vir 10:41 am |
| **Sept** | 23–Lib 3:25 am | 23–Lib 11:20 am | 23–Lib 5:10 pm | 23–Lib 9:04 pm | 23–Lib 2:58 am | 23–Lib 8:43 am | 23–Lib 2:25 pm | 23–Lib 8:17 pm | 23–Lib 2:36 am | 23–Lib 7:52 am |
| **Oct** | 23–Sc 12:31 pm | 23–Sc 6:03 pm | 23–Sc 11:53 pm | 24–Sc 5:51 am | 23–Sc 11:44 am | 23–Sc 5:31 pm | 23–Sc 11:18 pm | 24–Sc 5:07 pm | 23–Sc 10:55 am | 23–Sc 4:41 pm |
| **Nov** | 22–Sag 9:15 am | 22–Sag 3:21 pm | 22–Sag 8:55 pm | 23–Sag 2:54 am | 22–Sag 8:46 am | 22–Sag 2:36 pm | 22–Sag 8:28 pm | 23–Sag 2:14 am | 22–Sag 8:00 am | 22–Sag 1:48 pm |
| **Dec** | 21–Cap 10:17 pm | 22–Cap 4:08 am | 22–Cap 9:57 pm | 22–Cap 3:53 pm | 21–Cap 10:45 pm | 22–Cap 3:37 am | 22–Cap 9:34 am | 22–cap 3:18 pm | 21–Cap 9:04 pm | 22–Cap 2:53 am |

| | 1930 | 1931 | 1932 | 1933 | 1934 | 1935 | 1936 | 1937 | 1938 | 1939 |
|---|---|---|---|---|---|---|---|---|---|---|
| Jan | 20-Aq 1:33 pm | 21-Aq 7:18 pm | 20-Aq 1:07 am | 20-Aq 6:53 am | 20-Aq 10:37 am | 20-Aq 6:29 pm | 21-Aq 12:12am | 20-Aq 6:01 am | 20-Aq 11:59 pm | 20-Aq 5:51 pm |
| Feb | 19-Pis 4:00 am | 19-Pis 9:06 am | 19-Pis 3:29 pm | 19-Pis 9:16 pm | 19-Pis 3:02 pm | 19-Pis 8:52 am | 19-Pis 2:33 am | 18-Pis 3:21 pm | 19-Pis 2:20 am | 19-Pis 8:10 pm |
| Mar | 21-Ar 3:30 am | 21-Ar 9:40 am | 20-Ar 2:54 pm | 21-Ar 8:43 pm | 21-Ar 2:28 am | 21-Ar 8:19 am | 20-Ar 1:58 am | 20-Ar 7:45 pm | 21-Ar 1:43 am | 21-Ar 7:29 am |
| Apr | 20-Tau 3:06 pm | 20-Tau 8:40 pm | 20-Tau 2:28 am | 20-Tau 8:19 am | 20-Tau 2:00 pm | 20-Tau 7:50 pm | 20-Tau 1:31 pm | 20-Tau 7:20 pm | 20-Tau 1:15 pm | 20-Tau 6:55 pm |
| May | 21-Gem 2:42 pm | 21-Gem 8:15 pm | 21-Gem 2:07 am | 21-Gem 7:57 am | 21-Gem 1:35 pm | 21-Gem 7:25 pm | 21-Gem 1:08 pm | 21-Gem 6:57 pm | 21-Gem 12:51 pm | 21-Gem 6:27 pm |
| June | 21-Can 11:53 pm | 22-Can 4:28 am | 21-Can 10:23 am | 21-Can 4:12 pm | 21-Can 9:48 pm | 22-Can 3:32 am | 21-Can 9:22 am | 21-Can 3:12 pm | 21-Can 9:04 am | 22-Can 2:40 am |
| July | 23-Leo 10:42 am | 23-Leo 3:21 pm | 22-Leo 9:18 pm | 23-Leo 3:06 am | 23-Leo 8:42 am | 23-Leo 2:33 pm | 22-Leo 8:18 am | 23-Leo 2:07 am | 23-Leo 7:57 am | 23-Leo 1:37 pm |
| Aug | 23-Vir 4:27 pm | 23-Vir 10:10 pm | 23-Vir 4:06 am | 23-Vir 9:53 pm | 23-Vir 3:32 pm | 23-Vir 9:24 pm | 23-Vir 3:11 am | 23-Vir 8:58 am | 23-Vir 2:46 pm | 23-Vir 8:31 pm |
| Sept | 23-Lib 1:35 pm | 23-Lib 7:23 pm | 23-Lib 1:16 pm | 23-Lib 7:01 pm | 23-Lib 10:45 am | 23-Lib 6:38 pm | 23-Lib 12:26 am | 23-Lib 6:13 am | 23-Lib 12:noon | 23-Lib 5:50 pm |
| Oct | 23-Sc 11:25 pm | 24-Sc 4:15 pm | 23-Sc 10:04 am | 23-Sc 3:48 pm | 23-Sc 9:35 pm | 24-Sc 3:29 pm | 23-Sc 10:18 am | 23-Sc 3:06 pm | 23-Sc 8:54 pm | 24-Sc 2:46 am |
| Nov | 22-Sag 7:34 pm | 23-Sag 1:25 pm | 22-Sag 7:10 am | 22-Sag 10:53 pm | 22-Sag 6:44 pm | 23-Sag 12:35 pm | 22-Sag 6:25 pm | 22-Sag 12:17 pm | 22-Sag 6:06 pm | 22-Sag 11:59 pm |
| Dec | 22-Cap 8:40 am | 22-Cap 2:30 pm | 21-Cap 8:14 pm | 22-Cap 1:58 pm | 22-Cap 5:49 am | 22-Cap 1:37 pm | 21-Cap 7:27 pm | 22-Cap 1:22 am | 22-Cap 7:13 am | 22-Cap 1:05 pm |

| | 1940 | 1941 | 1942 | 1943 | 1944 | 1945 | 1946 | 1947 | 1948 |
|---|---|---|---|---|---|---|---|---|---|
| Jan | 20–Aq 11:44 pm | 20–Aq 5:34 am | 20–Aq 11:16 am | 20–Aq 5:20 pm | 20–Aq 11:09 pm | 20–Aq 4:55 am | 20–Aq 10:44 am | 20–Aq 4:23 pm | 20–Aq 10:18 pm |
| Feb | 19–Pis 2:04 pm | 18–Pis 7:59 pm | 19–Pis 1:39 am | 19–Pis 7:41 am | 19–Pis 1:28 pm | 18–Pis 7:15 pm | 19–Pis 1:10 am | 19–Pis 6:53 am | 19–Pis 12:37 pm |
| Mar | 20–Ar 1:24 pm | 20–Ar 7:21 pm | 21–Ar 1:03 am | 21–Ar 7:03 am | 21–Ar 12:49 pm | 20–Ar 6:38 pm | 21–Ar 12:34 pm | 21–Ar 6:13 pm | 20–Ar 11:57 am |
| Apr | 20–Tau 12:51 am | 20–Tau 6:51 am | 20–Tau 12:30 pm | 20–Tau 6:32 pm | 20–Tau 12:18 am | 20–Tau 6:08 am | 20–Tau 12:03 pm | 20–Tau 5:40 pm | 19–Tau 11:25 pm |
| May | 21–Gem 12:23 am | 21–Gem 6:23 am | 21–Gem 12:01 pm | 21–Gem 6:03 pm | 20–Gem 11:51 pm | 22–Gem 5:41 am | 21–Gem 11:34 am | 21–Gem 5:04 pm | 20–Gem 10:58 pm |
| June | 21–Can 8:37 am | 21–Can 2:33 am | 21–Can 8:08 pm | 22–Can 2:13 am | 21–Can 9:03 am | 21–Can 1:52 pm | 21–Can 7:45 pm | 22–Can 1:19 am | 21–Can 7:11 am |
| July | 22–Leo 7:34 pm | 23–Leo 1:26 pm | 23–Leo 6:59 am | 23–Leo 1:05 pm | 22–Leo 6:55 pm | 23–Leo 12:48 am | 23–Leo 6:37 am | 23–Leo 12:12 pm | 22–Leo 6:06 pm |
| Aug | 23–Vir 2:21 am | 23–Vir 8:30 am | 23–Vir 1:50 pm | 23–Vir 7:55 pm | 23–Vir 1:47 am | 23–Vir 7:36 am | 23–Vir 1:23 pm | 23–Vir 7:09 pm | 23–Vir 1:03 am |
| Sept | 23–Lib 11:46 pm | 23–Lib 5:33 am | 23–Lib 11:10 am | 23–Lib 5:12 pm | 23–Lib 11:02 pm | 23–Lib 4:50 am | 23–Lib 10:41 am | 23–Lib 4:29 pm | 23–Lib 10:22 pm |
| Oct | 23–Sc 8:39 am | 23–Sc 2:22 pm | 22–Sc 8:01 pm | 24–Sc 2:09 am | 23–Sc 7:57 am | 23–Sc 1:45 pm | 23–Sc 7:37 pm | 24–Sc 1:27 am | 23–Sc 7:19 am |
| Nov | 22–Sag 5:49 am | 22–Sag 11:38 am | 22–Sag 5:23 pm | 22–Sag 11:22 pm | 22–Sag 5:09 am | 22–Sag 10:56 pm | 22–Sag 4:47 pm | 22–Sag 10:38 pm | 22–Sag 4:29 am |
| Dec | 21–Cap 6:55 pm | 22–Cap 12:44 am | 22–Cap 6:31 am | 22–Cap 12:30 pm | 21–Cap 6:15 pm | 22–Cap 12:04 am | 22–Cap 5:54 pm | 22–Cap 11:44 am | 21–Cap 5:23 pm |

| | 1949 | 1950 | 1951 | 1952 | 1953 | 1954 | 1955 | 1956 | 1957 |
|---|---|---|---|---|---|---|---|---|---|
| Jan | 20-Aq 4:11 pm | 20-Aq 10:00 am | 20-Aq 3:53 pm | 20-Aq 9:38 pm | 20-Aq 3:22 am | 20-Aq 9:14 am | 20-Aq 3:03 pm | 20-Aq 8:49 pm | 20-Aq 2:43 am |
| Feb | 18-Pis 6:27 am | 19-Pis 12:16 am | 19-Pis 6:10 am | 19-Pis 11:57 am | 18-Pis 5:41 pm | 19-Pis 11:33 pm | 19-Pis 5:19 am | 19-Pis 11:05 am | 18-Pis 5:01 pm |
| Mar | 20-Ar 5:49 pm | 20-Ar 11:30 pm | 21-Ar 5:26 am | 20-Ar 11:14 am | 20-Ar 5:01 pm | 20-Ar 10:54 pm | 21-Ar 4:36 am | 20-Ar 10:21 am | 20-Ar 4:17 pm |
| Apr | 20-Tau 5:18 am | 20-Tau 11:00 am | 20-Tau 4:49 pm | 20-Tau 10:37 pm | 19-Tau 4:26 am | 20-Tau 10:20 am | 20-Tau 3:58 pm | 19-Tau 9:44 pm | 20-Tau 3:45 am |
| May | 21-Gem 4:51 am | 21-Gem 10:27 am | 21-Gem 4:15 pm | 20-Gem 10:04 pm | 21-Gem 3:53 am | 21-Gem 9:48 am | 21-Gem 3:25 pm | 20-Gem 9:13 pm | 21-Gem 3:09 am |
| June | 21-Can 1:03 pm | 21-Can 6:37 pm | 22-Can 12:25 am | 21-Can 6:13 am | 21-Can 12:noon | 21-Can 5:55 pm | 21-Can 11:32 pm | 21-Can 5:24 am | 21-Can 11:21 am |
| July | 22-Leo 1:58 pm | 23-Leo 5:30 am | 23-Leo 11:29 am | 22-Leo 5:05 pm | 22-Leo 10:53 pm | 23-Leo 4:45 am | 23-Leo 10:25 am | 22-Leo 4:20 pm | 22-Leo 10:13 pm |
| Aug | 23-Vir 6:49 pm | 23-Vir 12:24 pm | 23-Vir 6:22 pm | 23-Vir 12:03 am | 23-Vir 5:46 am | 23-Vir 11:37 am | 23-Vir 5:19 pm | 22-Vir 11:15 pm | 23-Vir 5:07 pm |
| Sept | 23-Lib 4:05 am | 23-Lib 9:44 am | 23-Lib 3:38 pm | 22-Lib 9:24 pm | 23-Lib 3:07 am | 23-Lib 8:56 am | 23-Lib 2:42 pm | 22-Lib 8:30 pm | 23-Lib 2:27 am |
| Oct | 23-Sc 1:04 pm | 23-Sc 6:48 pm | 23-Sc 12:37 am | 23-Sc 6:22 am | 23-Sc 12:07 pm | 23-Sc 5:58 pm | 23-Sc 11:44 pm | 23-Sc 5:35 am | 23-Sc 11:33 am |
| Nov | 22-Sag 10:17 am | 22-Sag 4:03 pm | 22-Sag 9:52 pm | 22-Sag 3:36 am | 22-Sag 9:23 am | 22-Sag 3:14 pm | 22-Sag 9:02 pm | 22-Sag 2:51 am | 22-Sag 8:45 am |
| Dec | 21-Cap 11:24 am | 22-Cap 5:14 am | 22-Cap 11:01 am | 21-Cap 4:44 pm | 21-Cap 10:22 pm | 22-Cap 4:25 am | 22-Cap 10:12 am | 21-Cap 4:00 pm | 21-Cap 9:49 pm |

| | 1958 | 1959 | 1960 | 1961 | 1962 | 1963 | 1964 | 1965 | 1966 |
|---|---|---|---|---|---|---|---|---|---|
| **Jan** | 20-Aq 2:20 pm | 20-Aq 2:20 pm | 20-Aq 8:11 pm | 20-Aq 2:02 am | 20-Aq 7:49 am | 20-Aq 1:55 pm | 19-Aq 7:43 pm | 20-Aq 1:30 am | 20-Aq 8:21 am |
| **Feb** | 18-Pis 10:49 pm | 19-Pis 4:38 pm | 19-Pis 10:26 am | 18-Pis 6:27 pm | 18-Pis 10:16 pm | 19-Pis 4:09 am | 19-Pis 10:25 am | 18-Pis 3:49 pm | 18-Pis 9:39 pm |
| **Mar** | 20-Ar 10:06 pm | 21-Ar 3:55 am | 20-Ar 9:43 am | 20-Ar 5:27 am | 20-Ar 9:30 pm | 21-Ar 3:20 am | 20-Ar 9:43 am | 20-Ar 3:05 am | 20-Ar 8:53 am |
| **Apr** | 20-Tau 9:28 am | 20-Tau 3:17 pm | 20-Tau 10:06 pm | 20-Tau 2:33 am | 20-Tau 8:51 am | 20-Tau 2:37 pm | 19-Tau 9:00 pm | 20-Tau 2:27 pm | 20-Tau 8:12 am |
| **May** | 21-Gem 8:52 am | 21-Gem 2:38 pm | 20-Gem 8:33 pm | 21-Gem 1:51 am | 21-Gem 8:17 am | 21-Gem 1:59 pm | 20-Gem 8:33 pm | 21-Gem 1:27 pm | 21-Gem 7:33 am |
| **June** | 21-Can 4:57 pm | 21-Can 10:50 pm | 21-Can 4:43 am | 21-Can 10:12 am | 21-Can 4:24 pm | 21-Can 11:04 pm | 21-Can 4:43 am | 21-Can 9:56 pm | 21-Can 3:33 pm |
| **July** | 23-Leo 3:51 am | 23-Leo 9:45 am | 22-Leo 5:38 am | 22-Leo 9:12 pm | 23-Leo 3:19 am | 23-Leo 9:00 am | 22-Leo 3:38 pm | 22-Leo 8:49 pm | 23-Leo 2:24 am |
| **Aug** | 23-Vir 10:47 am | 23-Vir 4:44 pm | 22-Vir 10:35 pm | 23-Vir 3:46 am | 23-Vir 10:13 am | 23-Vir 3:58 pm | 22-Vir 10:35 pm | 23-Vir 3:43 am | 23-Vir 9:18 am |
| **Sept** | 23-Lib 5:10 am | 23-Lib 2:09 pm | 22-Lib 8:00 pm | 23-Lib 1:26 am | 23-Lib 7:35 am | 23-Lib 1:24 pm | 22-Lib 8:00 pm | 23-Lib 1:06 am | 23-Lib 6:43 am |
| **Oct** | 23-Sc 5:12 am | 23-Sc | 23-Sc 5:03 am | 23-Sc 10:46 am | 23-Sc 4:41 pm | 23-Sc 11:30 pm | 23-Sc 5:03 am | 23-Sc 10:11 am | 23-Sc 3:52 pm |
| **Nov** | 22-Sag 2:30 am | 22-Sag 8:23 pm | 22-Sag 2:19 am | 22-Sag 8:10 am | 22-Sag 2:02 pm | 22-Sag 7:50 pm | 22-Sag 2:19 am | 22-Sag 7:30 am | 22-Sag 1:15 pm |
| **Dec** | 22-Cap 3:40 am | 22-Cap 9:35 am | 21-Cap 5:27 pm | 21-Cap 9:25 pm | 22-Cap 3:15 pm | 22-Cap 9:02 am | 21-Cap 3:27 pm | 21-Cap 8:41 pm | 22-Cap 2:29 pm |

| | 1967 | 1968 | 1969 | 1970 | 1971 | 1972 | 1973 | 1974 | 1975 |
|---|---|---|---|---|---|---|---|---|---|
| Jan | 20–Aq 1:05 pm | 20–Aq 6:54 pm | 20–Aq 12:30 am | 20–Aq 6:25 am | 20–Aq 12:14 pm | 20–Aq 6:00 pm | 19–Aq 11:49 pm | 20–Aq 5:47 am | 20–Aq 11:37 am |
| Feb | 19–Pis 3:25 pm | 19–Pis 9:11 pm | 18–Pis 2:47 pm | 18–Pis 8:43 pm | 19–Pis 2:28 am | 19–Pis 8:12 am | 18–Pis 2:02 pm | 18–Pis 8:00 pm | 19–Pis 1:51 am |
| Mar | 21–Ar 2:37 pm | 20–Ar 8:22 pm | 20–Ar 2:08 pm | 20–Ar 7:59 pm | 21–Ar 1:28 am | 20–Ar 7:22 am | 20–Ar 1:13 pm | 20–Ar 7:08 pm | 21–Ar 12:58 am |
| Apr | 20–Tau 1:56 am | 19–Tau 7:42 pm | 20–Tau 1:18 am | 20–Tau 5:16 am | 20–Tau 12:54 pm | 19–Tau 6:38 pm | 20–Tau 12:31 am | 20–Tau 5:19 am | 20–Tau 12:08 pm |
| May | 21–Gem 1:19 pm | 20–Gem 7:07 pm | 21–Gem 12:41 am | 21–Gem 6:32 am | 21–Gem 12:16 pm | 20–Gem 6:00 pm | 20–Gem 11:54 pm | 21–Gem 5:37 am | 21–Gem 1:25 pm |
| June | 21–Can 4:23 pm | 21–Can 1:13 am | 21–Can 6:55 am | 21–Can 2:43 am | 21–Can 8:21 am | 21–Can 2:07 am | 21–Can 8:01 am | 21–Can 1:38 pm | 21–Can 7:27 pm |
| July | 23–Leo 8:16 am | 22–Leo 2:13 pm | 22–Leo 8:05 pm | 23–Leo 1:38 pm | 23–Leo 7:15 am | 22–Leo 1:03 pm | 22–Leo 6:56 pm | 23–Leo 12:30 am | 23–Leo 7:23 am |
| Aug | 23–Vir 3:13 pm | 22–Vir 9:52 pm | 22–Vir 2:35 am | 23–Vir 6:35 am | 23–Vir 2:16 pm | 22–Vir 8:04 pm | 23–Vir 1:55 am | 23–Vir 7:29 am | 23–Vir 1:24 pm |
| Sept | 23–Lib 12:38 pm | 22–Lib 6:26 pm | 23–Lib 12:07 am | 23–Lib 5:59 am | 23–Lib 11:47 am | 22–Lib 5:34 pm | 22–Lib 11:22 pm | 23–Lib 4:59 am | 23–Lib 10:56 am |
| Oct | 23–Sc 9:44 pm | 23–Sc 1:30 am | 23–Sc 9:03 am | 23–Sc 3:05 pm | 22–Sc 8:53 pm | 23–Sc 2:42 am | 23–Sc 8:31 am | 23–Sc 2:12 pm | 23–Sc 8:07 pm |
| Nov | 22–Sag 7:05 pm | 22–Sag 12:59 am | 22–Sag 6:23 am | 22–Sag 12:25 pm | 22–Sag 6:15 pm | 22–Sag 12:04 am | 22–Sag 5:55 am | 22–Sag 11:39 am | 22–Sag 5:32 pm |
| Dec | 22–Cap 8:17 pm | 21–Cap 2:00 pm | 21–Cap 7:44 pm | 22–Cap 1:36 am | 22–Cap 5:26 am | 21–Cap 1:14 pm | 21–Cap 7:09 pm | 22–Cap 12:57 am | 22–Cap 7:47 am |

# 12

## Sagittarius: The Big Picture

Because the twelve signs of the zodiac represent twelve ways of being in the world, you will know about yourself and why *you* tend toward certain types of behavior and attitudes by knowing more about Sagittarius. If you read about the elements and qualities in "Defining Terms," for instance, you'll find out that you are one of the active, outgoing *fire signs,* and, as one of the *mutable signs,* you adapt easily to people and situations. You can "meet yourself" in the Sagittarian prototype described in "Twelve Places at the Table," and your big, benevolent planetary ruler, Jupiter, provides some excellent clues about the Sagittarian style.

However, even with these broad brush strokes, your Sagittarius portrait is still a bit abstract; to "see yourself" in totality, you need more of the background filled in. That means going back to some very important basics: your ninth-place position in the zodiac, your picture-symbol, the centaur-archer, and the "shorthand figure" or glyph that astrologers use to indicate Sagittarius when they draw up a horoscope. In Sagittarius, as in every astrological sign, these three factors link together, forming a strong "chain of meaning" that holds together everything that is Sagittarius.

When the sun reaches zero degrees Sagittarius on or about November 22, the days are becoming shorter and the nights longer. Ninth-sign Sagittarius marks the end of the fall season, and culminates with the winter solstice on December 22, the darkest point of the seasonal year and the beginning of the winter sleep. The paradox is that from earliest times this period has been one of joyful expectancy; the winter solstice is a time of celebration, because, once again, the earth will begin to "turn toward the light" and be reborn. Hanukkah is the Jewish "Festival of Lights," and the Christian Christmas has its roots in much earlier pagan celebrations that were also connected with divine births. In a sense, the winter solstice is the birthday of the sun. It is difficult for modern people to comprehend the momentous importance such points in a seasonal year had for cultures whose very life depended on the ability to survive from harvest in the fall to replanting in the spring. Therefore, as precursor of the winter solstice, Sagittarius is a sign connected with all things hopeful, optimistic and joyful.

Via its ninth-place position in the zodiac, Sagittarius symbolizes that period of human life in which the individual has gathered all his vital forces together (during the previous sign Scorpio), and is now ready to move out into the world, understand it, and bring a new latitude of vision to others. Sagittarius is the sign connected with law and order—not in the sense of repressive and punitive measures, but in the sense of organizing society into a working whole.

Sagittarius' picture-symbol, the archer-centaur, is one of the most appropriate in the zodiac for the sign it represents. The centaur is half-man, half-horse and represents the internal battle of the Sagittarian between wanting to be the most noble of humans and the desire for the most "bestial" things the world has to offer. The archer aims for the highest; the horse threatens to drag Sagittarius down to the lowest.

In myth and legend, Sagittarius appears in a number of forms. To the Babylonians, he was the archer-god of war, the strong one. In the Old Testament, Sagittarius appears as the tribe of Joseph. His father Jacob, prime minister and lawgiver to the Egyptian Pharoah, says of Joseph: "The archers have sorely grieved him . . . but his bow abode in strength. Joseph is a fruitful bough, whose branches run over the wall." As Joseph was favored, so is Sagittarius often considered a favored sign which is blessed with a special kind of luck.

The most famous "incarnation" of Sagittarius is the immortal centaur, Chiron. Unlike the other centaurs, who were rather crude, Chiron was gifted in philosophy and the arts. He was also a master and teacher to ancient greats like Jason and Asclepios (the great doctor who learned healing from Chiron). Well-meaning Chiron was accidentally wounded by a poisoned arrow Hercules was aiming at the "bad" centaurs, and suffered such severe pain that he asked to be relieved of his immortality on earth. Zeus, in reward for his great services to mankind, released Chiron into the heavens where he now resides as the constellation Sagittarius. In many ways, the "evolved" Sagittarian is the real-life embodiment of Chiron—wise, just, a great teacher, and "philosophical" in the best sense of the word. Like Chiron, Sagittarius exists on earth, but has an acute awareness of higher things.

The glyph or shorthand symbol astrologers use to indicate Sagittarius (see illustration) is also "an open book." It is quite evidently the arrow that the archer part of Sagittarius has at his disposal. The problem for the human Sagittarian is to aim the arrow in some definite direction, and not to scatter his/her shots. Sagittarius must also learn to use the arrow only when he/she needs it—and to remember that it is not intended as a weapon of war. It is Sagittarius' link with the higher aspirations of man and should be used as such. The good Sagittarian always aims at the truth, as well. The Sagittarian glyph is also interpreted as the parts of the body this sign is said to rule: the hips, thighs, and leg joints. Physical mobility is very important to the Sagittarian, because he/she does not like to be confined in any way. Interpreted in this manner, the symbol also says to the Sagittarian that his/her mission is a very active one, and that he/she is expected to cover a lot of territory, both mentally and physically, in the course of a lifetime.

# 13

## Sagittarius: Objectives and Obstacles

### A Game Plan for Being the Most Successful Sagittarius Under the Sun

Every astrological sign is a set of possibilities; being born under a particular sign does not guarantee you *are* or *will be* all those things that sign is capable of being. Nor would you want to. There are positive characteristics to be cultivated, as well as negative ones you can avoid or overcome. Living "à la carte"—selecting what you want from all the options available—is open to you, within the overall context of your sign.

You can, of course, order the "prix fixe" dinner by living your life as it comes without attempting to direct it. The choice is yours, which is one good reason it is incorrect to regard your astrological destiny as preordained. You are responsible for how you embody your sign and what results from that embodiment.

Astrologically speaking, your life as a sign is a journey with a starting point, the raw or "primitive" end of the side, and a destination, the evolved or "ideal" realization of that sign. Once again, you don't have to take the full trip; there are plenty of exits if you choose to use them, and few people are ever totally "finished." But if you at least know where you are going and what potential booby traps lie along the way, you will be way ahead of the game.

Regard the following as a "map" and use it in charting your course. The most successful way to be the best of your astrological sign is to work with it, in full knowledge of its up side and its down side. The happiest people of any astrological sign are those who aim high and are not afraid to stretch their understanding of themselves in order to reach their goal.

## Where Sagittarius Starts

In such a "fortunate" sign, even the worst of Sagittarians are rarely evil or malicious types. Ancient astrologers described Sagittarian faults as the kind that are "easily pardoned." The primitive or unevolved Sagittarian rarely hurts anyone other than him-/herself, although they may hurt themselves very badly. Astrological tradition tells us there are three potential levels for the Sagittarian: the gypsy, the student, and the philosopher. While many are middle-of-the-roaders, too many Sagittarians fall into the gypsy category. These are the people born under this sign who breeze through life, forming few attachments, never getting organized, and leaving chaos in their paths. Like the true gypsy, their main interest is in moving around, but rarely with a specific destination in mind. Often these Sagittarians also have a rough manner that is very unattractive. Constantly on the prowl, they develop very little loyalty to anyone or anything. In fact, a lot of Sagittarians—both male and female—can not only be promiscuous, but even cruel to romantic partners. Again, the intention is not to hurt, but the abrupt ending to relationships that is typical of this type of Sagittarian can leave others devastated.

The unevolved Sagittarian has any or all of the vices connected with excess, whether it's drinking, gambling, overeating, uncontrolled sexuality, or some other indulgence. Buried deep in this kind of Sagittarian is the desire for *understanding through experience*. However, most of them never get in touch with this critical part of their personality, and go on indulging themselves for the pure joy of it, often ending up down and out because of it. Here are some buzz words by which you can recognize the unevolved or primitive type of Sagittarian:

| | |
|---|---|
| Sloppy | Irresponsible |
| Wasteful | Insincere (but pleasant about it) |
| Escapist | Boisterous/boorish |
| Dogmatic | Undisciplined |
| Tactless | An exaggerator |

### Where Sagittarius Can Go

From the lowest form of Sagittarius, the wandering gypsy, to the highest form, the wise philosopher, is a mighty big leap, perhaps the biggest journey one can take in the zodiac. In some ways, the Sagittarian destiny is the hardest for anyone to get to on a practical level in life. Simply put, the destiny of the higher Sagittarian is to achieve an *understanding of the ultimate meaning of life.* To become the great philosopher/teacher like the wise centaur Chiron. For even the "best," however, life usually ends up being a ceaseless quest for understanding. But, the evolved Sagittarian, in expanding his awareness, goes after those experiences and activities that have real meaning, rather than empty pleasures. He/she approaches life with the zest and enthusiasm that is the Sagittarian birthright and doesn't shrink from any kind of experience, no matter how unfamiliar. The good Sagittarian is like a good explorer; he/she knows what he/she is looking for, and isn't afraid to seek in out-of-the-way places to find it. Though there are many Sagittarians involved in lifework of a physical nature, the true Sagittarian is a mental explorer, an armchair traveler who can take that leap of imagination and grapple with the most difficult concepts. It is also possible for the restless Sagittarian to curb his/her incessant need for mobility and form excellent relationships. However, he/she will also have reached a stage of self-understanding that is far above the average. Here are some buzz words by which you can recognize the "evolved" or higher Sagittarian type:

| | |
|---|---|
| Candid but tactful | Jovial/adaptable |
| Kind/compassionate | Dependable |
| Realistically optimistic | Generous |
| Versatile | Adventurous |
| Broadminded | Just and fair |

### How Sagittarus Can Get There

One of the most important inner strengths the Sagittarian can develop is his/her openness to new ideas. While in some it can be mere restlessness and a tendency to get bored very easily, the Sagittarian's need for new experience can be a blessing rather than a curse. It is very un-Sagittarian to get stuck in a rut, and the best of the sign know exactly when it's time to jump ship and go on to something new. If the Sagittarian is really honest with him-/herself, he/she will realize that the natural optimism of this sign is a feeling that life really does mean something and is worth doing something about. This sign has a built-in mechanism to dispel doom and gloom—both for him-/herself and others—and should make the most of this inner resource.

Sometimes life requires great courage in order not to turn one's back on it; the Sagittarian should learn to use his/her capacity to trust, and the great moral courage that comes with it. Most Sagittarians have some kind of goal or ideal, should identify it early on in life, and then use it as the guiding star that will always indicate where the shots of the archer should be aimed. That way, Sagattarius can maintain a sense of direction and have a reason to get up every morning, no matter how dark the day may be.

### Potential Pitfalls

It is all too easy for Sagittarians to be blinded by their own optimistic natures. It is sad but true that it is possible to be *too* trusting in the world we live in. Sagittarius is so rarely suspicious or hesitant about new people and new ideas that it is possible for Sagittarius to be totally defenseless against the manipulation and detrimental purposes of others. Hasty judgments are often bad judgments, and Sagittarius is particularly prone to make them. Similarly, the eager, optimistic Sagittarian can easily overextend him-/herself in a lot of directions, particularly the financial. A character in one of Charles Dickens' novels, Mr. Micawber, is the ultimate Sagittarian. No matter how flat broke he is, his attitude is "something will always turn up." Unfortunately, it doesn't always, and many a Sagittarian has found him-/herself holding an empty bag when they thought it would be full of gold. Don't get cynical, Sagittarius, but do get a little more realistic.

# 14

## Pairing Off with Sagittarius

### Your Compatibility with Other Signs of the Zodiac

Since there are only twelve signs of the zodiac, it would be unusual to go through life without having to interact with each of them at one time or another. Obviously, your astrological makeup is more complex than your Sagittarius sun sign, but there are some basic truths about how you tend to react when face to face with someone of another sun sign. If you have read about "The Geometry of Relationships," you already know that being a fire sign means Sagittarius relates more easily to certain elements than to others. Now, getting more specific, you will see what the odds are on your matchups with each of the other signs, including your own.

When people talk about "relationships," they are usually referring to the romantic kind, and there is no doubt that since time immemorial love has been observed to have a great deal to do with keeping the earth revolving in its orbit. However, we also have a lot of other personal interactions, from important ones, like boss-employee and parent-child to more casual ones, like waitress-patron, cabdriver-rider, and buddy-buddy. The general rules that follow apply in all cases; just change the language a little and do a bit of interpretation. You will find that there is more truth than poetry in the matter of astrology compatibility.

***Sagittarius with Aries***   There's a lot of volatility here, as in all fire-fire pair-offs. In this case, there is a real chance for a long-term relationship, mainly because Sagittarius will simply love Aries' "childish" ways, but not take a punitive atttude toward them. However, Sagittarius could get a little pedantic and authoritative, which Aries will have a problem with. All in all, however, you are two honest, sincere, friendly types who really deserve each other. This is good in business too.

***Sagittarius with Taurus***   You two are likely to get on each others nerves right from the start. For one thing, Taurus moves too slowly for you, and would rather stay in one place a lot of the time. Taurus, on the other hand, will find your breezy ways very annoying; he/she wants more certainty than you bring to the table. As a business partner, Taurus would be excellent for you, making sure you don't go overboard financially in your enthusiasm.

***Sagittarius with Gemini***   You are a deeper thinker, but you will admire Gemini's active, inquiring mind. As mutable signs, you also don't get hung up on little things that don't mean much in the larger scheme of things. However, unless one of you has a big dose of stability in his/her horoscope, you could be a rather variable pair who have a lot of trouble getting it together.

***Sagittarius with Cancer***   Take care in dealing with Cancer, particularly romantically. He/she is much shrewder than you and could end up breaking your honest heart. Not that Cancer would lie to you; the problem is that this highly emotional sign may finally decide you are not a safe enough bet, and call the whole thing off before you are ready for it. In the long run, it wouldn't work anyway—and you are able to take rejection with a philosophical attitude, for the most part.

***Sagittarius with Leo***    Though you are both fire signs, you may be rather put off by Leo's bombastic ways. You've got a few opinions of your own, and you don't like to be constantly upstaged. On the other hand, you two could have a wonderful time just playing around. For a mad, fun affair, you couldn't find a better partner. In business, you two would stimulate each other a lot—maybe even too much. You are both gamblers at heart, and you would understand each other's tendency to be a "high roller."

***Sagittarius with Virgo***    You would be very good for Virgo, and in some ways, he/she could be good for you. Sagittarius could open up a lot of doors the timid sign of Virgo is usually too scared to even knock on, and Virgo could help you to get your act together. If you can take Virgo's tendency to nag, and if he/she won't get bent out of shape by your footloose manner, all will go well. However, there are a fair number of ifs here, and you should proceed with caution.

***Sagittarius with Libra***    Though he/she may maintain a cool facade, Libra will be more than a little moved by you. After all, your fire-sign nature is just what air-sign Libra needs to warm up. No matter what your sex, you will find Libra a wonderfully gentle creature and moderate your ways accordingly. Together, you could be terrific. Remember, however, that when Libra takes a partner, he/she can't live alone anymore. Make sure you are sure.

***Sagittarius with Scorpio***    Scorpio is much too possessive for freedom-loving Sagittarius, but that isn't all the bad news. With your sense of fair play and open attitudes, you are likely to find Scorpio too overbearing and emotional. In some ways, you could learn a lot from each other, but it may not be worth the hurt you both could suffer in the process. As a team in business this would be great; Scorpio could provide just the right touch of practicality for your high-flying ideas.

***Sagittarius with Sagittarius***    This has been known to work, but only under some very special conditions—like open marriage. If such arrangements suit you, enter into a romantic relationship with your eyes open. However, even if you give each other plenty of room, you've still got the problem of two very high-powered individuals who could easily wear each other out. Why not shake hands and remain the best of friends?

***Sagittarius with Capricorn***    You could be very impressed by this individual who seems to know exactly where he/she is going. Capricorn will be fascinated by your ability to roll with the punches. However, in a permanent relationship you might find that your goals are too far apart, and that there is not a great deal of mutual agreement about what life is all about. And yet, like Scorpio, Capricorn would be another excellent business manager for you.

***Sagittarius with Aquarius***    This could be love at first sight—even if neither of you appears "smitten" right off. It may start out as the best of friendships, and gradually you will find you have your arms around each other. You are two excellent specimens of humanity if you live up to your true astrological natures. You two will take a lot of trips together, both the mental and the physical kind.

***Sagittarius with Pisces***    Where Pisces' twisting, turning mind puts some people off, you find it fascinating. At least here is someone who is willing to "explore" higher things. In the long run, however, Pisces is a bit *too* flaky for slightly flaky you, no matter how mature you both may have become. You've also got too much drive for easygoing Pisces, and he/she might not be able to keep up with you.

# 15

## The Sagittarius Sex Role Dilemma

One of the most important ways in which the twelve signs of the zodiac are divided is into "masculine" signs and "feminine" signs, and there are six of each. The reason is simple: As one sign follows the other in the zodiac, they alternate energies, much like the Yin/Yang principle of eastern philosophy. The universe is made up of opposites that complement each other; light and dark, hot and cold, black and white, hard and soft. One is not better than the other; rather, each is essential to the existence of its opposite. In other words, you can't have one without the other.

The six fire and air signs are "masculine," since fire and air are connected with *active, assertive, outgoing* energy.

| | |
|---|---|
| Aries | Gemini |
| Leo | Libra |
| Sagittarius | Aquarius |

The six water and earth signs are "feminine," because water and earth represent *reactive, inner-directed, receptive* energy.

| | |
|---|---|
| Taurus | Cancer |
| Virgo | Scorpio |
| Capricorn | Pisces |

To put it simply, *the masculine fire and air signs are positive, while the earth and water signs are negative.* To remain neutral and avoid placing a higher value on one or the other kind of energy (or sign) it is useful to think of a battery with positive and negative poles. Without both, it simply doesn't work.

Though the masculine-feminine division of the signs has nothing whatever to do with human physical sexuality or sexual preference, it has very important implications for human behavior. Bluntly put, women born into male signs can be more "masculine"/achieving/competitive than men born into female signs. Both men and women born into signs that match their own sex may overemphasize the behaviorial and attitudes connected with that gender. The "ideal" person, psychologically and metaphysically speaking, has a healthy mix of both masculine and feminine attitudes. Without at least some of both, we cannot be whole people able to encompass and understand the total range of human emotions, desires, drives, and goals. Since none of us is perfect, just about everyone could stand a bit more "gender blending." Your astrological sign offers some excellent clues about how you can accomplish that.

The Sagittarian sex role dilemma is particularly deep for both the males and the females born under this sign. Sagittarius is the third and last of the fire signs, and therefore the least "personal." The Sagittarian's fiery ardor is often directed to success and great causes in life rather than relationships. As a masculine sign, Sagittarius is outer- rather than inner-directed, so therefore even farther away from that part of us that is concerned with emotion and relationships. For Sagittarian women, the situation is potentially disastrous—unless they make a tremendous effort to get in touch with their feminine selves, and develop their capacity to be the nurturing, supportive people they are by virtue of their physical sex. Sagittarian men are so far away from their "inner woman" that they have a great deal of

127

difficulty relating to females, sometimes really prefer-ring the company of men, and regarding women as total sex objects. Therefore, Sagittarian men must also do a lot of soul-searching in order to balance their super-masculinity with that softer, more caring part of them that is really there. Keep these things in mind as you read the following Sagittarius portraits, and you will better understand the "why" of your Sagittarius behavior.

# 16

## The Sagittarian Female

### Better Buddy Than Sweetheart

Another good handle for the Sagittarian woman would be "Lady Luck." Many are born with such good mental and physical equipment that they seem to breeze through life, experiencing the very best. It sometimes seems as if their accomplishments are achieved effortlessly. This is, of course, rarely the case, but more than one Sagittarian female has asked herself in the middle of the night, "when is my lucky streak going to break?" However, in the very next mental breath, she might well ask, "but why can't I find somebody to love?" No matter how "feminine" a particular Sagittarian woman may be, there is something in her direct manner and sure movements that makes her seem much more like an adolescent boy than a full-grown woman. And though she really wants to be known for her intelligence and abilities, there is always a nagging part of her that worries and wonders why men don't appreciate her as a woman. One reason may well be that she developed anything but a good image of the female in her own childhood. Sagittarian women typically grow up in households where daddy was not only the boss, but also a man to be admired. Whatever his real accomplishments, the Sagittarian girl saw his position as far preferable to that of her mother, whom she often pitied rather than emulated. Tremendously likable, Sagittarian women usually have lots of friends of both sexes. But, when it comes to sex itself, they may so devalue their own femininity that they can't put it together with caring.

*As a child,* the Sagittarian girl was probably the apple of her father's eye—at least for a while. However, after her cute and cuddly first years are over, she may find it more difficult to get her father's attention. Many Sagittarian women feel emotionally deprived because of a "no win" childhood situation; being cute and cuddly does not come naturally to the Sagittarian girl. Conversely, if she trys to be like her "all-man" daddy, her tomboy ways are often misunderstood by both parents. On top of it, she may appear so competent, so sound that she is given independence before she is really ready for it. Sagittarian girls rarely have trouble in school; in fact, they often shine. They are also easily disciplined as long as their parents understand that their measures must always be fair and logical, and that the Sagittarian girl really wants an answer when she says, "Why must I?"

*As a young woman,* the Sagittarian female often rushes into the career world like a kid in a candy store, trying to decide which of many interesting directions she should apply her considerable talents. If she gets some good guidance and lands in the right spot, she often experiences instant success. Her biggest trouble in the business world is likely to be her "itchy feet"; Sagittarians of both sexes often feel like moving on as soon as they've perfected a job. The wise employer will continue to give the Sagittarian female more and more responsibility to keep her interested.

The "masculine principle" is so strong in the Sagittarian female that it can be used profitably for career development. However, unless she incorporates it with the woman she is, she will have a disappointing romantic life. Some young Sagittarian women (really wanting "intellectual" companionship) project such an unconscious sexuality through their body language that men assume they immediately want a physical relationship. Gradually this type of Sagittarian woman gets the idea that all men are interested in is sex and turns off altogether. The sad part is that what these females really want is the impossible "perfect male" just like dear old dad was (in her mind). Most men are totally confused by Sagittarian women, though they can't help but like them. Sagittarius is probably the friendliest sign in the zodiac in every respect. The women are so frank and outspoken, that they have a kind of awkward charm that is completely irresistible. The problem really is that they so resist their own femininity they can totally mess up the emotional side of their existence.

*As a mate,* the Sagittarian woman insists on doing her own thing. It's not that she will necessarily have extramarital affairs, but she will insist on freedom of mind and movement. Instinctively, the Sagittarian woman knows that if someone tries to restrict her, she will be miserably unhappy. Marriage does not come naturally to her, anyway, so a possessive mate would compound her problem. However, if she chooses her partner carefully and spells things out in advance, the Sagittarian woman can be the perfect life partner—at least for a strong, independent man. Resilient and optimistic, she is able to bounce back from any life crisis and plunge back into things with enthusiasm. She will be more than willing to take on her share; in fact, most Sagittarian wives automatically expect to combine marriage with a job or career. Sagittarian women almost never play emotional games either; if something is wrong, they will tell their mates about it in no uncertain terms. And, if she's come to terms with her femininity, she is a healthy sexual partner who will rarely say "I'm too tired." But the best part about the Sagittarian wife is that she is her own woman—and expects her mate to have the same strong sense of individuality that she has. She won't be a leaner, nor will she make great demands on her mate's time; she's much too busy with her many interests to ever turn into a nag.

*As a mother*, the Sagittarian woman is often a shock to her peers. They may have gotten used to the fact that housework is very low on her list of priorities, but they may regard her casual ways with her children as just short of neglect. Not that she won't spend time with her children; the Sagittarian woman will often find their company preferable to that of older, more inhibited people. However, what she really wants to do is play with them. If they get a little dirty, so what? If their clothes need a little patching, the Sagittarian mother's attitude is that her children will simply rip them again. Similarly, she will rarely force them to eat something simply because it is good or them. Sagittarian women enjoy life and want their children to enjoy it as well. However, underneath her playful approach is a deep, abiding love—and a conviction that her children are the greatest. She will help them to become even greater by teaching them that life is a wonderful adventure and that honesty and tolerance are the world's highest virtues.

# 17

## The Sagittarian Male

### Don Quixote

Like their Sagittarian sisters, Sagittarian men are often extremely popular and instantly liked by those they meet. Their honesty and enthusiasm can be contagious, and they often have a marvelous, wacky, slightly slapstick sense of humor. If a Sagittarian man has evolved, he also has a wonderful kind of "cosmic humor" that puts the world and all its foibles into comforting perspective. However, the Sagittarian male is far from perfect—especially if he has not spent some time getting acquainted with himself. He is so totally devoted to the "masculine principle" that he can be very one-sided. It is very difficult for many Sagittarian males to break through the wall between their all-male minds and that other half of all of us that really needs love and support and can give it to others. Not that he won't always help out a friend in need; if anything, these men can be too generous with their time and money. What he has a problem with is giving in the emotional sense. Many Sagittarian males grew up worshipping their fathers and wanting to be as successful and masculine as they were. Sagittarian men often choose the company of men over women and can be categorized as the "locker room type." Sports, outdoor activities, and other male interests are what really make such

Sagittarian men comfortable. As for women, they tend to separate sexual partners from friends, and apply a different set of standards to each. For most Sagittarian men, it is very difficult to put the sexual act—which is a fine sport—together with feelings of companionship and, though they don't like to use the term, romantic love.

*As a child,* the Sagittarian male is likely to be a terror— the proverbial "Peck's Bad Boy" who is always in trouble with his elders, but rarely for anything terribly serious. He is usually extremely active and fond of all kinds of rough sports; the practical joke is likely to be his signature. What the Sagittarius boy lacks in grace, he makes up in good humor and a generally straightforward, honest nature. Parents of Sagittarius boys must take care not to restrict them—either physically or mentally—unless there is real danger. The Sagittarius child who is hemmed in early in life can make up for it later on by "busting out all over"—not always in very productive directions. Sagittarius boys can be a real heartache for the clingy, overprotective mother (or father); the way to prove you love a Sagittarian boy is to leave him alone and let him go his own way.

*As a young man,* the Sagittarian male sets out into the world anxious to "score," in more ways than one. He'll seek out some kind of work that absorbs him, but doesn't tie him down. With his fresh outlook and winning ways, he will have little difficulty getting hired, and his quick mind and abundant energy will usually make him reasonably successful. One job is often not enough for him, and he'll often have something else "on the side"; after all, he needs a lot of cash to support his generous ways and usually abundant life-style.

Although he will rarely admit it, the young Sagittarian male is often very anxious about his own sexuality. He is so male-oriented that he often makes very fast friendships with his own sex; the feelings he has toward his male companions can be so strong they seem to him like "love." Most have no problem with heterosexual physical sex; in fact, some young Sagittarian men try to experience more sexual encounters than Don Juan. The problem is that he looks for sex with one woman and companionship with another. It is not unlike the Sagittarian male to have a female buddy who is just dying to become a lot more to him. Such relationships can spell a lot of heartache for the women involved, because they can't seem to engage Sagittarius totally. Though most Sagittarian males would rather die than hurt anyone, they can make an awful lot of women unhappy in the course of a lifetime.

*As a mate,* the Sagittarian man is finally able to put it together—usually. Ideally, he has gotten over his fear of emotion (which he tends to regard as a weakness) and has admitted that he really needs somebody to love and live with. A Sagittarian male can be the most "faithful" of husbands—at least in the mental sense. That is because he has found that one woman who has changed his idea about females. Because Sagittarius is such a restless sign, and because the men have such a need for adventure, the Sagittarian husband may be temporarily smitten from time to time, but home is really where his heart is, and he will always return.

These men, like their Sagittarian sisters, are delightfully upbeat, undemanding partners. A messy household will not upset him too much—as long as his wife has neglected it in favor of some pursuit they can talk about. The wife of a Sagittarian man should be forewarned that if she settles down into a dull routine, and becomes "dull" herself, it can spell death to the marriage. Sagittarian males don't require much in the way of creature comforts, but they can be totally turned off by a mate who lets household routine turn her into a drag.

*As a father,* the Sagittarian man may not come into his own until his children are a bit older. He can be terrified by a delicate little infant, and will be frank about saying he can't handle it, in any sense of the word. However, when his children are finally mobile, he will have no greater pleasure than romping and playing with them, and taking them on all kinds of excursions. He can also be a surprisingly strict disciplinarian. Like the Sagittarian mother, the Sagittarian father won't inhibit normal "kid stuff"; in fact, he'll just love their pranks and practical jokes. What he will demand from them is absolute honesty and fairness. And he will usually get it, because the Sagittarian brand of fathering is so open and nonpunitive that his children will not hesitate to tell him the truth.

# 18

# Sagittarius Help Wanted

## Selecting a Career/Your On-the-Job Style

A vitally important aspect of a successful Sagittarian game plan is making sure you land in the right job or career—i.e., the one that best suits your native talents and tendencies. It is more than a truism that people perform better doing what comes naturally. There are some "natural" careers for Sagittarius, and they have several common denominators. One is the principle of reaching and stretching, in both the mental and the physical senses. Another is figuring the odds, and the gambling shows up in many careers. It is not possible to list *all* the specific jobs a Sagittarian should do well, but there are some "Sagittarian images" that provide useful guidelines. Though you may not literally end up *doing* any of these things, if you try to conjure up an idea of what it takes to do the following jobs, you'll have a better handle on what kind of inner resources Sagittarian people have available to them for career success.

| | |
|---|---|
| Stockbroker/commodities traders | Space scientist/astronaut |
| Veterinarian (especially for larger animals) | Priest/clergyman |
| Coach or physical education Teacher | Jockey |

| Language scholar/teacher | Politician/lawmaker |
| Importer or exporter | Salesperson (of anything) |
| Lawyer/judge | Publisher/writer |

Equally important to finding the best job slot for you is understanding how your Sagittarius sun sign affects your modus operandi on the job and your potential for moving up. Every sun sign has certain "success skills" that can smooth and widen the career path, as well as "blind spots" that can cause roadblocks. The more you know about both, the better off you will be.

The typical Sagittarian's greatest success skill is likely to be his/her personality. The vast majority of Sagittarians exhibit an eagerness and a buoyancy of spirit that can convince any employer that he/she should be hired. Unfortunately, for some Sagittarians that eagerness and ambition can fade fairly quickly—especially if they get bored or feel closed in. It is important for any Sagittarian to learn to live with his/her need for movement and change. One practical suggestion is to get into a job or career where you are not chained to a desk eight hours a day and where you will receive constant stimulation from other people.

It may surprise some of you to see "priest/clergyman" on the list of Sagittarian careers. Astrologically, it makes a lot of sense, because Sagittarius and the ninth house that sign rules are connected with "higher" things and thoughts. However, even the religious role a Sagittarian might play has to have a social aspect. The contemplative life would be a horror for most born under this sign; the religious function they would best serve is as a counselor, especially to young people.

Another way the Sagittarian can avoid the potentially fatal trap of boredom is to have two jobs, and an uncanny number of people born under this sign actually do juggle two jobs, or have an outside interest that is both a passion and a revenue producer. No matter how unscholarly a particular Sagittarian may be, even he/she needs constant mental stimulation and a sense that something is really happening.

If they make rather restless employees, Sagittarians make excellent bosses, at least as far as their subordinates are concerned. Higher-ups may feel that the Sagittarian's management style is a bit too loose, but they will be impressed by the amount of work that actually gets done in that environment. Anyone who works for a Sagittarian must be prepared for the fact that he/she could care less about details. Most Sagittarians are great at dealing with the overall picture, but disastrous when it comes to tying up loose ends. The self-aware Sagittarian will make sure that his/her back-up personnel force includes at least a couple of tidy, practical earth signs.

"Retirement" is a word that sounds foreign to many Sagittarians. They are not workaholics for the most part, but this is a sign that regards stretching and achieving as a natural part of life. Many go on working in some form or other until their dying day. Sagittarius is a "lucky" sign in many respects, and not the least of them is the ability to remain refreshed and alert long after others have fallen by the wayside. That's because it's really not work they're doing; they are having a great time.

# 19

## How "Pure" a Sagittarius Are You?

### Your Moon Sign . . . Your Rising Sign

No one is a "pure Sagittarius"—or pure anything for that matter—when it comes to astrological signs. As you will learn when you read "Defining Terms," there are many factors in a horoscope that add up to the total person that is you. Yes, there are twelve basic personality types, according to the zodiac, but within those broad groups there are almost infinite variations.

Though you are a Sagittarius "at the core," and can count on the portrait of your sun sign to define you in essence, the two other horoscope factors that count most in your personality profile are your moon sign and your rising sign. Many people know their moon sign; anyone can quickly determine it via an ephemeris. If you know your birthtime at least within one hour, you can use the table in this book to find out what your rising sign is.

#### The Moon—Your "Dark Side"

Almost more than your sun sign, your moon sign indicates what makes you run. Most of the time, you do not know it yourself, because the moon is your subconscious, your "dark side" not because it is bad, but because it is hidden. When the meaning of your moon sign is added to your Sagittarius sun sign, it is a fuller picture and a better indicator of your probable personality. Here's how a Sagittarius sun sign mixes with each of the moon signs.

*Sagittarius sun sign/Aries moon sign*    This combination could result in a personality that's too hot to handle. All the fire sign characteristics are doubled in you, and you may be one of the world's more rebellious characters. On the other hand, you never lack energy and enthusiasm, and there are few things you will not dare to do—or at least try. You are honest to a fault.

*Sagittarius sun sign/Taurus moon sign*    This is a great combination for both material and emotional success. Your earth-sign moon gives you the reliability and stability Sagittarius sometimes lacks. The combination of Sagittarius' fiery warmth with the tenderness of Taurus makes for a very lovely person—one who is both sympathetic, and just. People really like you.

*Sagittarius sun sign/Gemini moon sign*    It may be impossible for you to stay in one place for any length of time; you are almost excessively active. You are also the perpetual student who can never get enough information or education. If you don't take firm control of your active and restless nature, you could suffer from nervous exhaustion at times.

*Sagittarius sun sign/Cancer moon sign*    Your imagination could easily run away with you if you're not careful. Your appreciation of both art and nature is intense, but you could go overboard in the direction of "sensationalism." Though your Sagittarian sun sign gives you an upbeat attitude, Cancerian doubts and worries can easily bring you down. Try to develop consistency in your attitudes.

*Sagittarius sun sign/Leo moon sign*    This is a splendid combination. You are a born leader with a very big heart of pure gold. Your danger is that you will feel love toward many, but not always get the same in return; try to protect your easily broken heart. You would be great in the theater, either as a dramatist or an actor.

**Sagittarius sun sign/Virgo moon sign**   You are far more discriminating than the typical Sagittarian and have a lot more refinement. You are very bright and express your ideas very clearly, but sometimes you are a bit too critical of others. Be wary of a tendency to get really down in the dumps, even depressed. Use the common sense you were born with to throw off those moods.

**Sagittarius sun sign/Libra moon sign**   Your Libra moon moderates the impulsive qualities in Sagittarius and makes you a very courteous person. You attract friends easily, and they are generally of the better sort, both socially and intellectually speaking. You've got quite a bit of ambition, and it may run in the direction of the arts, where you could excel.

**Sagittarius sun sign/Scorpio moon sign**   You are a lot less naive than the "typical" Sagittarian; in fact, you could even be a bit devious at times. You've got plenty of energy and persistence, but your temper could be a very bad one, and you could love to argue for argument's sake. There are much better things to do with your mind, like becoming the very successful executive you could be.

**Sagittarius sun sign/Sagittarius moon sign**   You are the ultimate Sagittarian and will experience many changes throughout your lifetime. Though your social attitudes are reasonably conservative, you yourself could be quite undisciplined, and may have to make a major effort to get it together. Your wonderfully philosophical attitude makes you a wonderful friend.

***Sagittarius sun sign/Capricorn moon sign*** Whatever field you enter, your ambition could easily drive you to the top because you've got a large dose of practicality as well as imagination. You could tend to take too much responsibility on yourself or assume authority where it hasn't been granted to you. A religious career might draw you.

***Sagittarius sun sign/Aquarius moon sign*** You simply love any kind of mystery and delight in figuring out complicated things that totally defeat others. You are a rather peaceful type, but enterprising too. However, a close relationship with a member of the opposite sex may be difficult for you to form. Public life is a natural for you.

***Sagittarius sun sign/Pisces moon sign*** Your biggest enemy may be lack of initiative. No matter how good your ideas, they are never going to get off the ground unless you get up some steam. In general, your personal life should be very happy, and you may have excellent relationships with those you love. In some ways, you are a more passive than active performer in the business world.

## Your Rising Sign—Know Your Cover

The third of the "big three" astrological factors is your rising sign, which you can think of as an *overlay* to your sun sign. Although it does not carry the psychological weight your moon sign does, your rising sign is also "unconscious" because it is a mode of external behavior that comes so naturally to you that you may not be aware of it. In a sense, your rising sign is your cover. It can temporarily mask that sign, especially when people first meet you. Here's what happens to Sagittarius when you lay a rising sign over "typical" Sagittarian behavior:

**Sagittarius with Aries rising**    You probably have enough energy for two people and tend to bowl people over when you meet them. Hold back a little.

**Sagittarius with Taurus rising**    Chances are you enjoy a lot of the more pleasurable experiences of life, and are a real social person. Don't go overboard.

**Sagittarius with Gemini rising**    This combination makes for a chatterbox; you don't have to give all your opinions on first meeting.

**Sagittarius with Cancer rising**    You are a real "softy" in every sense of the word. Just don't get overly emotional with everyone you meet.

**Sagittarius with Leo rising**    You could easily be the class clown type; know your audience before you go into your slapstick routine.

**Sagittarius with Virgo rising**    You may express yourself with such precision that there doesn't seem to be room for argument; ease up a bit.

**Sagittarius with Libra rising**    You are the perfect host or hostess—even when it isn't your party. Nice going!

**Sagittarius with Scorpio rising**    People just *know* there's somebody absolutely fascinating behind that reserved exterior. You've got a great "act" if you learn how to use it.

**Sagittarius with Sagittarius rising**    This combination makes for one of the most outgoing, friendly types in the zodiac. Just make sure you don't appear insincere.

**Sagittarius with Capricorn rising**    You could easily become pompous and opinionated; don't always be so sure of yourself (or appear to be).

***Sagittarius with Aquarius rising***    This can be a very "lofty" combination. You could appear too aloof; come down off that cloud.

***Sagittarius with Pisces rising***    You are a real smooth talker and probably exude more charm than most. Make sure you let people know how honest you really are.

# 20

# Find Your Rising Sign

It is easier than many people think to find out your rising sign. One reason is that it is based on "universal" or "sidereal" time—the measure used in space travel. To ascertain your rising sign, look through the following chart and locate the birthdate nearest your birth date; look across and locate the time nearest your birth time. Remember that if daylight saving time was in effect at your birth, you must subtract one hour from the time stated on your birth certificate. In the section for your date and time, you will find an abbreviation for the sign that was rising when you were born. For instance, if your birthdate is June 12 at 9:30 a.m., your rising sign is Leo; if you were born on the same date at 9:30 p.m., your rising sign is Capricorn.

You will notice that the *year* you were born does not affect your rising sign. However, the geographical latitude does. These tables are calculated for the middle latitudes of the United States. If you were born far to the south, it is wise to look at the sign that *follows* your rising sign as well. If you were born far to the north, check out the *previous* sign.

# Rising Signs—A.M. Births

| | 1 AM | 2 AM | 3 AM | 4 AM | 5 AM | 6 AM | 7 AM | 8 AM | 9 AM | 10 AM | 11 AM | 12 NOON |
|---|---|---|---|---|---|---|---|---|---|---|---|---|
| Jan 1 | Lib | Sc | Sc | Sc | Sag | Sag | Cap | Cap | Aq | Aq | Pis | Ar |
| Jan 9 | Lib | Sc | Sc | Sag | Sag | Sag | Cap | Cap | Aq | Pis | Ar | Tau |
| Jan 17 | Sc | Sc | Sc | Sag | Sag | Cap | Cap | Aq | Aq | Pis | Ar | Tau |
| Jan 25 | Sc | Sc | Sag | Sag | Sag | Cap | Cap | Aq | Pis | Ar | Tau | Tau |
| Feb 2 | Sc | Sc | Sag | Sag | Cap | Cap | Aq | Pis | Pis | Ar | Tau | Gem |
| Feb 10 | Sc | Sag | Sag | Sag | Cap | Cap | Aq | Pis | Ar | Tau | Tau | Gem |
| Feb 18 | Sc | Sag | Sag | Cap | Cap | Aq | Pis | Pis | Ar | Tau | Gem | Gem |
| Feb 26 | Sag | Sag | Sag | Cap | Aq | Aq | Pis | Ar | Tau | Tau | Gem | Gem |
| Mar 6 | Sag | Sag | Cap | Cap | Aq | Pis | Pis | Ar | Tau | Gem | Gem | Cap |
| Mar 14 | Sag | Cap | Cap | Aq | Aq | Pis | Ar | Tau | Tau | Gem | Gem | Can |
| Mar 22 | Sag | Cap | Cap | Aq | Pis | Ar | Ar | Tau | Gem | Gem | Can | Can |
| Mar 30 | Cap | Cap | Aq | Pis | Pis | Ar | Tau | Tau | Gem | Can | Can | Can |
| Apr 7 | Cap | Cap | Aq | Pis | Ar | Ar | Tau | Gem | Gem | Can | Can | Leo |
| Apr 14 | Cap | Aq | Aq | Pis | Ar | Tau | Tau | Gem | Gem | Can | Can | Leo |
| Apr 22 | Cap | Aq | Pis | Ar | Ar | Tau | Gem | Gem | Gem | Can | Leo | Leo |
| Apr 30 | Aq | Aq | Pis | Ar | Tau | Tau | Gem | Can | Can | Can | Leo | Leo |
| May 8 | Aq | Pis | Ar | Ar | Tau | Gem | Gem | Can | Can | Leo | Leo | Leo |
| May 16 | Aq | Pis | Ar | Tau | Gem | Gem | Can | Can | Can | Leo | Leo | Vir |
| May 24 | Pis | Ar | Ar | Tau | Gem | Gem | Can | Can | Leo | Leo | Leo | Vir |
| June 1 | Pis | Ar | Tau | Gem | Gem | Can | Can | Can | Leo | Leo | Vir | Vir |
| June 9 | Ar | Ar | Tau | Gem | Gem | Can | Can | Leo | Leo | Leo | Vir | Vir |
| June 17 | Ar | Tau | Gem | Gem | Can | Can | Can | Leo | Leo | Vir | Vir | Vir |
| June 25 | Tau | Tau | Gem | Gem | Can | Can | Leo | Leo | Leo | Vir | Vir | Lib |
| July 3 | Tau | Gem | Gem | Can | Can | Can | Leo | Leo | Vir | Vir | Vir | Lib |
| July 11 | Tau | Gem | Gem | Can | Can | Leo | Leo | Leo | Vir | Vir | Lib | Lib |
| July 18 | Gem | Gem | Can | Can | Can | Leo | Leo | Vir | Vir | Vir | Lib | Lib |
| July 26 | Gem | Gem | Can | Can | Leo | Leo | Vir | Vir | Vir | Lib | Lib | Lib |
| Aug 3 | Gem | Can | Can | Can | Leo | Leo | Vir | Vir | Vir | Lib | Lib | Sc |
| Aug 11 | Gem | Can | Can | Leo | Leo | Leo | Vir | Vir | Lib | Lib | Lib | Sc |
| Aug 18 | Can | Can | Can | Leo | Leo | Vir | Vir | Vir | Lib | Lib | Sc | Sc |
| Aug 27 | Can | Can | Leo | Leo | Leo | Vir | Vir | Lib | Lib | Lib | Sc | Sc |
| Sept 4 | Can | Can | Leo | Leo | Leo | Vir | Vir | Vir | Lib | Lib | Sc | Sc |
| Sept 12 | Can | Leo | Leo | Leo | Vir | Vir | Lib | Lib | Lib | Sc | Sc | Sag |
| Sept 30 | Leo | Leo | Leo | Vir | Vir | Vir | Lib | Lib | Sc | Sc | Sc | Sag |
| Sept 28 | Leo | Leo | Leo | Vir | Vir | Lib | Lib | Lib | Sc | Sc | Sag | Sag |
| Oct 6 | Leo | Leo | Vir | Vir | Vir | Lib | Lib | Sc | Sc | Sc | Sag | Sag |
| Oct 14 | Leo | Vir | Vir | Vir | Lib | Lib | Lib | Sc | Sc | Sag | Sag | Cap |
| Oct 22 | Leo | Vir | Vir | Lib | Lib | Lib | Sc | Sc | Sc | Sag | Sag | Cap |
| Oct 30 | Vir | Vir | Vir | Lib | Lib | Sc | Sc | Sc | Sag | Sag | Cap | Cap |
| Nov 7 | Vir | Vir | Lib | Lib | Lib | Sc | Sc | Sc | Sag | Sag | Cap | Cap |
| Nov 15 | Vir | Vir | Lib | Lib | Sc | Sc | Sc | Sag | Sag | Cap | Cap | Aq |
| Nov 23 | Vir | Lib | Lib | Lib | Sc | Sc | Sag | Sag | Sag | Cap | Cap | Aq |
| Dec 1 | Vir | Lib | Lib | Sc | Sc | Sc | Sag | Sag | Cap | Cap | Aq | Aq |
| Dec 9 | Lib | Lib | Lib | Sc | Sc | Sag | Sag | Sag | Cap | Cap | Aq | Pis |
| Dec 18 | Lib | Lib | Sc | Sc | Sc | Sag | Sag | Cap | Cap | Aq | Aq | Pis |
| Dec 28 | Lib | Lib | Sc | Sc | Sag | Sag | Sag | Cap | Aq | Aq | Pis | Ar |

# Rising Signs—P.M. Births

| | 1 PM | 2 PM | 3 PM | 4 PM | 5 PM | 6 PM | 7 PM | 8 PM | 9 PM | 10 PM | 11 PM | 12 MIDNIGHT |
|---|---|---|---|---|---|---|---|---|---|---|---|---|
| Jan 1 | Tau | Gem | Gem | Can | Can | Can | Leo | Leo | Vir | Vir | Vir | Lib |
| Jan 9 | Tau | Gem | Gem | Can | Can | Leo | Leo | Leo | Vir | Vir | Vir | Lib |
| Jan 17 | Gem | Gem | Can | Can | Can | Leo | Leo | Leo | Vir | Vir | Lib | Lib |
| Jan 25 | Gem | Gem | Can | Can | Leo | Leo | Leo | Vir | Vir | Lib | Lib | Lib |
| Feb 2 | Gem | Can | Can | Can | Leo | Leo | Vir | Vir | Vir | Lib | Lib | Sc |
| Feb 10 | Gem | Can | Can | Leo | Leo | Leo | Vir | Vir | Lib | Lib | Lib | Sc |
| Feb 18 | Can | Can | Can | Leo | Leo | Vir | Vir | Vir | Lib | Lib | Sc | Sc |
| Feb 26 | Can | Can | Leo | Leo | Leo | Vir | Vir | Lib | Lib | Lib | Sc | Sc |
| Mar 6 | Can | Leo | Leo | Leo | Vir | Vir | Vir | Lib | Lib | Sc | Sc | Sc |
| Mar 14 | Can | Leo | Leo | Vir | Vir | Vir | Lib | Lib | Lib | Sc | Sc | Sag |
| Mar 22 | Leo | Leo | Leo | Vir | Vir | Lib | Lib | Lib | Sc | Sc | Sc | Sag |
| Mar 30 | Leo | Leo | Leo | Vir | Vir | Vir | Lib | Lib | Sc | Sc | Sc | Sag |
| Apr 7 | Leo | Leo | Vir | Vir | Lib | Lib | Lib | Sc | Sc | Sc | Sag | Sag |
| Apr 14 | Leo | Vir | Vir | Vir | Lib | Lib | Sc | Sc | Sc | Sag | Sag | Cap |
| Apr 22 | Leo | Vir | Vir | Lib | Lib | Lib | Sc | Sc | Sc | Sag | Sag | Cap |
| Apr 30 | Vir | Vir | Vir | Lib | Lib | Sc | Sc | Sc | Sag | Sag | Cap | Cap |
| May 8 | Vir | Vir | Lib | Lib | Lib | Sc | Sc | Sag | Sag | Sag | Cap | Cap |
| May 16 | Vir | Vir | Lib | Lib | Sc | Sc | Sc | Sag | Sag | Cap | Cap | Aq |
| May 24 | Vir | Lib | Lib | Lib | Sc | Sc | Sag | Sag | Sag | Cap | Cap | Aq |
| June 1 | Vir | Lib | Lib | Sc | Sc | Sc | Sag | Sag | Cap | Cap | Aq | Aq |
| June 9 | Lib | Lib | Lib | Sc | Sc | Sag | Sag | Sag | Cap | Cap | Aq | Pis |
| June 17 | Lib | Lib | Sc | Sc | Sc | Sag | Sag | Cap | Cap | Aq | Aq | Pis |
| June 25 | Lib | Lib | Sc | Sc | Sag | Sag | Sag | Cap | Cap | Aq | Pis | Ar |
| July 3 | Lib | Sc | Sc | Sc | Sag | Sag | Cap | Cap | Aq | Aq | Pis | Ar |
| July 11 | Lib | Sc | Sc | Sag | Sag | Sag | Cap | Cap | Aq | Pis | Ar | Tau |
| July 18 | Sc | Sc | Sc | Sag | Sag | Cap | Cap | Aq | Aq | Pis | Ar | Tau |
| July 26 | Sc | Sc | Sag | Sag | Sag | Cap | Cap | Aq | Pis | Ar | Tau | Tau |
| Aug 3 | Sc | Sc | Sag | Sag | Cap | Cap | Aq | Aq | Pis | Ar | Tau | Gem |
| Aug 11 | Sc | Sag | Sag | Sag | Cap | Cap | Aq | Pis | Pis | Ar | Tau | Gem |
| Aug 18 | Sc | Sag | Sag | Cap | Cap | Aq | Aq | Pis | Pis | Ar | Tau | Gem |
| Aug 27 | Sag | Sag | Sag | Cap | Cap | Aq | Pis | Ar | Tau | Tau | Gem | Gem |
| Sept 4 | Sag | Sag | Cap | Cap | Aq | Pis | Pis | Ar | Tau | Gem | Gem | Can |
| Sept 12 | Sag | Sag | Cap | Aq | Aq | Pis | Ar | Tau | Tau | Gem | Gem | Can |
| Sept 20 | Sag | Cap | Cap | Aq | Aq | Pis | Pis | Ar | Tau | Gem | Gem | Can |
| Sept 28 | Cap | Cap | Aq | Aq | Pis | Ar | Tau | Tau | Gem | Gem | Can | Can |
| Oct 6 | Cap | Cap | Aq | Pis | Ar | Ar | Tau | Gem | Gem | Can | Can | Leo |
| Oct 14 | Cap | Aq | Aq | Pis | Ar | Tau | Tau | Gem | Gem | Can | Can | Leo |
| Oct 22 | Cap | Aq | Pis | Ar | Ar | Tau | Gem | Gem | Can | Can | Leo | Leo |
| Oct 30 | Aq | Aq | Pis | Ar | Tau | Tau | Gem | Can | Can | Leo | Leo | Leo |
| Nov 7 | Aq | Aq | Pis | Ar | Tau | Tau | Gem | Can | Can | Leo | Leo | Leo |
| Nov 15 | Aq | Pis | Ar | Tau | Gem | Gem | Can | Can | Can | Leo | Leo | Vir |
| Nov 23 | Pis | Ar | Ar | Tau | Gem | Gem | Can | Can | Leo | Leo | Leo | Vir |
| Dec 1 | Pis | Ar | Tau | Gem | Gem | Can | Can | Can | Leo | Leo | Vir | Vir |
| Dec 9 | Ar | Ar | Tau | Gem | Gem | Can | Can | Leo | Leo | Leo | Vir | Vir |
| Dec 18 | Ar | Tau | Gem | Gem | Can | Can | Can | Leo | Leo | Vir | Vir | Vir |
| Dec 28 | Tau | Tau | Gem | Gem | Can | Can | Leo | Leo | Vir | Vir | Vir | Lib |

# 21

## Sagittarius Astro-outlook for 1986

You may have to curb your innate wanderlust a bit in 1986, freewheeling Sagittarius. Home, family and things close by are going to claim a fair amount of your time and interest. If there are dramatic changes, they will most likely involve domestic conditions, and a move is highly likely. It will definitely promote greater harmony within your circle. With Saturn in your sign, you are surely going to take on additional responsibilities and display much more concern with financial security than you have, at least in the recent past.

With regard to finances: You will probably be ready to sacrifice for others, but you should not let your desire for extra income lead you into any get-rich-quick schemes. Exercise caution about anything that seems too good to be true, because it probably is. In this area of life, as in all, realize you might be too idealistic and trusting at this particular time.

Self-expression is the key to good fortune this year, and you should have any number of opportunities to exercise your talents (especially if they are artistic in any way). For some, a family wedding or other kind of major gathering is likely. As for general style: This is one year you will find yourself more able to hold your tongue and thereby keep the friendship of others—which is sometimes strained by your innate frankness.

April is an excellent time to begin a new project and

expect good results. February, August, and November could easily bring an intense involvement or the deepening of an existing relationship. For more details, consult the daily forecasts in the pages ahead.

## 22

**Fifteen Months of Day-by-Day Predictions**

# O C T O B E R   1 9 8 5

*Tuesday, October 1 (Moon in Taurus)*    Keep on asking questions until you are absolutely sure you have the right answers. You will be able to make a sure move only when you know the true intentions and motivations of others. In your personal sphere, you are likely to get a lot of TLC today; enjoy it.

*Wednesday, October 2 (Moon in Taurus)*    You may feel like chucking everything today, but you will not be able to; responsibility is at the top of the list today. However, if you are persistent, you will make a lot of headway—and feel a lot better for it. Don't forget some recent health resolutions.

*Thursday, October 3 (Moon Taurus to Gemini 8:26 a.m.)*    Be willing to let go of a losing proposition; that way you will be able to cut your losses. Take a low-key approach to most things today. You may meet someone who will become a close friend in the future; you should have absolute confidence in this person's sincerity.

*Friday, October 4 (Moon in Gemini)*    You may be especially communicative today—especially in your personal relationships. It is a time to speak out about what you are willing to give in return. In other kinds of

151

"contracts," you should be equally forthright. Someone has an excellent impact on your business situation. You now have a wider professional circle.

**Saturday, October 5 (Moon Gemini to Cancer 8:42 p.m.)**   It is a day to listen more than talk; the more you observe, the better off you will be. Absorb all the information you can, but avoid a direct confrontation that can force your hand. Time is on your side. You may find some clues in the number 2.

**Sunday, October 6 (Moon in Cancer)**   You should get an excellent return on your investment of time today. What you accomplish will give you great satisfaction. Someone may be on your case about your being extravagant; explain that it is all in everyone's best interest. At least according to you. In another area, you may have to have split-second timing today.

**Monday, October 7 (Moon in Cancer)**   Today, it is you who decides to take a long, hard look at your financial situation. You realize you have got to build a stronger foundation in order to see your money grow. Avoid excesses of any kind. Be alert for something that happens behind closed doors.

**Tuesday, October 8 (Moon Cancer to Leo 6:38 a.m.)** Today, you have a shift in priorities, and now turn your attention to "higher things." In fact, you may be questioning some of your own values and attempting to elevate them. At the same time, you may be considering a journey—even if it is one of the mind. A confusing message comes in, and you should not overreact.

**Wednesday, October 9 (Moon in Leo)**   Be prepared to be especially flexible today, because some plans could be turned upside down. It may annoy you that you are the one who has to make the adjustment, but realize it is easier for you than for someone else. A reconciliation will come later in the day. The lucky number is 6.

*Thursday, October 10 (Moon Leo to Virgo 1:24 p.m.)*
You may need some time alone to sort out the pieces of a puzzle. Don't fear the unknown; be willing to look into your emotional depths to get a more mature outlook. When you come out of this mood, you will be a lot more sure of yourself—and of what you want.

*Friday, October 11 (Moon in Virgo)*   Today, you reemerge into the outer world, ready to deal with things as they are. And they are rather good. Along with some extra duties comes some extra recognition—and possible financial reward. However, don't turn into a workaholic. Leave some time for love and romance.

*Saturday, October 12 (Moon Virgo to Libra 2:38 p.m.)*   Prepare your statement carefully before you speak today; people will be listening to every word. You may have to do some sugar-coating in order to get your ideas across. Don't worry; you can usually make things sound extremely good, even if they aren't. You might be asked to volunteer for a charitable endeavor today.

*Sunday, October 13 (Moon in Libra)*   You really won your case yesterday, and today it pays off in the form of admiration and affection from others. In fact, you may be absolutely intriguing to a particular person—are you intrigued? Something you have wanted for a long time suddenly becomes available; snap it up!

*Monday, October 14 (Moon Libra to Scorpio 2:50 p.m.)*   Be conservative, and do some waiting now; it is important to see which way the wind is blowing. You can build some good will close to home with a sensitive friend who wants your advice. Be generous with it. One of your wishes is granted—isn't it nice?

*Tuesday, October 15 (Moon in Scorpio)*   You should accept the limits of your situation cheerfully today; in fact, you are better off not extending yourself now.

153

Move slowly and carefully, and some of your past errors will be both forgiven and forgotten. It should be a great relief. The lucky number today is 3.

**Wednesday, October 16 (Moon Scorpio to Sagittarius 2:25 p.m.)**    Play it close to the vest today; it is unwise to reveal too much. In fact, refuse to bite at an obvious ploy to obtain private information from you. You must think about the welfare of others today—possibly parents or other older relatives. Be especially attentive and kind.

**Thursday, October 17 (Moon in Sagittarius)**    As the moon is in your sign now, you can expect more favorable responses to your request. You should be able to pick up on some small and subtle clues that are dropped today; if you analyze them correctly, you will be able to see a trend and get there ahead of everyone else. Take care not to be tripped up by a tricky person—possibly a Gemini.

**Friday, October 18 (Moon Sagittarius to Capricorn 3:37 p.m.)**    You can obtain harmony without sacrificing much of your independence; you should be willing to make some sort of concession. Though it may bug you, you should get in and say "yes"—even if you consider it an excessive demand. The person who does the pushing could be a Taurus or a Scorpio.

**Saturday, October 19 (Moon in Capricorn)**    If you are realistic, you will be able to shake off some vague fears that have been bothering you. It should be obvious that they exist only in your mind. If you give your creativity free reign, you can vastly improve your earning potential. Listen to your intuition.

**Sunday, October 20 (Moon Capricorn to Aquarius 8:04 p.m.)**    You may seem rather cruel and distant to someone who wants to get close to you; if you are interested, you must appear so. You are very much in

154

control—where both emotions and money are concerned. Be ready to back your words with action.

*Monday, October 21 (Moon in Aquarius)* You will get the chance to put your idea forward; don't blow it. Do your homework carefully, and get all your facts straight. Remember where you put everything today; it would be very easy to misplace something and drive yourself crazy trying to find it.

*Tuesday, October 22 (Moon in Aquarius)* Be willing to listen to some new ideas, even if they do not mesh completely with your own. The subject may be your own immediate environment, and the problem may be your personal habits versus someone else's. Keep the lines of communication open, and you will have no problem. Let your love for someone else override petty concerns.

*Wednesday, October 23 (Moon Aquarius to Pisces 3:35 a.m.)* Take a careful inventory of all your practices now; it is essential to be efficient in order to be secure. You will be able to reach an understanding with someone older who is not always "in synch" with your ideas. In fact, you should take one piece of advice—about being more discriminating than you are. The lucky number today could be 2.

*Thursday, October 24 (Moon in Pisces)* Have the courage of your own convictions and hold to your position. Though it may sound trite, the motto of the day should be "Try, try again." Keep your sense of humor and realize that your big break is just around the corner. The lucky number today is 3.

*Friday, October 25 (Moon Pisces to Aries 2:09 p.m.)* You could be a bit too abrupt and alienate some people today. Realize that others are only trying to help with what they believe is solid advice. You should listen to some of it—because it could be invaluable to your rebuilding program. A change of scenery is likely.

*Saturday, October 26 (Moon in Aries)*    A delightful change of pace should be the order of the day. You may become involved with a fast-talking individual who claims to admire you very much; though it is pleasant, don't overreact. You are particularly susceptible to flattery now, so you must take care to protect yourself against anything but the "real thing."

*Sunday, October 27 (Moon in Aries)*    Someone you made a promise to a while back comes and insists that you honor it now. You should, and without grumbling. In general, you should be feeling rather happy and revitalized; communicate your feelings to others who can benefit by them.

*Monday, October 28 (Moon Aries to Taurus 2:11 a.m.)*    Protect yourself against someone who wants something for nothing. You can hold your own and do not have to back down. Spend some time figuring out ways to improve your fitness and stamina; you may need them in the weeks ahead. Steer clear of any backstage maneuvers.

*Tuesday, October 29 (Moon in Taurus)*    You can get the job done better if you accept the help of someone who offers it; don't turn this person off. Realize how important it is to turn in excellent work now, and you will be more willing to rely at least a little bit on someone else. Cooperation is the key all day long, and 8 is the lucky number.

*Wednesday, October 30 (Moon Taurus to Gemini 2:36 p.m.)*    If you maintain a slow and steady pace, you will be able to complete something—and in record time. Some of your health resolutions are beginning to pay off already; don't you feel better? It is important to see

156

the whole picture; a consultation with a realistic friend—possibly an Aries—could be very beneficial.

**Thursday, October 31 (Moon in Gemini)**    Don't think you will be considered too pushy if you insist on getting something in writing; most people accept the fact that it is the only way to protect yourself in such matters. Legal rights of all kinds are in the spotlight now; that includes impersonal contracts. Marriage may be up for discussion.

# NOVEMBER 1985

**Friday, November 1 (Moon in Gemini)**    The ball is definitely in your court today; plan your return shots carefully. You can succeed at a power play, but you must be willing to accept the new responsibilities that are part of the package. Realize that you will have a much greater opportunity to cash in on your talents—and you will be in good shape.

**Saturday, November 2 (Moon Gemini to Cancer 3:12 a.m.)**    It's going to take a lot of persistence to finish something you have started. If you don't, however, you will really get down on yourself—so it is worth the effort. Meanwhile, you may have to stake out your territorial rights. Someone may be trying to encroach on them. Get involved in a community group if you are asked.

**Sunday, November 3 (Moon in Cancer)**    Someone thinks you are absolutely super and would make the best partner in the world. The subject could be love or business. Be sure to take a look at the whole picture before you commit to anything. Your lucky number today could easily be 1.

**Monday, November 4 (Moon Cancer to Leo 3:12 a.m.)** Avoid making a hasty decision today, and don't force any issues. Wait patiently, and this tricky time will pass. Someone else may be rather upset today as well; it is up to you to smooth the waters. You can do it if you apply the light touch.

**Tuesday, November 5 (Moon in Leo)**   Today, you are able to take a much more philosophical attitude toward current events in your life. You see one subject in a whole new light, and you are able to figure out a game plan. Somebody is right in there pitching for you, and it should make you feel a lot more competent. Don't overdo physical activity today.

**Wednesday, November 6 (Moon Leo to Virgo 9:34 p.m.)**   Don't trust anyone else with the details today; this is one time you must do it yourself. If you stay on track, you will make it—and even make it big. If you have any confusion on a technical point, seek a professional opinion. You aren't expected to know everything yourself. The number 4 could be lucky today.

**Thursday, November 7 (Moon in Virgo)**   You do not have to simply accept things quietly. If you face the issue and take direct action, you can greatly improve your advantage. Your dynamic new ways may be particularly attractive to others, and you should get a very positive response. Regard the whole thing as an "advertisement" for yourself.

**Friday, November 8 (Moon in Virgo)**   It is possible that you are trying to impress someone now. That means you want your environment to be a favorable reflection on you. What that may mean is some quick adjustments and "patch-up" decorating. Don't go overboard, however; be your sloppy Sagittarian self, and you will come out smelling like a rose.

**Saturday, November 9 (Moon Virgo to Libra 1:14 a.m.)**   Today, you may simply want to be alone, but it may be very difficult to get any kind of privacy. For one thing, someone who is under a great deal of pressure may seek you out for advice and counsel. Be willing to give it, because your charitable act will pay off later on. You really are a good person! Something makes you realize that one of your fondest wishes is literally coming true.

*Sunday, November 10 (Moon in Libra)* A casual acquaintance suddenly turns into a true benefactor, which proves that you never know what can happen! With this help, and your serious attitude, you will reach the top with little difficulty. People expect a lot of you, but you should appreciate their confidence in you.

*Monday, November 11 (Moon Libra to Scorpio 1:53 a.m.)* For some of you, a casual, platonic relationship may be changing into something else—much more highly charged. For others, it may be an ideal or cause that is suddenly becoming a lot more important to you. In either case, waste no time in getting on with things. There may be an exchange of secrets today; be sure that you at least keep the confidence.

*Tuesday, November 12 (Moon in Scorpio)* You may be trying to do too much at one time; realize you do not have infinite energy. An unforeseen obstacle may require some fancy maneuvering on your part. Don't sweat it! There is always another day. The lucky number today is 1.

*Wednesday, November 13 (Moon Scorpio to Sagittarius 1:12 a.m.)* If you have given yourself time to catch up and plan your next move, today you should be ready to move forward—fast! Your psychological outlook should be excellent and free from energy-draining emotions. A very dedicated person will aid you in getting what you want now. The lucky number today should be 2.

*Thursday, November 14 (Moon in Sagittarius)* Today, you should jump in with both feet and participate to the fullest. Your timing should be excellent and your enthusiasm running high. You may have to take a short side trip, but it should be more fun than work. You may have a delightful episode with another Sagittarian or possibly a Gemini. The person is invaluable in helping you make a plan.

**Friday, November 15 (Moon Sagittarius to Capricorn 1:10 a.m.)**    Your patience may be tested today, but don't overreact. It may grind you to have to stay within the rules, but the self-discipline will do you no harm. In fact, you really are putting yourself in a better position to earn—and acquire the things you want. Complaining will only make the situation worse.

**Saturday, November 16 (Moon in Capricorn)**    Some quick changes call for ready answers; have them right at your fingertips. There may be some very fast-paced but enlightening communication between you and someone else today—you will enjoy the verbal give and take a great deal. An issue of personal property may arise; don't argue with people you love.

**Sunday, November 17 (Moon Capricorn to Aquarius 3:54 a.m.)**    This is one of those times when you are sure you know better than anyone else what is good for you—stick to your guns. You can be extremely resourceful in situations like this, and today you can prove it. You may have a sentimental reunion with someone you have not seen in a while—it could be a Taurus or a Libra. The number 6 could be extremely lucky today.

**Monday, November 18 (Moon in Aquarius)**    Get absolutely clear on what you want out of a situation before you enter into it. In fact, before even dipping in your little toe, you must get down to the nitty-gritty about what it is you believe. That may mean casting off some secret fears you have been ashamed to tell anyone about. Don't be afraid to share with a close confidant now.

*Tuesday, November 19 (Moon Aquarius to Pisces 10:04 a.m.)* You may find you have some tough competition today, but don't lose heart. If you use a straightforward approach, you can be a big winner today—both on the job and in a love relationship. The more you believe in yourself, the more someone else will believe in you.

*Wednesday, November 20 (Moon in Pisces)* Now you are ready for a major step; have confidence in yourself! You have done your homework well, and listened carefully to everyone's opinions. Now it is up to you. However, don't turn down a helping hand from a generous person—possibly an Aries or a Libra.

*Thursday, November 21 (Moon Pisces to Aries 8:00 p.m.)* Jump at what sounds like a golden opportunity today; it very well could be. The important thing is to take the initiative and act immediately. Realize you are on firm ground. In another matter, take the concerns of an older family member into consideration before arranging things the way you want them.

*Friday, November 22 (Moon in Aries)* Your love of freedom is especially strong today; in fact, you may feel like completely bursting loose. It's okay as long as you know your limits. Enjoy an active day with a lot of interaction with interesting people. You deserve it! And you will gain some valuable new insights.

*Saturday, November 23 (Moon in Aries)* You may feel like skimming the surface today rather than digging deep; it's okay as long as you realize the details will have to be dealt with later. Just be sure to put things down on paper. You get a nice "thank-you note," though it may not be in the form of a letter. What you learn proves to you that your efforts on someone else's behalf have paid off.

*Sunday, November 24 (Moon Aries to Taurus 8:37 a.m.)* A job well done will give you great satisfaction now; be sure that you get it. Stick to the practical today; there will be time to test out your theories later on. You may get involved in a rather amusing situation where flirting is fun—and actually becomes a challenge to your creativity. Enjoy!

**Monday, November 25 (Moon in Taurus)**    Creative change is the order of the day. Don't hesitate to toss out some old habits in favor of a new regime. You will feel like a new person. In another matter, be willing to spend of yourself to get what you want. And pay some attention to your physical state—especially the matter of fitness and diet. Could you stand some improvement?

**Tuesday, November 26 (Moon Taurus to Gemini 9:02 p.m.)**    You are instrumental in removing a disturbing influence from the scene; greater harmony is the result. It should give you confidence in your ability to handle others. If you are a true Sagittarian, that should be one of your strong points. The emphasis today is on the welfare of others—tomorrow belongs to you.

**Wednesday, November 27 (Moon in Gemini)**    An honest, serious talk behind closed doors could be the best way to handle a delicate situation. If you shout, you will not get your point across. Remember, not everyone is as open and aboveboard as you are; you may have to play by someone else's rules. The lucky number today is 7.

**Thursday, November 28 (Moon in Gemini)**    This day you are able to turn in a stunning, quality performance. You impress people—even yourself. Even though you are able to branch out in certain areas, an affair of the heart calls for patience. Plan your moves carefully, and you can come out a winner. It is not wise to "lean on" someone close to you.

**Friday, November 29 (Moon Gemini to Cancer 8:59 a.m.)**    You may be having second thoughts about something and considering a new beginning. You do not drop people lightly, but this is one time you may have to do so. You realize there are others who need you a lot more. An excellent pal—possibly an Aries—would be a good person to consult in this matter.

**Saturday, November 30 (Moon in Cancer)**      Stability and security are what you desire now—in love as well as business. You are not in a risk-taking mood. Your managerial abilities become obvious in the way you handle some joint funds. Someone recognizes them, and gives you a big compliment. Take it to heart.

# DECEMBER 1985

**Sunday, December 1 (Moon Cancer to Leo 8:04 p.m.)** There are few real, genuine opportunities—one presents itself to you today. The scope is large, and so should be your thinking. However, realize this will take time—and be willing to spend that time in order to build up something of real substance. Avoid signing something you are not sure of.

**Monday, December 2 (Moon in Leo)**      You get a surge of energy today, and should put it to use in some tangible way. There is something that needs doing, and you should be able to put your back into it now. Someone may try to do a number on you today; be alert to his/her wily ways. Accept only what has lasting value.

**Tuesday, December 3 (Moon in Leo)**      Someone else's patience may be tried today while you take it slow and steady and get your act together. Refuse to be rattled. In fact, insist on finishing something before you begin something else. It can wait! The lucky number today is 2.

**Wednesday, December 4 (Moon Leo to Virgo 4:38 a.m.)**      Now your waiting pays off, and you can prove

163

it to the person who was bugging you yesterday. Just don't get smug! Research of all kinds is favored now, as is all written material. If there is something of that nature you must do, this is a good time to do it. In fact, your artistic abilities are at a high—and you should be able to do it with flair.

**Thursday, December 5 (Moon in Virgo)**    Keep your priorities straight and your long-term goals in clear focus. Don't let anyone throw you off the track. Your past performance and solid reputation are excellent advantages now; do not hesitate to use them. A Leo could inspire you—but be rather annoying as well. Let it roll off your back.

**Friday, December 6 (Moon Virgo to Libra 9:44 a.m.)** Prestige, honors, and even a possible promotion are indicated. Use this excellent day to your advantage. One way might be by welcoming a change in scenery and a new social situation. Though it is not in your nature to be shy, sometimes you do hesitate before meeting new faces. A party-loving friend may have cause for celebration—and ask you to celebrate with him/her. Join the party!

**Saturday, December 7 (Moon in Libra)**    Today, you want to do one thing, someone else wants to do another; it could lead to a battle of wills. However, since you will win out in the end, don't force things. Home should be a source of happiness and well-being now. You may be very concerned with its physical appearance—as well as your own. Spend some time freshening things up.

**Sunday, December 8 (Moon Libra to Scorpio 1:05 p.m.)**    You could easily get a distorted view of reality now; quietly observe and evaluate what you see. It is important not to have any illusions about anything. You are feeling a little unsettled, but someone arrives who helps you sort little things out. It is a sensitive person—possibly a Pisces—and he/she is able to make you see where you are in error.

**Monday, December 9 (Moon in Scorpio)**     Complaints are a luxury you cannot afford at this time; watch your tongue—and your actions as well. There is a struggle going on—possibly behind the scenes—but you will ultimately benefit. Lie low until the "storm" passes; there is calmer weather coming!

**Tuesday, December 10 (Moon Scorpio to Sagittarius 1:11 p.m.)**     You break out into the open today, emotionally speaking. Things seem much brighter—and they are. You are able to focus your interests on the outer world and impress people with some hidden talents you suddenly display. Even you are amazed! The lucky number today should be 9.

**Wednesday, December 11 (Moon in Sagittarius)**     Again you are in an outgoing, adventurous mood. Don't waste time getting started, but don't get carried away either. Your energy is high, but it must be controlled. People who like people are drawn into your orbit and play significant roles.

**Thursday, December 12 (Moon Sagittarius to Capricorn 1:03 p.m.)**     You may have to go on a fact-finding mission before you begin a new project; it is necessary in order to ensure success. Someone you met recently is becoming a better and better friend. You will discover you have an excellent new ally. Consider the needs of family—especially older family—when you consider your own. Listen to someone with sound advice.

**Friday, December 13 (Moon in Capricorn)**     The changes that come today are welcomed. Everything is rather upbeat, with the emphasis on lots of activity—both mental and physical. However, try not to get confused; the best way is to define your range of interests. Income and personal resources are in the spotlight today.

*Saturday, December 14 (Moon Capricorn to Aquarius 1:39 p.m.)* You might consider this a dull day—at least at the beginning. There are some matters of money and accounts that must be taken care of, so try to get them out of the way fast. Then you will be free to enjoy a sociable time with some gregarious people like yourself. You may find one is an Aquarius or a Leo—both of whom are excellent foils for your excellent sense of humor. Number 4 should be lucky today.

*Sunday, December 15 (Moon in Aquarius)* The key to pleasure today is to express yourself in some "creative" way. It could even be on a home do-it-yourself project. A casual something you say gets a very warm response—much warmer than you expected. You are impressed. You should seek quality in everything today— from people to the materials you work with.

*Monday, December 16 (Moon Aquarius to Pisces 6:21 p.m.)* Things just seem to fall into your hands today—right things. Wherever you are, you are able to be very effective, even on a shopping trip, which you may take with a discriminating friend or neighbor. A phone call or a written message comes in that says "yes." It should lift your spirits.

*Tuesday, December 17 (Moon in Pisces)* You may be feeling a little fatigued today; if possible, lie low and let others do the leg work. Someone is willing to negotiate on your behalf, and it lightens your burden. You've been a bit upset or puzzled about a relationship, but now everything clears up and it is a relief. You realize your fears and worries were unfounded.

*Wednesday, December 18 (Moon in Pisces)* In spite of the fact that there are those who call you a "flake," you are really quite dependable. Now that dependability in your past performance brings rewards. You have a right to congratulate yourself. One of your relationships is beginning to get more intense; don't let it scare

166

you off. There is a possibility of a change in your status—that is, marital status—and you should be open to the possibility.

**Thursday, December 19** *(Moon Pisces to Aries 2:55 a.m.)* Faraway places with strange-sounding names may appeal to you now. You would like to leap over a lot of barriers, including the language barrier. Communication is the key in everything you do now, and that includes affairs of the heart. You are making progress.

**Friday, December 20** *(Moon in Aries)* You are able to get everyone to agree to a spontaneous change in plans today. The result is delightful—for everyone involved. Your emotional responses are particularly strong right now, and you run the risk of going out on a limb for someone you care about. Just be sure you have a "safety net." The lucky number today could be 1.

**Saturday, December 21** *(Moon Aries to Taurus 3:09 p.m.)* Slow down your pace in order to get greater enjoyment out of all your sense pleasures today—including food and recreation. There should be a nice, secure, homey atmosphere around you now; it is excellent for restoring your sense of security. Enjoy all the festivities, but leave time for rest.

**Sunday, December 22** *(Moon in Taurus)* If you go after all the fun that is there for the asking, you could easily overdo and end up overstimulated. Put the accent on quality over quantity in social engagements. There is a lot to do, but you get a lot of help from an energetic person. Don't forget someone who is confined and not able to join in the festivities.

**Monday, December 23** *(Moon in Taurus)* In spite of the holiday mood, you must get back to basics today and deal with some necessities. You may have to put service to others over your own personal enjoyment today—but you should be glad to do so. Don't neglect some important details that come in a message you receive; they will be important later on. You may be involved with a Taurus or a Scorpio today—either one of whom could appear a bit "pushy."

**Tuesday, December 24 (Moon Taurus to Gemini 3:46 a.m.)**    Do some creative thinking today, and you will discover the way to delight those you love. Variety is definitely the spice of life—no one knows that better than you. Even with all the excitement in the air, you should not overlook a rather serious matter of partnership. Set aside time to talk and to improve your understanding of some of the issues involved.

**Wednesday, December 25 (Moon in Gemini)**    Honest communication is one of the best gifts you receive. It creates harmony for those close to you and brings true joy at this time of the year. Your warmth and enthusiasm attract everyone—including some unexpected guests. Celebrate to your heart's content!

**Thursday, December 26 (Moon Gemini to Cancer 3:41 p.m.)**    The most productive thing you can do today is lie back and get your act together. As you watch the events unfold naturally, you will see why this is the best posture. One of your relationships is taking on a new look—and you may be seeing someone in a new light. Take it all in and wait before you make your move.

**Friday, December 27 (Moon in Cancer)**    Now you can move into high gear and take some decisive action. However, call upon some past experience to see exactly where you should make your breakthrough; you can score some major points if your timing is exact. The number 8 may be lucky today.

**Saturday, December 28 (Moon in Cancer)**    You may be feeling rather dreamy today, but there will be little time to dream. A practical approach will solidify the recent gains you made. If you are feeling a bit insecure, your anxieties fall away when you discover that one whose opinion is important to you totally approves of your actions. Strategic help may come from another corner as well.

**Sunday, December 29 (Moon Cancer to Leo 1:51 a.m.)** Don't wait for others to come to you today; if you do, an opportunity will simply pass you by. Something important to your overall development happens today—it is possibly a matter of travel or education. Here, too, ask a lot of questions and volunteer for "front-line" activity.

**Monday, December 30 (Moon in Leo)** By all means, complete what has been started today; that includes something that may have been started by someone else. You may resent it, but you will not regret it. As much as it ties you up today, it will free you up in the future. Make contact with a Cancer or a Capricorn— either one of whom could be very helpful in promoting your objectives now. The lucky number today could be 2.

**Tuesday, December 31 (Moon Leo to Virgo 10:06 a.m.)** You close out the year on an up-note. You feel like reaching out and you are highly optimistic— which is what you should be at this time. Enjoy your freedom from anxiety today, and resolve to keep it this way in the coming year. You can accomplish great things. Happy New Year!

# JANUARY 1986

**Wednesday, January 1 (Moon in Virgo)** The year for Sagittarius starts out on a high note. In your socializing you could easily run into someone who will be a big help in your career life. At the very least, ambition will be very much on your mind today, and you may be thinking about a rather serious job commitment. For some Scorpios, the serious attitude is toward a long-term relationship.

**Thursday, January 2 (Moon Virgo to Libra 3:45 p.m.)** Something has been hanging fire, and this is a good day to wrap it up totally. After that, you will be free to reevaluate just where you are going in life, and to look at the big picture. If you mix with people who are open-minded, you will find that they are a great source of inspiration. One in particular may be an Aries, and you should make an effort to get to know him/her better.

**Friday, January 3 (Moon in Libra)** Your independent attitude upsets someone today—or possibly more than one. Realize that if you don't give this matter more attention, you could easily lose someone. If you can't be there, at least be nice. Some Sagittarius will be feeling very original and ready to make a new start; make sure you are sure of your direction.

**Saturday, January 4 (Moon Libra to Scorpio 7:44 p.m.)** This is a much better day for getting along with people—particularly those very close to you. Most Sagittarians will be feeling rather home-oriented this weekend, and should spend as much time as possible with family. In some cases, a special celebration is in the picture. Sit back and take a much more passive than an active role today.

**Sunday, January 5 (Moon in Scorpio)** You may sense a touch of intrigue in the air today, and you are right. However, no one is really withholding anything from you. Don't spread yourself too thin by rushing from one thing to another—even mentally. This is an excellent time to utilize your cheerful disposition to cheer someone else up.

**Monday, January 6 (Moon Scorpio to Sagittarius 9:46 p.m.)** You could be feeling rather fenced in by cir-

170

cumstances today. Much as you dislike it, you are going to have to concentrate on detail work today and get some routine matters out of the way. Don't let it throw you, because a much freer time is coming. Be willing to work behind the scenes.

*Tuesday, January 7 (Moon in Sagittarius)*    Things are looking up considerably, and you should feel like kicking over the traces today. When you do, you will express yourself extremely well. For some Sagittarians, the time is right to get in touch with a member of the opposite sex and clear up a misunderstanding. Try a little heart-to-heart talk; just be sure you come off as totally sincere.

*Wednesday, January 8 (Moon Sagittarius to Capricorn 10:42 p.m.)*    Since you are very much in the spotlight now, you may realize you have not been paying enough attention to your appearance lately. Admit that you can get a little sloppy sometimes—and correct things. Sagittarians with artistic or musical talent can use it to create greater harmony in their environment. The lucky number today is 6.

*Thursday, January 9 (Moon in Capricorn)*    Some financial confusion could cause you needless worry; resolve not to get into this situation again. Do not be fooled by someone who promises you something for nothing, because there is simply no such thing. Try to keep your mind on "higher things" today because you will do better with them than "wordly things."

*Friday, January 10 (Moon in Capricorn)*    You are much more able to be realistic today—especially monetary things. Some Sagittarians will be prompted to ask for the raise they think they have earned. Don't be surprised if you get it. Others may be thinking of buying or selling for profit; long-term gains are very possible now. For best results, team up with a Capricorn.

*Saturday, January 11 (Moon Capricorn to Aquarius 12:01 a.m.)*     Those calls and letters may keep on coming today, as you find yourself in contact with many people. You should be in a rather giving mood and not be expecting too much in return. Don't undersell yourself however. And do not be taken advantage of by people who really need you, but are not willing to give in to your needs. Sometimes you can be a bit of a sucker.

*Sunday, January 12 (Moon in Aquarius)*     This is an excellent day to communicate in a clever, original way. If you have been thinking about a writing project, begin it now. You may find yourself smack in the middle of a group of flamboyant, dramatic types—the kind you like best. You may be asked to take the lead in organizing something. A Leo can be a lot of fun.

*Monday, January 13 (Moon Aquarius to Pisces 3:39 a.m.)*     If you had your way, you probably would not want to stir out of the house today. If you are lucky and can do it, stay home and let someone baby you. If you must go out into the world, let someone else take the lead, don't force any issues. Try your luck with number 2.

*Tuesday, January 14 (Moon in Pisces)*     Now you come back to life with a surge of energy and a desire to reach beyond your current boundaries, both mentally and physically. Even if all that is not really possible now, you can bring the world to yourself by reading and study. Isn't it nice to feel revitalized?

*Wednesday, January 15 (Moon Pisces to Aries 11:03 a.m.)*     Don't expect too much excitement today; do expect to get a lot accomplished. Patience and fortitude will be required to overcome some minor obstacles. Realize that you are rebuilding now and that things will be a lot sturdier after you do.

*Thursday, January 16 (Moon in Aries)*    You will have a much longer leash today, and be ready for all kinds of fun and games. Some people you come in contact with now could change your thinking; it could be particularly beneficial to your love life. Which could easily stand some rekindling at this time. The lucky number today is 5.

*Friday, January 17 (Moon Aries to Taurus 10:14 p.m.)*    Most Sagittarians will be in the mood to pamper themselves a bit today. Some will feel like doing it with "the sweets of life." Others will feel in the mood for a more cultural gambit. Music and art can really soothe Sagittarius' sometimes rather frazzled nerves. You could be helpful in settling a dispute today.

*Saturday, January 18 (Moon in Taurus)*    You may not be exactly clear about what is expected of you now, and you may find yourself stewing over the matter rather than attempting to clear it up. A few pointed questions will quickly reveal what the problem is. In the course of this day, some Sagittarians may find that they have been mistaken about someone that they idealize. It should be a lesson in being more realistic.

*Sunday, January 19 (Moon in Taurus)*    Today your head will be a lot clearer and you will have a much more clear-cut view of your duties and responsibilities. Now it is possible to show someone who is important to you just how much you can be trusted to follow through on things. You can expect some significant rewards today, particularly of the emotional kind. Your lucky number today is 8.

*Monday, January 20 (Moon Taurus to Gemini 11:12 a.m.)*    This is an excellent day for some personal public relations activity. Wherever you go, people will immediately pick up your positive vibes. It's possible that some Sagittarians have been selling themselves short; there may be more demand for your special talents than you have been aware of. It's important to be ready to break with the past in some way.

*Tuesday, January 21 (Moon in Gemini)*     The accent is on romantic developments in most Sagittarians' lives. Even if a relationship has been around for a long time, it will get a lot more mellow at this time. However, in trying to come closer to someone else, do not come on too strong or appear too eager. A relaxed but sincere approach will win the day.

*Wednesday, January 22 (Moon Gemini to Cancer 11:14 p.m.)*     Once again the emphasis is on your relationship life, but today it is less likely to be smooth. You may have overdone it, and are feeling a bit jumpy. However, don't make any rash moves. Let the ball stay in the other person's court. Later in the day, the situation will blow over and there will be peace again.

*Thursday, January 23 (Moon in Cancer)*     It is unlike you to take anything overly seriously—including yourself. Today it is particularly important to keep your sense of proportion. Getting overly analytical about anything—particularly a relationship—will not pay off now. Try to team up with someone relaxed—possibly another Sagittarian—and find your footing again.

*Friday, January 24 (Moon in Cancer)*     This is a good day to pay bills, balance your checkbook, and bring things up to date financially. A turn of events could put your mind squarely on money, and on achieving greater stability in your financial life. Someone may suggest a practical way to handle things, and you should listen carefully. Remember, this is a joint effort. Your lucky number is 4.

*Saturday, January 25 (Moon in Cancer)*     This is a rather unsettled day, and you may feel the effects. If at all possible, you should try to get a change of scenery. But not one that is too costly. Sagittarians are generally rather flexible, and now they should be more than ready to adjust to constantly changing situations. An exchange of ideas with a romantic partner will considerably clear the air.

**Sunday, January 26 (Moon in Leo)**   This full moon may find you in conflict between personal obligations and your desire to get away from it all. If you put your mind to it, you should be able to resolve a sticky situation in time to get some free time for yourself. You are going to have to work at keeping all your relationships on an even keel now.

**Monday, January 27 (Moon Leo to Virgo 3:51 p.m.)** Sagittarians may be uncharacteristically quiet today, but plenty will be going on in their minds. This is one of those days when Sagittarius can begin to hatch some really fabulous ideas. For the moment, they may not be too practical, but they do have long-term possibilities. Though it's OK to "escape" now, just don't romanticize things or people too much. A Pisces could be a great sounding board now.

**Tuesday, January 28 (Moon in Virgo)**   Now you come back into the practical world, and should be willing to deal with matters both large and small. A tough problem has no easy answers, but you will be able to solve it. Apply both your brains and some "elbow grease." Your lucky number today is 8.

**Wednesday, January 29 (Moon Virgo to Libra 9:10 p.m.)**   Many Sagittarians will be evaluating their career slot right now, and some will be thinking about cutting out. The reason is that the current situation is simply too limiting. Don't be afraid to strike out, however, you can stay right where you are and make things better, if you take a larger view of the situation. In a personal matter, try to be very forgiving.

**Thursday, January 30 (Moon in Libra)**   No matter what group you find yourself in, you can be—will be—

the leader. Some Sagittarians can expect to make a romantic coup. Whatever you do today, don't be afraid to show your style and come on fairly strong. The lucky number is 1.

*Friday, January 31 (Moon in Libra)* Sagittarians generally have a lot of hunches, and today you can trust one particular one. In some cases, it is wisest to take a passive rather than active role. Feelings are more important and more comfortable for you than logic now; it's OK to follow that route today. Someone older may give you a pat on the back and contribute to your sense of well-being.

# F E B R U A R Y   1 9 8 6

*Saturday, February 1 (Moon Libra to Scorpio 1:19 a.m.)* Many Sagittarians have to make a decision which has long-term effects; don't let petty fears and doubts cloud your vision. If you rise above small things and look at the overall view, you will be able to see clearly what needs to be done. However, it is important to keep your decisions and your plans to yourself right now. Don't spill it to an Aries.

*Sunday, February 2 (Moon in Scorpio)* You are going to have to find some constructive outlet for your energy and your aggressiveness today. Otherwise, you could find yourself in the middle of a royal battle. If necessary, continue to be secretive and to work privately. You will derive the most benefit from that modus operandi today. The lucky number is 1.

*Monday, February 3 (Moon Scorpio to Sagittarius 4:31 a.m.)* Now the moon moves into your own sign, and pushes you into the limelight. However, even though you feel highly energized, try to be a bit conservative before you rush into anything new. There are many possibilities here, and you must choose among them wisely. Don't neglect people who are important to your emotional security, but do bank on your intuition.

*Tuesday, February 4 (Moon in Sagittarius)* The accent is squarely on you today, and how you project yourself to the world. Be sure you are sure of your own self-image before you "go public." Someone will find you are a kindred soul now, and it could be an interesting relationship. Most Sagittarians will be feeling rather conscious of their image now; perhaps a shopping trip is in order.

*Wednesday, February 5 (Moon Sagittarius to Capricorn 7:02 a.m.)* Some practical matters are going to demand your personal attention now, and you will not be able to turn them over to anyone else. You might as well settle down to routine, and hard work—a solid approach is the only thing that will get results. Some Sagittarians should be aware of the need for diet and exercise. Self-discipline is in order today, if you are to get anywhere.

*Thursday, February 6 (Moon in Capricorn)* Now you feel like busting out and you should be able to do so. The accent is on change and variety. Also a possible surprise source of income that is suddenly revealed. Your words are golden today and could actually take off. Write them down. Someone who loves you could be very generous now.

*Friday, February 7 (Moon Capricorn to Aquarius 7:35 a.m.)* Someone may try to high pressure you today, or manipulate you. The subject will be money. It is important to be as diplomatic as possible and to work in a spirit of compromise. You two can strike a harmonious balance. Some Sagittarians should consider giving another a token of affection—possibly simply a bouquet of flowers.

*Saturday, February 8 (Moon in Aquarius)*    An important agreement is on the agenda; it is wise not to sign anything or agree to anything until you have all the facts and figures straight. Don't take anything for granted and do read between the lines. Realize that your head is a bit in the clouds, and you could possibly be fooled. Your lucky number is 7.

*Sunday, February 9 (Moon Aquarius to Pisces 11:32 a.m.)*    This is a much better day to say, "yes, I agree." You will be much more businesslike, enterprising, and ambitious. For some Sagittarians, an agreement means more responsibility and a look ahead to the future. Just do be certain that you are not biting off more than you can chew. Some Sagittarians will be very impressive to someone who is in a position to further their ambitions.

*Monday, February 10 (Moon in Pisces)*    Refuse to let anyone hold you back now; it's possible that someone close to you is limiting your growth. Not deliberately, but out of a mistaken sense of responsibility. Show that you are very able to handle things yourself. One way would be by completing something that's been hanging fire for a long time. Expect to meet a rather electrifying person who could spark your imagination.

*Tuesday, February 11 (Moon Pisces to Aries 6:21 p.m.)*    This is a day of high energy and lots of originality. You should be ready to make that bold new start or take that chance. In many areas, you can depend on your personal appeal to make you a winner. Some Sagittarians will find themselves smack in the middle of a romantic adventure—possibly right on their own home ground. The lucky number is 1.

*Wednesday, February 12 (Moon in Aries)*    Someone younger or less experienced may need some good advice now. Your protective instincts should be quite strong, and you should follow them. By staying relaxed and using a touch of imagination, you can turn a highly creative project—and get lots of applause. However, be willing to share things with others—including the making of decisions.

**Thursday, February 13 (Moon in Aries)**     Once again, you are highly charged, but you should take care not to scatter your forces in too many different directions. A very bright, witty person could stimulate your imagination—but possibly lead you astray as well. Take advantage of multiple opportunities for social life and entertainment. But realize that you can't do it all.

**Friday, February 14 (Moon Aries to Taurus 5:38 a.m.)**     It will quickly become clear that "the party's over" and that now is the time to get back down to work. Your possibly unsettled behavior pattern could unsettle other people today; make an effort to bring yourself down to earth. Be willing to wrestle with details—and try your luck with number 4.

**Saturday, February 15 (Moon in Taurus)**     A good heart-to-heart talk may be needed to clear the air today. The way to handle a possible dispute is to open up the lines of communication. Also, be flexible and willing to change your way of doing things. It is unlike you to be too rigid, and to insist on any particular routine. Take a lesson in flexibility from a Gemini.

**Sunday, February 16 (Moon Taurus to Gemini 5:17 p.m.)**     You could easily be tempted to overdo today. Your excesses could take any number of forms, including too many good foods or too much expensive entertainment. Enjoy, but do not endanger your physical or mental health. Your lucky number is 6.

**Monday, February 17 (Moon in Gemini)**     If you are puzzled about one of your relationships, you are probably reading more into it than is really happening at the moment. If you sit back and watch and let the other person take the lead, you will get a clear picture of what is really going on. All Sagittarians should force themselves to be realistic now—particularly about the potential of certain partnerships.

**Tuesday, February 18 (Moon in Gemini)**   You are in line for sharing in the prestige of someone else now; take it with good grace and do not be envious. Also, do not neglect your own responsibilities. Some Sagittarians should consult a pro who has a proven record of good advice. Others should tune in when there is talk about expanding the household in one way or another.

**Wednesday, February 19 (Moon Gemini to Cancer 7:39 a.m.)**   It will be clear to some Sagittarians by now that they must raise their expectations—and stop spoiling someone else by giving in to his/her every whim. This is a give-and-take relationship, and you may have been giving too much. If you let things go too far, you could find things falling apart. The key is to understand what makes you tick and what your needs really are. They could overwhelm you later on. The lucky number is 9.

**Thursday, February 20 (Moon in Cancer)**   A powerful physical attraction could come along and sweep you off your feet now. If you want it, this is the time for a sizzling romance. In all areas, this is the time for action and picking up where you left off. Whether it's love or some other kind of adventure, be ready for it. A Leo may be very much in the picture.

**Friday, February 21 (Moon Cancer to Leo 3:25 p.m.)** The emphasis is on joint finances and security. Someone may be pressuring you to think about savings for a rainy day. You should be willing to admit that it sometimes really does rain. Be willing to talk things over in a friendly way, to show that there's no hard feelings. This is one of those times you can depend on one of your famous hunches. You may seem to have ESP.

*Saturday, February 22 (Moon in Leo)*    Most Sagittarians will be too restless to sit at home now and will want to kick over the traces in some way or another. Social life should be particularly interesting, and you could even find yourself indulging in a little light-hearted flirtation. There's nothing wrong with it, as long as you both realize it's going nowhere. Your lucky number is 3.

*Sunday, February 23 (Moon Leo to Virgo 11:58 p.m.)* This should be a rather quiet Sunday, and a good one for sitting back and figuring out where you are going. It may become obvious that in order to reach that goal, you are going to have to do something practical about it. One thing might be further study. Don't try to get someone else to do things now; your personal attention is required.

*Monday, February 24 (Moon in Virgo)*    During this full moon, many Sagittarians will find themselves in the middle of a conflict—most possibly between home and career. In many cases, a sudden turn of events will create a new opportunity. Look into it and learn all you can, but be ready to talk it over with someone who is very important to you personally. In other cases, the emphasis today is on romance, and it can be exciting.

*Tuesday, February 25 (Moon in Virgo)*    Some Sagittarians are going to have to use a lot of diplomacy on the job today. It could be that someone in authority is not quite pleased. You can create an atmosphere of harmony around you if you are willing to make adjustments. Some of you may have to actually change your way of doing things—or your location. Don't neglect your artistic talents now. Your lucky number is 6.

*Wednesday, February 26 (Moon Virgo to Libra 4:07 a.m.)*    You could be the "hopeless romantic" today, causing you to withdraw into your own thoughts and away from the crowd. It's important to realize that no one person can fulfill all the needs in your life; if you expect them to, you are going to be disappointed. Be willing to join in the fun and games, even if you don't really feel like it.

**Thursday, February 27 (Moon in Libra)**    You should really bounce back today and have renewed energy. Your focus should be on bringing your dreams and hopes down to the level of practical reality, which you can do. Make a positive step by contacting someone in a position to help you. The backing you need will be there. Your lucky number is 8.

**Friday, February 28 (Moon Libra to Scorpio 7:06 a.m.)**    Now's the time to weed out people in your circle who are simply a drain on you, and give little in return. Sometimes you are a bit too indulgent with people. When you broaden your social scope, you will meet new friends who are a lot more pioneering, and a lot more success-oriented. You are generally optimistic, and you can be so with certainty now.

# MARCH 1986

**Saturday, March 1 (Moon in Scorpio)**    Romantically involved Sagittarians may find themselves in the middle of a rather dramatic scene today. Someone will let you know in no uncertain terms how much he/she cares—and wants to make sure you do too. On another front, the only thing that can hold you back today is your own lack of self-confidence. Don't let those fears and self-doubts overwhelm you—be bold and share your generous personality with others. Your lucky number is 1.

**Sunday, March 2 (Moon Scorpio to Sagittarius 1:51 a.m.)**    Make this a day for a lot of R&R, because a much busier, more taxing time is coming. Most Sagittarians will want to stay right on their own home ground today, because it will seem like an inviting retreat. You may hear a rumor that has been circulating and realize that it needs to be put to rest. Speak up. However, it is important not to force any issues.

**Monday, March 3 (Moon in Sagittarius)**    With the moon in your own sign, your cycle is high, and your popularity is widespread. Everyone will seem to want you on their team today—and you should dress and feel your self-expressive best. Anything new is worth trying today—no matter how adventurous. In your light-hearted mood, you will want a companion who thinks like you.

**Tuesday, March 4 (Moon Sagittarius to Capricorn 12:56 p.m.)**    You may find it rather difficult to keep your mind on your work today, but it is important to catch up on important details. Realize that this is a time of testing, and you will be judged by how carefully you speak, and how well turned-out you look. It's important to focus on all those little grooming details you sometimes tend to forget. Your lucky number is 4.

**Wednesday, March 5 (Moon in Capricorn)**    If you want a real bargain, you are going to have to compare prices before you buy. And possibly break new shopping territory. The key to any kind of transaction today is to be discriminating and to ask as many questions as you can. On the personal side, be willing to share your ideas and to make some kind of sentimental gesture. A Taurean could be very important.

**Thursday, March 6 (Moon Capricorn to Aquarius 4:42 p.m.)**    You may feel an urge to totally change your environment. Look into the expenses of various projects before you make any radical changes. The things worth investing in are those that will create greater harmony by being equally important to everyone.

*Friday, March 7 (Moon in Aquarius)*    It's possible for you to overreach now; see a situation as it really is before you go out on a limb. When you know the real facts about someone you admire, you may revise your opinion a bit. Take every opportunity to display your artistic talents.

*Saturday, March 8 (Moon Aquarius to Pisces 7:48 p.m.)*    It's important not to make any promises today unless you really intend to deliver. You are going to be tested on your sense of responsibility, and you must come up to the mark—especially if you want a relationship to last. In a business move, you will look good and gain a lot of prestige as a result. The lucky number is 8.

*Sunday, March 9 (Moon in Pisces)*    Someone around may be getting overly dependent on your company. You may have to reevaluate some of your close relationships and possibly loosen some ties in order for both of you to grow healthy psychologically. Your ideas and opinions deserve a wider audience.

*Monday, March 10 (Moon in Pisces)*    You could be especially sensitive today, in the best sense of the word. That means you should follow a hunch you have and investigate a new opportunity to get in on the ground floor of something. Your natural optimism will be well-rewarded now. An Aquarian would be an excellent person to talk things over with.

*Tuesday, March 11 (Moon Pisces to Aries 5:03 a.m.)* This is an excellent day for a stroll down Memory Lane. Nostalgia for the past is highlighted, as are all kinds of sentimental feelings. However, in a romantic matter, take a wait-and-see attitude—particularly before forcing your attentions on anyone else. Your lucky number today is 2.

*Wednesday, March 12 (Moon in Aries)*    You could feel that life is a three-ring circus today. It's great to be popular, but you may have trouble deciding on what direction to go in. In some cases, Sagittarians should be willing to laugh at their own foibles. If you've done something silly, be willing to admit it.

**Thursday, March 13 (Moon Aries to Taurus 3:04 p.m.)** You are going to have to put your back into a project today if you want to get it off the ground. It's possible to do so without stifling your spontaneity. The rule for the day is to learn the rules before you break them. Don't let any little things escape your attention, and you will be way ahead.

**Friday, March 14 (Moon in Taurus)** Some exciting things may be happening in your work life. In some cases, new equipment or new procedures will rekindle your interest. And your energy. A fast-talking person may attempt to change your mind, and you should be willing to listen. Don't tie yourself down to any one way of doing things. Your lucky number is 5.

**Saturday, March 15 (Moon in Taurus)** Sharing work with others will make things go faster and get you free of things early in the day. In some cases, a remodeling project or possibly a change of residence becomes a topic of high interest. Be willing to give a little in your typical Sagittarian fashion. A Libra or a Taurus really has much better taste than you do.

**Sunday, March 16 (Moon Taurus to Gemini 3:23 a.m.)** Someone who has some of the same values you do can be a great source of inspiration now. However, remember that no one is perfect—not even the person you love most. Partnerships and one-on-one relationships of all sorts are in the spotlight. See them as they really are.

**Monday, March 17 (Moon in Gemini)** Someone will help you if you show that you are willing to help yourself. You are not generally a dependent type, but sometimes you can slough off responsibility too easily. In all things, show that you are serious today.

**Tuesday, March 18 (Moon Gemini to Cancer 4:04 p.m.)**  You are better off finishing things than starting them right now. There are some valuable lessons to be learned from your current experience, and you should make an effort not to overlook them. If you feel a little strapped, realize that your cash flow will flow more easily in the near future. The lucky number is 9.

**Wednesday, March 19 (Moon in Cancer)**  Some Sagittarians can expect a rather generous gift now. Others should take a new look at their financial resources, and possibly make some changes. If you want to impress someone, be willing to make some rather drastic changes in your style.

**Thursday, March 20 (Moon in Cancer)**  Your security needs will be at the top of your mind today. It's an excellent time to open a new bank account or start some new money-saving habits. If you've got a money problem, don't brood over it, but share your concerns with other people. Then resolve to enjoy what you have. The lucky number is 2.

**Friday, March 21 (Moon Cancer to Leo 2:38 a.m.)**  Some Sagittarians may be looking forward to taking off for the weekend. However, don't let that distract you from what needs to be done today. On the other hand, if you feel you have more to handle than you are comfortable with, maintain a light touch and a sense of humor. You will come through with flying colors.

**Saturday, March 22 (Moon in Leo)**  Get set for a "rapid-fire" day in which all your shots could hit the mark. However, take care to keep solid ground under your feet, because your head could be a bit up in the clouds. One thing you could be concentrating on is a plan for future "adventure"—possibly a trip to a rather exotic place. Don't let a friendly exchange of ideas (possibly with another Sagittarian) escalate into a dispute.

**Sunday, March 23 (Moon Leo to Virgo 9:39 a.m.)** Now you really can throw off those restrictions and find life a lot more enjoyable and interesting. For some Sagittarians, love is at the top of the list today. In some cases, you may be carrying on a long-distance love affair. Expect the distance to close very soon. Your lucky number is 5.

**Monday, March 24 (Moon in Virgo)** Someone at the top is going to be a bit moody today, and you will have to handle him/her with care and diplomacy. However, it should be easy for you, and you should be able to promote harmony wherever you are. Keep your ears open for someone with a rather distinctive voice; he/she could be important in your future. Some Sagittarians will be celebrating a special occasion.

**Tuesday, March 25 (Moon Virgo to Libra 1:22 p.m.)** If you set your standards too high, you may be disappointed. There is no such thing as the perfect job—or the perfect person. Make the most of what you have, and be the best that you can be within your current circumstances. You may be a bit too dreamy today, and should attempt to see the situation as it actually is.

**Wednesday, March 26 (Moon in Libra)** The full moon could easily put you in a rather scattery frame of mind. Don't let people distract you into wasting time; you can make some significant gains today. Those long-term dreams simply won't come true if you don't do something tangible about them.

**Thursday, March 27 (Moon Libra to Scorpio 3:05 p.m.)** Join forces with other people in a rather large-scale venture. You can accomplish a lot more with group action than with personal action today. Don't hide your ideas behind a touch of shyness; you may be surprised at how acceptable they are. Check with an Aries.

*Friday, March 28 (Moon in Scorpio)* You are heading for a major breakthrough, but you may have to work quietly behind the scenes until you are recognized. Keep thinking those original thoughts and letting those creative talents flower. Some of you find yourselves involved in a secret love affair. The lucky number is 1.

*Saturday, March 29 (Moon Scorpio to Sagittarius 4:20 p.m.)* You may find yourself feeling a bit impatient today—both with people and your current situation. Trust your intuition to give you the answers and reassurances you need; no one else is likely to do it for you today. You will be more comfortable at home than in the outside world.

*Sunday, March 30 (Moon in Sagittarius)* As the moon breaks through into Sagittarius, your social life picks up momentum. Now you can break out of that rut and do something daring and different. Pay extra attention to how you look today, and "dress for success." You'll be glad you did. The lucky number is 3.

*Monday, March 31 (Moon Sagittarius to Capricorn 6:25 p.m.)* You are going to have to force yourself to settle down to the work week. A more Spartan attitude toward the pleasures of life is necessary. This is one of those days you can find excitement and fulfillment even in the most routine activities. By the end of the day, you should have a real feeling of accomplishment. The lucky number is 4.

# APRIL 1986

*Tuesday, April 1 (Moon in Capricorn)* Even though your mind may be very much on money today, it is not a day to begin a new financial program. Concentrate on figuring out how you can save rather than how you can spend. Time to hold on to what you have and to appreciate it for what it is. Some Sagittarians may receive a bonus of some sort.

**Wednesday, April 2 (Moon Capricorn to Aquarius 10:11 p.m.)**   Your money worries may seem temporarily solved today, and that could put you in a very optimistic mood. However, it could make you splurge more than you should. It's OK to be generous and outgoing, but don't go overboard. A witty, brainy person could very well be attracted to you today.

**Thursday, April 3 (Moon in Aquarius)**   You may feel chained to your desk or wherever you have to work today, which is of course something that Sagittarius dislikes intensely. You are wise not to complain to yourself or anyone else. Realize you are going through a testing time to show what you can really do. Take up every challenge and master it. Your lucky number is 4.

**Friday, April 4 (Moon in Aquarius)**   Get ready for the feeling of release and a sudden change. No matter what else happens, you are going to have some really brilliant ideas. Capture them on paper before they get away. Romance could be right under your nose.

**Saturday, April 5 (Moon Aquarius to Pisces 4:03 a.m.)**   You may have the burden of responsibility for harmony thrust squarely upon you. But your generally sunny disposition should see you through—along with everyone else. Do something to make life better for everyone, like adding a special touch of beauty or planning for a special entertainment. If you are alert, you will be able to settle a dispute even before it starts.

**Sunday, April 6 (Moon in Pisces)**   As a Sagittarian, you are generally willing to give people the benefit of the doubt. However, now you may be going too far in that direction. Realize that not everyone is as frank and outspoken as you are, and that someone may be hiding something from you. Try to get away from it all for at least a few minutes today.

**Monday, April 7 (Moon Pisces to Aries 12:12 p.m.)** You could be a bit pushy today, just to get what you want. Realize you could overplay your hand. Some new kind of enterprise—possibly a love relationship—can get underway if you really work at it. Your lucky number today is 8.

**Tuesday, April 8 (Moon in Aries)** This is one of those days you can rise above the ordinary and create a very special mood around you. If you put aside your own self-doubts, you can inspire everyone around you to great heights. Don't hesitate to express yourself in some way today; it could attract a rather dynamic person to you. Possibly an Aries.

**Wednesday, April 9 (Moon Aries to Taurus 10:36 p.m.)** Whether you've got a new love or an old love, life could become very romantic today. Mainly because of your daring mood. You are definitely ready for action, not just talk. Take advantage of your personal magnetism and go after what you want.

**Thursday, April 10 (Moon in Taurus)** If someone challenges you today, don't feel you have to respond. You can win by letting someone else take the lead—and possibly look foolish. A relaxed, warmhearted attitude will create a buffer zone around you and ease you through the day. Your lucky number today is 2.

**Friday, April 11 (Moon in Taurus)** The key word for you today could be "enjoyment." Whatever you have to do, you will do it with a lighthearted attitude. However, if you had your "druthers," you would put play above work. However, don't overlook a new job opportunity that could be right at your fingertips.

*Saturday, April 12 (Moon Taurus to Gemini 10:51 a.m.)*    You may have to revamp your personal plans for the weekend and handle some important duties that are suddenly thrown in your lap. Just grit your teeth and see them through, rather than running off at the first invitation. Your reward will definitely come, and your feeling of accomplishment will be only part of it.

*Sunday, April 13 (Moon in Gemini)*    You may have to do some fast talking today to settle a dispute that develops. Whatever else happens, keep the lines of communication open. No matter how strong the provocation is, you should maintain a low profile and be willing to be flexible. Let someone else make the decisions.

*Monday, April 14 (Moon Gemini to Cancer 11:42 p.m.)*    Someone around you will simply not be willing to compromise today; you are going to have to be gentle with him/her. As much as you feel you are over-extending yourself, you are going to have to make the necessary adjustment. Be glad that your live-and-let-live personality allows you to do this. Your lucky number is 6.

*Tuesday, April 15 (Moon in Cancer)*    Your rather dreamy attitude about finances simply won't work now; that becomes obvious when joint finances come into the spotlight. Resolve to avoid pie-in-the-sky situations that promise a lot but deliver a little. Don't jump at the first offer someone makes you. Tomorrow's decision will be better than today's.

*Wednesday, April 16 (Moon in Cancer)*    The emphasis is on successful transactions and on increase in income. Yesterday's snags are suddenly untangled. For some Sagittarians a serious love affair is very much in the picture. You may be feeling particularly emotional about it today. Your lucky number is 8.

191

*Thursday, April 17 (Moon Cancer to Leo 11:10 a.m.)*
Some Sagittarians have been too willing to let someone else hang on their coattails. It's time to let go of people who drain you—emotionally or financially. Be very clear-minded in your evaluation of a relationship. Remember, it's your future.

*Friday, April 18 (Moon in Leo)* Travel and expanded opportunities of all kinds are likely now. New faces and new places are what life should bring at this particular time. If nothing drops in your lap, go out and seek additional leadership opportunities. There are few if any roadblocks in your way.

*Saturday, April 19 (Moon Leo to Virgo 7:24 p.m.)* Memories of the past may strongly influence you today—and play a large part in future planning. Just make sure that sentiment does not cloud your logic. In making an important decision, seek the advice of someone older. And don't insist that something has to happen today.

*Sunday, April 20 (Moon in Virgo)* Don't turn down any invitation today, no matter how uninteresting it seems at first. You are slated to meet someone who can further your ambitions. You also could be challenged by someone's views—someone new to your circle. You can handle the differences with a light touch and a sense of humor. The lucky number today is 3.

*Monday, April 21 (Moon Virgo to Libra 11:50 p.m.)* Much as you may wish this day were more exciting, your attention will be fixed on routine matters. However, in your own quiet way, you will be advancing your own interests, and your prestige, in your present career situation. It's important to focus on a practical approach to every problem you encounter; by doing so, you will impress someone at the top who absolutely loves detail types. Later on, when you are more secure, you will be able to show your true colors.

*Tuesday, April 22 (Moon in Libra)* A heart-to-heart talk could lead to much greater understanding between you and someone else you consider rather important. As a matter of fact, once you comprehend how someone really feels, your admiration could turn into love. In everything, be flexible and willing to change your schedule at a moment's notice. Your social life may demand it.

*Wednesday, April 23 (Moon in Libra)* You may find yourself smack in the middle of a heated discussion today, possibly over a gathering that you or your family are planning. This is one of those times that you are going to have to show everyone else how to cool it and let things roll off their backs. The way that you usually can. Your thoughts, hopes and wishes will be centering around those people closest to your heart. It is one of those days when you do more for others than you do for yourself. The lucky number is 6.

*Thursday, April 24 (Moon Libra to Scorpio 1:15 a.m.)* This full moon could easily find you embroiled in a rather confusing situation. You could even call it a bit of intrigue. Keeping a secret today could be rather difficult but realize that it is necessary, particularly to protect your own interests. There are no easy answers today, and your wisest course is to look within for inspiration. A Pisces person could help you in this regard.

*Friday, April 25 (Moon in Scorpio)* A really big chance could come your way today in the form of a person who is willing to back you. However, realize that you are going to have to keep things rather confidential—particularly if you are going to keep the respect you have for this person. Self-doubts will only hold you back now; try to display your strength and your ambition. The lucky number today is 8.

*Saturday, April 26 (Moon Scorpio to Sagittarius 1:16 a.m.)* When the moon moves into Sagittarius, you

193

move into the driver's seat. Be sure to take advantage of this high in your lunar cycle to forge ahead in a large-scale project. Some Sagittarians may have found that their vision is a bit limited recently; now is the time to put petty matters behind you. Pioneering tactics are called for.

**Sunday, April 27 (Moon in Sagittarius)**    You should be feeling like a new you. Even your appearance could be changed, and you will positively vibrate with renewed vitality. In the recent past you have shown some promise; now is the time for you to fulfill that promise. Do not hesitate to express yourself today, in whatever manner comes easiest to you. In a marriage relationship or a love affair, you can score a lot of points with your most important person.

**Monday, April 28 (Moon Sagittarius to Capricorn 1:41 a.m.)**    In a financial situation, you can easily play for time now. It is important to examine all aspects of this matter and to go with a rather conservative approach. You can depend on your intuition today, but be a bit leery of your logic. For best results, listen to someone who offers excellent advice. It could be a family member. Your lucky number is 2.

**Tuesday, April 29 (Moon in Capricorn)**    You could be feeling rather expansive today in several respects. For one thing, you could be in a mood to treat everyone else. OK, but realize it will get expensive. Anything new will have great appeal to you today, and you should be in a rather lighthearted mood. Don't waste your time on small matters; you should open up your mind as far as it will go. Another Sagittarian may be involved.

**Wednesday, April 30 (Moon Capricorn to Aquarius 4:06 a.m.)**    You will be ready for a more settled routine today. Now is the time to catch up on all kinds of loose ends—particularly with regard to financial matters. No matter how tempted you are to cut corners,

194

stick to what needs to be done. You are in a mood to be amused, but realize that this could easily lead to trouble. Stay on the straight and narrow.

# MAY 1986

*Thursday, May 1 (Moon in Aquarius)*    This is one of those days you are able to spread a lot of joy around you. Wherever you go, communicate your ideas and your way of looking at things. You can help a lot of people. A lot of interesting offers may come your way, but don't stretch yourself too thin. Make a visit to someone who is expecting you. Your lucky number is 3.

*Friday, May 2 (Moon Aquarius to Pisces 9:30 a.m.)* OK, now it's time to get back down to business. Apply yourself in a disciplined fashion to something that requires your full attention. One particular phone call could be very important; respond to it in a businesslike fashion. Though it may seem like a drag, you will have to review and revise something you have already done. Realize you are building on a more solid base.

*Saturday, May 3 (Moon in Pisces)*    If you are feeling a bit down, get together with someone who is bright, witty and fun to be around. The scene could be your very own home ground, and you could suddenly pull together a rather good group of people for spontaneous fun. No matter what else happens, more can happen. Expect change, variety—and possibly even romance.

*Sunday, May 4 (Moon Pisces to Aries 8:01 p.m.)* Don't get your back up when someone lays down the law in no uncertain terms; it could be a parent or other authority figure. If you rebel, you will be giving the expected response—and starting a whole new problem. Get away by yourself, and you will see how you can restore harmony on the home front. In some more serious cases, a whole change of routine or possibly even residence is the ultimate answer. Your lucky number is 6.

**Monday, May 5 (Moon in Aries)** The world of fantasy may seem very real to you today, or at least you will wish it were real. In some cases, there is the danger of falling in love with someone who doesn't even know you exist. Other escapist tactics are also possible. Some of them are less damaging. It is important to realize that you have a lot of sympathy and compassion to share with others.

**Tuesday, May 6 (Moon in Aries)** Today a more realistic attitude should prevail and should help you win the admiration of someone who admires your style. In some cases, hard work is due to be rewarded with some kind of increase. And definitely more prestige. Some Sagittarians are taking a much more serious attitude about romance.

**Wednesday, May 7 (Moon Aries to Taurus)** Put your back into your work today, because you should be able to complete a great deal. If someone appears to envy you or makes a petty remark, don't take it seriously, particularly if it comes from a fellow employee. Realize that you've got what it takes and are going places. You are better off associating with people who understand your real potential.

**Thursday, May 8 (Moon in Taurus)** On this day, your mind is so clear, you should be able to see forever. Opportunities you never recognized before are right there before you, and you should be able to pounce on them with renewed vitality and zest. Your work sphere is particularly emphasized now. However, you can also expect a member of the opposite sex to be magnetized by your presence. Your lucky number is 1.

*Friday, May 9 (Moon Taurus to Gemini 5:26 p.m.)*
Now is time to slow down the pace and rest on your laurels a bit. This is a time for patient waiting rather than anxious self-assertion. Some Sagittarians will feel a definite need for a "security blanket" and will draw to themselves people who are nurturing, gentle, and affectionate. Enjoy the warmth.

*Saturday, May 10 (Moon in Gemini)*    Other people may take the lead today, but you should not feel stifled by this. You should be willing to gear your actions and reactions to moods of other people. However, if you keep a cheerful manner and a readiness to take off on exciting adventures, you will find that you are much appreciated.

*Sunday, May 11 (Moon in Gemini)*    You can quickly dispatch some unpleasant but necessary chores if you team up with someone who is in the same industrious frame of mind that you are. There are certain limitations to your actions today, and it is important to recognize them. That way, you will not be overly upset by the necessity to tend to the basics in a mountain of details. Your lucky number is 4.

*Monday, May 12 (Moon Gemini to Cancer 7:18 a.m.)*
Now is the time to open up and say what you need. There are people who are ready to help you and share their resources with you. In one particular case, you could really have your whole way of thinking about a relationship totally transformed when you come closer and achieve a new rapport. At all costs today, remain flexible.

*Tuesday, May 13 (Moon in Cancer)*    Give in to that urge to indulge someone you love today. It could be costly, but it will pay off great dividends of affection. Your own immediate circle is the most comfortable place for you to be now, and could be the antidote to

197

some possibly shaky and insecure feelings. Your lucky number is 6.

**Wednesday, May 14 (Moon Cancer to Leo 6:15 p.m.)** You could be especially sensitive to the needs of others today; in fact, you are so tuned in, you appear to have ESP. However, do not make any rash moves in the financial area. You are all too likely to fall for a pie-in-the-sky proposition now. Wait until your mind clears before you talk serious business.

**Thursday, May 15 (Moon in Leo)**    Realize that you have what it takes to make it in a successful long-term business venture. However, also realize you need a lot more information—as well as help and support. This is a time you might consider other training in order to advance yourself. Someone rather unlikely suddenly becomes a serious romantic prospect.

**Friday, May 16 (Moon in Leo)**    Take a long-range view about developing your talents now; if you limit your thinking, you will definitely limit your future. Be willing to explore every new idea and investigate every new prospect. One way to expand your current boundaries is by associating with someone who is way ahead of you in terms of future thinking. He/she is very good for you.

**Saturday, May 17 (Moon Leo to Virgo 3:45 a.m.)** Today you should be willing to take a whole new look at your career direction. Ask yourself if you are blindly following a path someone else has marked out for you—or striking out with originality in your own direction. You may not like the answer. However, if you used today's vitality and personal magnetism, you can take a giant step forward in your professional life today. A Leo could be inspiring.

**Sunday, May 18 (Moon in Virgo)**    Don't dismiss a casual conversation you have today as unimportant;

even a family contact could prove valuable in moving your cause forward. However, in most things you can wait for the world to come to you today. Meanwhile, let your emotions and your intuition be your guide, and really trust your own feelings now. You may see someone else getting all the glory, but you can bask in its reflected glow. Your lucky number is 2.

*Monday, May 19 (Moon Virgo to Libra 9:41 a.m.)* Accept a rather unusual and unexpected social invitation today. It could lead to some very interesting things. Your personality should have some special sparkle today, and it should be a help in impressing others with your potential for success. Something could easily pique your intellectual curiosity today and you should pursue it by all means.

*Tuesday, May 20 (Moon in Libra)* If you stick with the right people, you can be in a much better spot to turn your dreams to reality. A good solid approach and practical methods will win the day. If you are tempted to escape from routine or to cut corners, you will be the loser. Don't gloss over any detail!

*Wednesday, May 21 (Moon Libra to Scorpio 12:02 p.m.)* Any Sagittarian can easily expect a very romantic adventure today. For some, it will combine all the things you desire—including mental rapport. Even if that is not your scenario, you can expect a surprising social encounter with interesting developments. At least one thing that happens today will encourage your willingness to express yourself—and possibly even to travel. The lucky number is 5.

*Thursday, May 22 (Moon in Scorpio)* If at all possible, escape to a "secret retreat" today. The only way you can avoid disharmony is to seal yourself off—preferably with someone simpatico. If total seclusion is not possible, go all out and pamper yourself. Give yourself "the works," including an excellent meal and good music. If possible, throw in a little romance.

**Friday, May 23 (Moon Scorpio to Sagittarius 11:57 a.m.)** This may be a very difficult full-moon period for Sagittarius. For one thing, you may feel rather isolated—particularly by events—and somewhat sorry for yourself. Realize that you have the choice of looking within for spiritual values or wallowing in self-doubt. This is definitely one time you should choose the higher path.

**Saturday, May 24 (Moon in Sagittarius)** With the moon in your own sign, the world is suddenly full of sunshine and promise for the future. Some Sagittarians may even feel like swearing eternal love to someone who has really been by your side for quite a time. Others may be on the lookout for someone new to fulfill that role. The lucky number today is 8.

**Sunday, May 25 (Moon Sagittarius to Capricorn 11:15 a.m.)** Don't waste any time or energy on someone who keeps draining you with too many demands and gives little in return. This is an excellent time to reevaluate your relationships and to put some of them on a new footing. You may realize that some new acquaintances are more interested in your growth than in holding you back. This is progress!

**Monday, May 26 (Moon in Capricorn)** A little extra cash could easily be burning a hole in your pocket. You may be tempted to spend it recklessly and then regret it later on. If you must "show off" do it with words and gestures. Now you should be thinking about ways of increasing your income rather than ways of dissipating it. Don't let a Leo lead you astray.

**Tuesday, May 27 (Moon Capricorn to Aquarius 12 noon)** Today you may pull in your horns and become a lot more conservative. For one thing, you will

e much more willing to budget and to cling to what-
ver security you have. The influence of someone
lder—or at least wiser—could be responsible. You may
lso have looked at your assets and decided they are
ot up to snuff. Good thinking!

*Wednesday, May 28 (Moon in Aquarius)*     You may
eel a strong need for change and adventure now.
However, you may have to satisfy it with some rather
hort trips and some rather small talk. Your wit
nd humor should be in top form. Those who write
r teach can get their message across quite stunningly
ow. However, don't scatter your energies too reck-
essly. Your lucky number is 3.

*Thursday, May 29 (Moon Aquarius to Pisces 3:54 p.m.)*
There's no way you can get out of it; there is a lot of
work to be done today. In fact, you may be the one who
et it pile up. Only a practical, solid approach will get
you through looking good. Your best course is to make a
schedule and stick to it. You can accomplish what you set
out to do if you refuse to allow yourself to be distracted.

*Friday, May 30 (Moon in Pisces)*     Responsibility is
he keynote of the day once more, even though you
wish there were more fun on the calendar. Some rather
heavy obligations need to be gotten out of the way.
However, if you clear up practical matters quickly, you
can still get in some fun later on. Your wisest course is
o stay close to your own home base. Your lucky number is 5.

*Saturday, May 31 (Moon Pisces to Aries 11:43 p.m.)*
You may awake with a tremendous amount of energy and decide to put it into your domestic surroundings. Even simply rearranging the furniture will give
you that new look that is so important to you right now.
There is a touch of sentiment and romance to this
entire day, and you should end it on a very happy note.
The lucky number today is 6.

# JUNE 1986

**Sunday, June 1 (Moon in Aries)**    Someone may take you up on a promise you made recently and you should be ready to carry through on it. In some cases, it will be children or young people who say "let's go." No matter what else happens today, you will count it among the better "play days" you have had this year. An Aquarian could be an excellent buddy.

**Monday, June 2 (Moon in Aries)**    A conversation you get into today could have rather serious consequences—and some rather deep meaning. In some cases, you will make the discovery that someone has remarkably similar interests and tastes. It could be a situation of falling in love "mind first" and of then deciding there is a strong physical attraction as well. That's not all bad!

**Tuesday, June 3 (Moon Aries to Taurus 10:45 a.m.)** If you run into some opposition to your plans today, don't argue. Diplomacy and sweet talk are the ways to save the day. However, you are going to have to be more sensitive to the needs and feelings of others than you are inclined to be. It might be a good idea to plan a special treat or a special dinner. Your lucky number is 6.

**Wednesday, June 4 (Moon in Taurus)**    The emphasis is definitely on work, health, and practical matters today. If you use your imagination, you can find some new ways to do old things—and to streamline your procedures. Some Sagittarians may have a touch of hypochondria today and imagine some minor ills, or some minor slights. Realize this is counterproductive. Come back to reality and see the situation as it really is.

**Thursday, June 5 (Moon Taurus to Gemini 11:20 p.m.)**    Step forward with confidence today no matter where you are. Realize that your ideas and your words

202

will be heard and that you could easily receive a pat on the back from someone who counts. Your prestige is definitely on the rise and your lucky number is 8.

**Friday, June 6 (Moon in Gemini)**    You could easily be asked to give more than you receive today. Give in to it and go with the flow. However, if you feel that someone is asking too much of you, and that you are expected to be totally selfless, you may have to evaluate the relationship. Do not permit someone else to limit you or put you down.

**Saturday, June 7 (Moon in Gemini)**    You are definitely expanding your emotional horizons now and revising your thoughts about relating to others. It's quite clear to you now that you do not have to be a puppet or a doormat, and that you have no strings on you. With your physical magnetism so high, you will attract someone who is both generous and romantic. Good for you!

**Sunday, June 8 (Moon Gemini to Cancer 12:16 p.m.)** The focus shifts to financial considerations and security. You will feel most comfortable if you maintain the status quo today, and do not make waves or force issues. In some cases, someone will come through at the last minute with the help you need. It could be someone in the family. Your lucky number is 2.

**Monday, June 9 (Moon in Cancer)**    Don't confuse physical attraction with real love. It would be easy now, because you are both popular and eager for adventure. Just keep things light and maintain your sense of humor where a member of the opposite sex is concerned. Things will develop naturally in due time.

**Tuesday, June 10    (Moon in Cancer)**    Now it's time to settle down to a much more routine existence. That means, pay the bills and bring records up to date. It's important to know exactly where you stand financially. In some cases, you are going to have to show that you are a solid citizen with integrity by following through on an earlier promise. Your lucky number is 4.

**Wednesday, June 11 (Moon Cancer to Leo 12:11 a.m.)** You are generally a rather spontaneous type, so it won't be hard to say yes to a spur-of-the-moment proposition you get today. Be willing to stray off the beaten track a bit for adventure. In most cases, you will feel as though the weight of the world has lifted off your shoulders and you will feel free to do the unexpected. A Gemini or a Virgo could be an excellent companion.

**Thursday, June 12 (Moon in Leo)** A message comes in from someone at a distance, and it changes the complexion of your day. And your mood. You realize you can look beyond the immediate for inspiration and happiness and peace of mind as well. In another situation, you can be the one to settle a long-standing dispute by being your charming self. Just try to be diplomatic.

**Friday, June 13 (Moon Leo to Virgo 10:18 a.m.)** It would be all too easy for you to goof today. Your head is somewhere in the clouds and you could lose ground because of it. Check, check and double-check all your plans for errors or omissions. And don't fall prey to a sob story you hear from a stranger—or even someone you know very well. Caution is a keynote for the day.

**Saturday, June 14 (Moon in Virgo)** Someone may ask you to step into a leadership role today, and you should realize that it could be fun. The added responsibility will be well worth the "power and glory" you receive. No matter what today's particular scenario is for any particular Sagittarian, you will be able to display a businesslike manner and impress some impressive people. Your lucky number is 8.

*Sunday, June 15 (Moon Virgo to Libra 5:38 p.m.)* This is an excellent time to get your message across and widen your sphere of influence. If you advertise yourself and reach out with greater self-expression, you will be amazed at the results you get. Those who have been limiting you are about to step out of the picture, and you might want to give them an extra shove. A rather fiery, dynamic type will be there to give you advice.

*Monday, June 16 (Moon in Libra)* You should be willing to take the initiative in making a new friendship today. This is the time for action in every respect, and for daring to make your dreams come true. Your rather special style and supermagnetism will attract members of the opposite sex now. Handle with care! Your lucky number is 1.

*Tuesday, June 17 (Moon Libra to Scorpio 9:36 p.m.)* You could easily run into some resistance today and you should draw back without forcing the issue. A passive role is the right one to assume today. In many cases, you will feel like being babied, spoiled, or pampered a bit. Make sure you find someone to do it. Pay attention to a sneaky feeling you have about someone; you are probably right.

*Wednesday, June 18 (Moon in Scorpio)* You are going to have to laugh at yourself today. It will be good for you, and should dispel some of your fears and self-doubts. Realize that the answers you are seeking are probably right in your own backyard rather than out there in the world. It's an excellent time to read and meditate and think about things rather deeply.

*Thursday, June 19 (Moon Scorpio to Sagittarius 10:36 p.m.)* Once again, you may be feeling a bit uneasy. Instead of fighting your feeling, settle down to routine and catch up with all kinds of details. If you just keep plugging along, you will be able to overcome a major obstacle. By the end of the day, you will feel as if you are coming out of the woods. Your lucky number is 4.

**Friday, June 20 (Moon in Sagittarius)** With the moon in Sagittarius, no one can tie you down now. No matter what you do, you will find yourself experiencing a change of scenery—and possibly even a romantic involvement. At the very least, you will be involved with a rather talkative, very charming member of the opposite sex who thinks you are positively super. It could be a Gemini.

**Saturday, June 21 (Moon Sagittarius to Capricorn 10:00 p.m.)** This month's full moon could easily put you in a romantic mood. In many cases, the setting will be your own home ground—and you will be in a frame of mind to settle differences between you and your loved one. It is possible to arrive at a compromise and turn gloom and doom into sweetness and light.

**Sunday, June 22 (Moon in Capricorn)** Hang onto your money today in every sense of the word. You could easily be in a rather unrealistic mood where finances are concerned. If you raise your sights beyond mundane matters, you will do much better. It is an excellent time to enjoy the beauty of nature and put your mind on "higher things." A Pisces could be particularly understanding.

**Monday, June 23 (Moon Capricorn to Aquarius 9:50 p.m.)** You should begin the work week with a serious attitude toward bettering your place in the world. It is important to follow up on your ambitions, and not to lose heart. There are definitely ways you can add to your income and also utilize your real talents more effectively. Seek them out! Your lucky number is 8.

**Tuesday, June 24 (Moon in Aquarius)** Someone may have been overly dependent on you lately, and now it is time for a heart-to-heart talk. You should both realize that you may be holding each other back by cutting off outside contact. If necessary, many Sagittarians are going to have to make a break with the past. It's all in the interests of greater growth.

**Wednesday, June 25 (Moon in Aquarius)**    Put aside routine chores and strike out to make that daring move you have been half afraid to attempt. It could be as simple as writing a letter or placing a phone call that will initiate something. Today you can count on your own creativity and your personal charisma to put you way ahead. Your lucky number is 1.

**Thursday, June 26 (Moon Aquarius to Pisces 12:12 a.m.)**    Today you may feel like pulling into your shell and escaping from the outside world. You will be extra emotional and sensitive. It's OK to indulge yourself, but don't brood over it. Someone older has the advice and inspiration you need right now, and you should seek him/her out. It could be a Cancer.

**Friday, June 27 (Moon in Pisces)**    You definitely will not be bored today; in fact, you may be dashing off in so many directions that you will have to keep your sense of humor ready. In all your running around, don't overlook the fact that good fortune could be right in your own backyard. Focus on some property matters you have been overlooking. In other cases, start studying that subject that interests you.

**Saturday, June 28 (Moon Pisces to Aries 6:35 a.m.)**    Realize that people are watching you today and that you must set a good example for them. That means not running out on a promise or obligation—particularly to a young person. It is not a time to back down on anything. Get some vigorous exercise to shake off those slightly uneasy feelings.

**Sunday, June 29 (Moon in Aries)**    Today a party mood will take over. In some cases, a quick change of plans could leave you absolutely breathless and enchanted! Someone could easily walk on the scene who shares your interests, and wants to get interested in you. It could all be very romantic for now.

*Monday, June 30 (Moon Aries to Taurus 4:54 p.m.)* This is the day to light up someone's life—even your own. That means, beautify your surroundings, no matter where you are. You should be extremely sensitive to anything that smacks of disharmony and be ready to set it to rights. This also applies to your close relationships. Why not plan a special celebration? Your lucky number is 6.

# J U L Y   1 9 8 6

*Tuesday, July 1 (Moon in Taurus)* You should be active, energetic and full of ideas for changes in the way you do things at work. In fact, you can set a good example by being willing to change with the times. No matter how unpopular, you can put your personal views across with wit rather than with emotional demands. Your lucky number is 5.

*Wednesday, July 2 (Moon in Taurus)* It is definitely a time to freshen up your surrounding and add some special touches. It will lift your spirits as well as the spirits of those around you. As a matter of fact, it could head off an argument that is brewing. Tact and diplomacy will also aid your cause. There is someone who is very loyal to you and you should let him/her know that you appreciate it.

*Thursday, July 3 (Moon Taurus to Gemini 5:32 a.m.)* Something is rather baffling today and it could be one of your relationships. Could it be that you are asking too much? Or perhaps sending out confusing signals? Try to put aside your own rather sensitive feelings now and listen to the problem of someone else. You are much better at giving than taking.

**Friday, July 4 (Moon in Gemini)**     Now the tables may be turned, and someone may be expecting more from you than you are willing to give. It's time for a long talk, and perhaps a compromise whereby you each adjust to the other's viewpoint. The day could end on a rather successful note—if you try for it. The lucky number is 8.

**Saturday, July 5 (Moon Gemini to Cancer 6:19 p.m.)** Once again, the focus is on your needs as compared to the needs of another. However, things should be righting themselves. On another front you will gain more by teaming up with pioneering types than those who are too scared to go forward. Show that you can rise above petty issues and petty people, and refuse to be confined to small minds.

**Sunday, July 6 (Moon in Cancer)**     Many are entering a new phase—one in which the generosity of another person will be very helpful to your advancement. In many cases, your renewed vitality is apparent. It could help you immensely in love and romance. Now's the time to be daring and to state your real desires to someone who is important in your life. It could be a Leo.

**Monday, July 7 (Moon in Cancer)**     Hold onto your cash today. This is definitely a time for saving rather than spending. However, there may be some real bargains—and grabbing them off could symbolize your commitment to security and safety. Someone older has good financial advice and you should listen.

**Tuesday, July 8 (Moon Cancer to Leo 5:56 a.m.)**     The urge to travel could interrupt some routine schedule that you had planned. Those who can't simply take off should seek out mental experiences that broaden their horizons and people who are at least able to talk in a different dimension. It is important to expand your consciousness now. Your lucky number is 3.

**Wednesday, July 9 (Moon in Leo)**   Some kind of different attention is necessary today. That means that your urge for freedom could definitely be restricted, and you could be a bit hemmed in. Don't give in to the temptation to pass the buck and let someone else take over your work. Only you can do it. Those who are studying anything will find this an excellent time.

**Thursday, July 10 (Moon Leo to Virgo 3:50 p.m.)** O.K., now you can cut out and indulge your love of adventure. All should try to maintain a flexible schedule because there could be many changes of plan. In some cases, there will be a very satisfying interchange of ideas with a member of the opposite sex. He/she is "creative" enough to earn your respect.

**Friday, July 11 (Moon in Virgo)**   It is important to see both sides of a story today. That is the only way to maintain harmony—inside as well as outside of you. It is not wise to be stubborn or to refuse to compromise. If you play the game, money could come your way.

**Saturday, July 12 (Moon Virgo to Libra 11:40 p.m.)** You may be more in the limelight today than you would like to be. If you are looking for privacy and time to concentrate on personal issues, you may be disappointed. However, realize that others look up to you and regard you as a role model. Go along with it for now. Your lucky number is 7.

**Sunday, July 13 (Moon in Libra)**   If you are involved in any kind of group, now's the time to make a name for yourself. There could be a significant meeting of the clan today. If you are willing to accept a leadership role, even if it means a lot of work, you will find it very satisfying. And ultimately rewarding. Ask a Capricorn.

*Monday, July 14 (Moon in Libra)*    You had better take a second look at a relationship that is restricting your freedom of movement. In some cases, it is possible that the wish to help someone else may be doing more harm than good. Realize that if you simply serve as a crutch, you will hinder someone else's growth. Try to widen your circle now.

*Tuesday, July 15 (Moon Libra to Scorpio 4:58 a.m.)* Someone who stays in the background can really benefit you now. In some cases, he/she will be providing the resources you need. In other cases, it will be a secret romance that bolsters your spirits. Many are heading for a major breakthrough now and should brush off some ideas that they have been sitting on for a while. The lucky number is 1.

*Wednesday, July 16 (Moon in Scorpio)*    You could be uncharacteristically touchy today, and aware of all the nuances of your feelings—as well as the feelings of others. To some, ESP experiences are even possible. However, you may not be totally comfortable today, so look for comfort and security wherever you can find it.

*Thursday, July 17 (Moon Scorpio to Sagittarius 7:34 a.m.)*    Everything feels a lot better today, and you should be able to breathe a sigh of relief. Some should even prepare for either travel or another brand new experience. Circumstances will be much less limiting now. It's highly possible that you will encounter a kindred soul who has a lot of the same interests that you do. Follow up on this.

*Friday, July 18 (Moon in Sagittarius)*    If you apply yourself steadily and seriously today, you can accomplish a great deal. Duty is definitely calling. In some cases, you may have to go back and redo something you have already done; be sure to see this project through! The lucky number is 4.

*Saturday, July 19 (Moon Sagittarius to Capricorn 8:10 a.m.)* Now you can relax and enjoy the attentions of a rather special member of the opposite sex. The two of you may have a lot of catching up to do, and comparing of notes on experiences and ideas. You should feel a great weight lift off your shoulders—especially in the presence of this person. A Gemini could easily be in the picture.

*Sunday, July 20 (Moon in Capricorn)* The accent is definitely on money and everything that money can buy. Some Sagittarians may be considering important purchases—probably in connection with home improvement. It's important to be willing to make some adjustments, even if they are not totally your cup of tea. Peace and harmony are worth it.

*Monday, July 21 (Moon Capricorn to Aquarius 8:17 a.m.)* You could dream some rather impossible dreams today—particularly about money and other expectations. Don't let emotions cloud your judgment now, particularly in a financial transaction. Count your change in every sense of the word, and don't expect something for nothing. Get some sober advice.

*Tuesday, July 22 (Moon in Aquarius)* You should be ultra-serious when you make promises now or seal agreements. This is no time to enter into anything lightly. In some cases, an ambitious business venture can well succeed, with the right person's backing it. Don't be afraid to ask. Love and marriage are under very good aspects now.

*Wednesday, July 23 (Moon Aquarius to Pisces 9:59 a.m.)* You could easily find "high adventure" right in your own backyard today. In some cases, it will be of a romantic nature. Someone around you may be dwelling in the past, and you should not let it get you down. Instead, go with a fiery, dynamic type who talks your language and could take your heart by storm. Your lucky number is 9.

**Thursday, July 24 (Moon in Pisces)**    You may be full of razzle-dazzle now, but you are also going to have to display how solid you are. Your reputation depends on it. Some Sagittarius will entertain in a rather unique manner; your home could easily be the center of a lot of attention right now. The lucky number is 1 today.

**Friday, July 25 (Moon Pisces to Aries 3:02 p.m.)**    It is important not to force any issues today, but to maintain an attitude of watchful waiting. Be as receptive as possible to the ideas of others. Some of you will feel a very strong need for proof of affection now; you can get it without being overbearing. Your lucky number today is 2.

**Saturday, July 26 (Moon in Aries)**    Most likely you will be feeling very much in the mood for fun—and freedom. Just don't stray too far off the beaten track. In some cases, there will be a clash of ideas and a love affair could be threatened. Realize that you are being a bit reckless now with both money and love.

**Sunday, July 27 (Moon in Aries)**    You can easily overcome a major obstacle if you refuse to get flustered, and agree to settle down to details. It's important now to conquer your restlessness and your need for change and excitement. Realize that you can get a lot more of lasting value by being a patient plodder now, much as you may dislike it.

**Monday, July 28 (Moon Aries to Taurus 12:11 a.m.)** You can be very influential in your place of business today. It should be easy to convince those who work with you that new ways are better than the old. If necessary, put your ideas in writing. They will carry a lot of weight. All kinds of exciting developments are indicated today including romance. A Gemini may be involved.

*Tuesday, July 29 (Moon in Taurus)*   A gentle manner and a tactful approach will be your best assets today. That is, if you are really serious about selling yourself or promoting your own interests now. Your desire for perfection is strong now, but you should not let it overrule your creativity. The lucky number is 6.

*Wednesday, July 30 (Moon Taurus to Gemini 12:19 p.m.)*   You are better off maintaining a low profile now. Let someone else take over the major decisions and be the visible one. As for you, you will be much too easily influenced because of your rather dreamy mood and your unrealistic attitude toward life now. For marrieds, realize that it could be detrimental to your relationship. See the situation as it really is.

*Tuesday, July 31 (Moon in Gemini)*   By all means get out and meet the public today; there are many ways in which you can establish greater prestige for yourself. Some will find that ambitious undertakings get the backing they need now; that's because you have shown others how reliable you can be. Good for you! Your lucky number is 8.

# A U G U S T   1 9 8 6

*Friday, August 1 (Moon in Gemini)*   Don't allow a domestic situation to get out of control. If you play the passive accommodating role, it will work. Simply refuse to be flustered by differences of opinion or outbursts from someone else. However, you should try to tone down your Sagittarian directness. Your lucky number is 6.

*Saturday, August 2 (Moon Gemini to Cancer 1:04 a.m.)*   Joint finances need a lot of looking at now; you may have been living on wishful thinking. If you put things in concrete terms, money matters will come into focus. This is no time for vague generalities. Shop if you must, but don't fall for any bargains that seem to be true, they probably are.

**Sunday, August 3 (Moon in Cancer)**    Both love and money are under better aspects today. In fact, an affair of the heart could be getting a lot more serious and a lot more interesting—mainly because you are more willing to commit yourself. See what happens when you don't run away from responsibility? The physical side of love is important now—as is a Capricorn.

**Monday, August 4 (Moon Cancer to Leo 12:26 p.m.)** Keep your eye on the big picture and the long-term outcome of something. If you get bogged down in what's happening for the moment, you will lose your perspective. However, it's important to double-check all details before you embark on any kind of venture. Realize that you are rising above a petty situation and that you are the much bigger person. Your lucky number is 9.

**Tuesday, August 5 (Moon in Leo)**    It's time for new beginnings and perhaps the cutting off of old ties. Something dramatic and spectacular could possibly totally revise your current scene. Be willing to think original thoughts, and refuse to be limited by the past. In some cases, a romantic adventure is highly possible.

**Wednesday, August 6 (Moon Leo to Virgo 9:44 p.m.)** If you insist on dwelling on regrets about the past, you will slow yourself down considerably. This is no time for nostalgia. Those who try to "go home again" will find that it is not possible. However, it's important to acknowledge your indebtedness to those who have been important to you; however, just don't let it make you give up your long-range goals.

**Thursday, August 7 (Moon in Virgo)**    Your popularity is your greatest asset now—particularly in making a career move. You will find that many are willing to help you move up the ladder. It's a day you can expect to be in the spotlight, so dress the part. Whatever else happens, your sense of humor and witty manner will impress someone important.

*Friday, August 8 (Moon Virgo to Libra 5:05 a.m.)* It's time to settle down. Try to stick to a routine today and schedule your time. If you take a solid approach and show how serious you really can be, you will benefit immensely. Your pay may be purely emotional, but it is well worth it. An Aquarian or a Leo could figure prominently.

*Saturday, August 9 (Moon in Libra)* Now the restrictions lift and the invitations should come pouring in. For some a casual get together turns out to be the scene of an exciting development—possibly in the field of romance. Any Sagittarius can expect to be face to face with someone who encourages his/her self-expression now. And wants to share ideas. The lucky number is 5.

*Sunday, August 10 (Moon in Libra)* You may have to smooth over a disagreement before it starts today, and it may take all the tact you can muster. On the other hand, a lot of pleasurable things are indicated, including good food, good friends, and good music. Your home may be the very best place for entertainment now.

*Monday, August 11 (Moon Libra to Scorpio 10:36 a.m.)* Realize that wishful thinking never made dreams come true. If others don't live up to your expectations, you should consider whether or not you have been realistic. However, there's no point in feeling sorry for yourself. Instead, listen sympathetically to someone else's problems. The lucky number is 7.

*Tuesday, August 12 (Moon in Scorpio)* It should be easy for you to pull strings from behind the scenes today. Just don't get overly manipulative. Someone whose success you greatly admire will share some of his/her secrets with you; it could easily help you get ahead. Don't let self-doubt or fears hold you back now.

**Wednesday, August 13 (Moon Scorpio to Sagittarius 2:17 p.m.)** Many Sagittarians are undergoing a change in consciousness now. That means taking a broader, more altruistic viewpoint toward life; for some, there may be real involvement in good works and good causes. It is important to let go of a past involvement that is causing you to eat your heart out. It only holds you back.

**Thursday, August 14 (Moon in Sagittarius)** Now you can step forward with confidence, because you are in a high lunar cycle and can call your own shots. In one way, your originality sets you apart from the crowd. In another way, your personal magnetism draws a lot of people to you. Expect greater rapport with someone very interesting. Your lucky number is 1.

**Friday, August 15 (Moon Sagittarius to Capricorn 4:22 p.m.)** Diet, exercise, and security needs should be at the top of your list today. In some cases, it would be wise to retreat from the public light—no matter how much you are enjoying it. Your moods and emotions could sway you a bit now, and you may need to get a firm grip on yourself. Let someone older be a good companion now.

**Saturday, August 16 (Moon in Capricorn)** An extravagant mood could overtake you today, so it's important to watch your spending. That means, don't be too ready to grab the check or to entertain others too lavishly. However, it's a good time to do some personal revamping—particularly with the idea of winning someone's heart and mind. You can do it!

**Sunday, August 17 (Moon Capricorn to Aquarius 5:44 p.m.)** Spend some time assessing your current financial situation and bringing records up to date. It's one of those days you will be able to zero in on the facts and figures, and come to some practical, detail-oriented new procedures for handling your money. You may need that. Your lucky number is 4.

*Monday, August 18 (Moon in Aquarius)* Your mind may be racing today, and it may be difficult for you to hold on to one idea before you get another one. Try to get your thoughts down on paper. Someone compounds the situation by doing a lot of fast talking; however, the scenario may be a romantic one so you will not mind. Just don't get overly stimulated.

*Tuesday, August 19 (Moon Aquarius to Pisces 7:52 p.m.)* This month's full moon could bring tensions and high emotions in your domestic sphere. If you find yourself caught between two factions, do not feel that you have to side with either. In fact, you can easily play the role of peacemaker. It could be as simple as suggesting some distractions.

*Wednesday, August 20 (Moon in Pisces)* You may feel a real urge to escape your responsibilities today; in some cases, you will really want to run away from it all. If you can, do spend some time with nature or some other kind of soothing environment, like music or art. If you delve deeply, you can discover the truths that lie within you. A Pisces could be an excellent soulmate now.

*Thursday, August 21 (Moon in Pisces)* Now you are back to reality, and much more able to cope with what needs to be done. Good fortune could be right in front of you today, in the form of something connected with real estate or property. For many, a love affair is deepening and there may be talk of settling down. The lucky number today is 8.

*Friday, August 22 (Moon Pisces to Aries 12:27 a.m.)*
Some vigorous physical activity may be what you need today—and what you desire. Whatever else you have to do, be sure to give your body some kind of workout. You may get a real creative lift by mingling with people who have very different backgrounds or talent than you do. Take it all in!

*Saturday, August 23 (Moon in Aries)* There is a great emphasis on love and romance now. In fact, some will find themselves "walking on air," especially when a rather generous individual decides to show them off all over town. Be sure to dress for the occasion, to show how original and witty you can be. Your lucky number is 1.

*Sunday, August 24 (Moon Aries to Taurus 8:36 a.m.)*
The focus continues on pleasure, as well as fun and games. However, there is a slightly lower keynote to the day. Why not allow that and let yourself enjoy some good company and some good food. Later on, you may have to do some nurturing for a loved one who is feeling a little down. You can afford to spread some joy around.

*Monday, August 25 (Moon in Taurus)* Even if you appear to settle down to work today, your mind and your heart are likely to be somewhere else. In fact, it may be obvious to others, which means your suggestions for changes in the work routine may not be taken seriously. Be willing to maintain your sense of humor, and to laugh at yourself, which may be necessary.

*Tuesday, August 26 (Moon Taurus to Gemini 8:00 p.m.)* Depending on how you play it, you could spend the day wailing about the obstacles to your progress, or you can settle down and overcome them through patient work and attention to detail. If you choose the latter course, you will prove yourself—and end up bask-ing in the glow of compliments for a job well done. The lucky number is 4.

**Wednesday, August 27 (Moon in Gemini)** You may find yourself busy adjusting to the whims and desires of someone else today—someone you love. It may be the only way to keep a problem from erupting. In another matter, learn the story behind the story before you criticize anyone. It's an excellent time for a heart-to-heart talk, which may be the key to progress.

**Thursday, August 28 (Moon in Gemini)** Once again, you may have to maintain a low profile and a big smile in order to keep the peace. Even if you must bite your tongue, don't just simply say how you really feel. That would be counterproductive now. Instead, try to "kill someone with kindness" plus a little sentiment, music, and romance.

**Friday, August 29 (Moon Gemini to Cancer 8:40 a.m.)** You may feel like retreating into your shell today. You can be alone without really feeling lonely now. However, don't waste time being in love with an illusion rather than a real person. Count your blessings and reassess your values; life is not all that bad. Your lucky number is 7.

**Saturday, August 30 (Moon in Cancer)** This is a time for joint decisions. Because you have your act together, you can make some good moves—particularly in the financial area. You now have faced reality and know exactly where you stand. You should feel very heartened by support of family members or authority figures who demonstrate how much they believe in you. Tangibly.

**Sunday, August 31 (Moon Cancer to Leo 8:08 p.m.)** Many Sagittarians are about to close a chapter on a part of the past that has been holding them back. Make a clean break. Others should refuse to carry a burden

220

that is not really theirs; you have enough problems clearing up your own obligations and debts. Team up with inspirational people who take a fairly broad view of life.

# SEPTEMBER 1986

*Monday, September 1 (Moon in Leo)*     Even though you may feel a real need to get away from it all, you may not be able to because of important commitments. However, allow yourself to indulge in a "voyage of the mind." You may visit some pretty amazing places. Now's the time to emphasize higher things and to associate with people who give you a life rather than those who can prove to be a drag.

*Tuesday, September 2 (Moon in Leo)*     It may be obvious by now that you are going to have to get additional training or education before you can make a significant career move. If you show you are serious and ready to learn, you may find current employers more than willing to help. It's important to make a commitment to the future now, and to get your act together. A Capricorn or a Cancer could be very helpful in this regard.

*Wednesday, September 3 (Moon Leo to Virgo 5:06 a.m.)*     It should be easy for you to tell the difference between what really matters and what is simply a straw in the wind. By latching on to important ideas as well as important people, you could really forge ahead now. However, realize that you've got to put your back into it and broaden your horizons at the same time. The lucky number is 9.

*Thursday, September 4 (Moon in Virgo)*     For many, a new phase begins today. As you show your initiative and your willingness to lead, you will impress the right people. A little bit of self-promotion wouldn't hurt either. Outside the work sphere, your charisma could easily draw someone to you who is both generous and romantic.

*Friday, September 5 (Moon Virgo to Libra 11:33 a.m.)*    It may seem as if obligations are overwhelming you today. There is no doubt that concerns of others will take precedence over your own plans today. However, you will not be uncomfortable as you draw back from the spotlight. In fact, you will feel rather secure in the company of those you know and trust. Take care not to force any issues today. Your lucky number is 2.

*Saturday, September 6 (Moon in Libra)*    A lighter, brighter mood will make this a more pleasant day if a rather restless one. Your urge will be to take off in some direction, wherever there are friends and fun. You are right to indulge your intellectual curiosity now, and to mingle with people who have a very different perspective than you do. However, don't scatter your forces too widely.

*Sunday, September 7 (Moon Libra to Scorpio 4:15 p.m.)*    Today you've really got your act together, and should be able to cut through a lot of red tape in order to get a group moving in the right direction. You will be at the center of activity. Some things you simply must do yourself and should not delegate authority to anyone else. An Aquarian could play a key role.

*Monday, September 8 (Moon in Scorpio)*    Someone could slip you a secret message today, and it could totally change the complexion of an affair of the heart. You are good at keeping your feelings hidden in this matter, but make sure that the person who matters most knows how you feel. No matter what your situation, it is an excellent time to exchange ideas with someone else and not hold back. Your lucky number is 5.

*Tuesday, September 9 (Moon Scorpio to Sagittarius 7:40 p.m.)* You may have to listen to somebody else's problems and do what you can to solve them. At best, you can seek a compromise. If you show a lot of affection and are extremely generous with someone, a rather touchy situation could clear up miraculously. Try a little tenderness—and a nice gift as well.

*Wednesday, September 10 (Moon in Sagittarius)* You may look better on the outside than you feel on the inside today. With the moon in Sagittarius, you are entering on a new cycle, but you may not be as sure of your new direction as you could be. Keep tuned in to your inner voice, and some kind of psychic experience could help clarify your situation. A lucky number is 7.

*Thursday, September 11 (Moon Sagittarius to Capricorn 10:28 p.m.)* Now you know where you are going in no uncertain terms. You are definitely in the driver's seat, and a leadership position could be thrust upon you. Be sure to react with responsibility and confidence. At the same time, your love life should be thriving, and the future should look bright. Your lucky number is 8.

*Friday, September 12 (Moon in Capricorn)* It may seem as if money is simply flowing through your fingers now, but in your generous mood you are spending on others as easily as you are on yourself. It's great to be a do-gooder, but you must remember that you can't buy love—or loyalty. Try to rise above petty motives and take the broad view. That is, if you want true happiness. An Aries could play a major role.

*Saturday, September 13 (Moon in Capricorn)* A secure financial position is within your grasp—if you develop some original ideas that come to you today. Don't pass them off as unworkable. It is very possible to promote big schemes and dreams, and to get in on the ground floor of an exciting new venture. Don't hang back. Your lucky number is 1.

**Sunday, September 14 (Moon Capricorn to Aquarius 1:07 a.m.)**    You may feel as though everyone is trying to manipulate you now. If you feel pushed, don't push back. A show of love and affection will accomplish a lot more than a show of force. If you try, you can really enjoy a quiet, homey day—full of good food and other good things.

**Monday, September 15 (Moon in Aquarius)**    If you want to feel free today, spend your time getting around and gathering information. Don't hesitate to express your ideas either because you can show how sharp you really are. All kinds of research are favored today as well as educational projects. When you meet people today, use your sense of humor, because it can be your greatest asset.

**Tuesday, September 16 (Moon Aquarius to Pisces 4:27 a.m.)**    An awful lot of practical things may seem to need doing today and demand your attention. Realize they cannot be put off. In many cases, you have let the details pile up and only a disciplined routine can cut them down to size. Yes, you've got hard work in front of you, but the rewards will be well worthwhile.

**Wednesday, September 17 (Moon in Pisces)**    Now you are ready for a change, and you will get it. In fact, some will get a whole new perspective on life and love. If you keep your schedule flexible, you will be able to goof off a bit and find some fun. Those who feel inclined should extend an invitation to that very interesting person they've been wanting to get together with. Your lucky number is 5.

**Thursday, September 18 (Moon Pisces to Aries 9:32 a.m.)**    The full moon emphasizes a sharp conflict between your personal and your public life. You will be pulled in two directions, and you could feel rather uneasy. If you go in the direction of loyal family members, you will feel the most support. A Taurus, a Libra, or a Scorpio could play a significant role.

**Friday, September 19 (Moon in Aries)** Your expectations for love and romance may exceed the reality of the situation. However, you don't have to end up alone simply because you set your sights too high. Instead, play a waiting game and someone will come to you. There are other forms of escape.

**Saturday, September 20 (Moon Aries to Taurus 5:25 p.m.)** Many Sagittarians will find that a love affair is intensifying now. However, you should also be coming to grips with reality. For some, that means thoughts of settling down or adding to your family. Long-term commitments are definitely indicated now. As is passion. Your lucky number is 8.

**Sunday, September 21 (Moon in Taurus)** Today you may experience the joy of service to others. In some cases, your special skills will help just the right person at just the right moment. All should be able to rise above selfish needs and desires today. Some will glimpse new fields to conquer and will be associating with pioneering types. Your lucky number is 9.

**Monday, September 22 (Moon in Taurus)** With your inventive ways, you will be able to get around a lot of busy work today by devising some exciting and interesting new ways of doing things. For many, it is a chance to display leadership and to show that you have a real sense of adventure. It could bring opportunities your way. A Leo, an Aquarian, or another co-worker will show how much he/she admires your personal style.

**Tuesday, September 23 (Moon Taurus to Gemini 4:13 a.m.)** Let someone else take the lead today, no matter what your sphere of operation. You will be much too vulnerable emotionally to take any risks, in fact, what you really need today are words of love and affection that assure you all is well. Try to get in touch with your inner feelings and you may be surprised at how much you can comfort yourself. Your lucky number is 2.

**Wednesday, September 24 (Moon in Gemini)**    Now a much lighter mood will take over. You are ready to meet people and to get involved in a lot of activity—possibly too much. In some cases, your independent spirit will flair up and get in the way of cooperation, which is desperately needed. Be willing to see the other person's point of view and to investigate alternatives.

**Thursday, September 25 (Moon Gemini to Cancer 4:44 p.m.)**    The key to cooperation now is to talk money sensibly to someone else. You should have a rather practical view of life now, and it will help a great deal. Show how sturdy you can be by paying bills and bringing records up to date. You know you can be disciplined when it is really necessary.

**Friday, September 26 (Moon in Cancer)**    You can avoid misunderstandings in one of your key relationships by being absolutely frank and open, which is your usual style. However, this time you may have to be even more so. If you really probe for information, you may find out something rather surprising which will change your whole point of view. In most cases, the desire for togetherness will overcome differences of opinion.

**Saturday, September 27 (Moon in Cancer)**    For some Sagittarians, their impulsive spending habits are now a cause for dissension in the family. It is important to be reasonable in this regard. It is also important to keep your mouth shut if you can't say something pleasant. Now as never before you must be willing to see both sides of a situation. Do something nice for everyone to ease the tension.

**Sunday, September 28 (Moon Cancer to Leo 5:39 a.m.)** Now you can break out of a rut and feel absolutely refreshed. The key is to mix with people and ideas very different from your own. This is a particularly subjective time, but you will benefit by seeing the subtleties of a situation. And then by trying to be objective about it. Your lucky number is 7.

**Monday, September 29 (Moon in Leo)** This is a great time to make some long-range plans that will move you ahead in your career. For many an encounter with a rather successful person will act as a catalyst to spur you on. It is important to start thinking about success in slightly different terms; money isn't everything. Let a Capricorn show you the way.

**Tuesday, September 30 (Moon Leo to Virgo 1:57 p.m.)** Your mental horizons continue to expand, and you may even be thinking about some further education—or at least a course. Refuse to be tied down by the past or by old ideas that people try to saddle you with. Many will have an excellent opportunity to express themselves and to grow in a very meaningful way. Your lucky number is 9.

# O C T O B E R   1 9 8 6

**Wednesday, October 1 (Moon in Virgo)** Now is the time to pull out all the stops where your career is concerned. Past efforts will now pay dividends and you will get the approval you want from someone at the top of the ladder. However, you must take some positive steps and show that you mean business. That is the only way to greater prestige and greater income. Your lucky number is 8.

*Thursday, October 2 (Moon Virgo to Libra 8:03 p.m.)* Someone is holding you back, but he/she will soon drop out of the picture. Therefore, you should not involve yourself in any petty squabbles. It is important to end your indecision about your direction in life, and to start making some long-range plans. First step is to finish off a big project.

*Friday, October 3 (Moon in Libra)* There are definite indications that someone who comes into your life now may totally transform it. Many are shifting their affiliations from one group to another. It is a positive step. In every way, groups are assuming a greater importance in your life. The lucky number is 1.

*Saturday, October 4 (Moon Libra to Scorpio 11:35 p.m.)* The pace will slow down a bit, and you will be able to take time out to catch up on some personal relationship matters. Don't get overbearing, however, because you can win your way through diplomacy. Some Sagittarians will find themselves in the middle of a special celebration that brings them in contact with people they haven't seen for a while. Relax and enjoy.

*Sunday, October 5 (Moon in Scorpio)* Your mind may be overflowing with creative ideas today, because your subconscious is very active. This may mean total confusion—or a real opportunity. The key is to take time out and separate the wheat from the chaff. Resist the urge to scatter your energies in a lot of meaningless activity.

*Monday, October 6 (Moon in Scorpio)* This is one of those days you gain a lot of satisfaction from sticking to a steady routine. You will feel you have accomplished something. Try not to be distracted by interruptions, because more than you realize you are laying foundations for future gain. Some confidential matters require careful handling, so don't neglect any details or be tempted to be indiscreet. Your lucky number is 4.

*Tuesday, October 7 (Moon Scorpio to Sagittarius 1:48 a.m.)*    With the moon in your own sign, you are ready for an exciting change of pace, and you will get it. Some will get a once-in-a-lifetime chance to show how skillful they can be and how eloquently they can express themselves. Don't blow it! A short trip could easily be on the calendar.

*Wednesday, October 8 (Moon in Sagittarius)*    You should be feeling good, so you will want to look your best as well. In some cases, that means paying a lot more attention to personal appearance. It's possible you have been neglecting yourself, as you have taken care of others. Realize you do not have to become a doormat, even if you want everybody to be happy. Let a Libra or a Taurus show you how to treat yourself.

*Thursday, October 9 (Moon Sagittarius to Capricorn 3:52 a.m.)*    It will be all too obvious that you get what you pay for. Don't get hooked by a bargain that seems too good to be true, because it is. In all financial matters, you may be a bit hazy or confused today. You are far better off dealing with intangibles than material matters now. Hold off on a major decision.

*Friday, October 10 (Moon in Capricorn)*    Now you can step forward in confidence in a business matter. This is an excellent time to make an investment of time or money or to put one of your pet theories to work. Never fear, you will receive the backing you need from someone who has it. Your lucky number is 8.

*Saturday, October 11 (Moon Capricorn to Aquarius 7:45 a.m.)*    Stop wasting time with people who drain you and have little to offer in return. Instead, get in touch with people who are doing big things and making positive changes in their own lives. And perhaps the lives of others. An Aries would be an excellent companion.

*Sunday, October 12 (Moon in Aquarius)*    You don't have to stray very far from your own home ground to have some excitement today. In some cases, there will be a very significant meeting with a very significant person; it could start your life off in a whole new direction. The likelihood is that it will be a romantic partner. Your lucky number today is 1.

*Monday, October 13 (Moon Aquarius to Pisces 11:03 a.m.)*    Be very careful when you speak today, because your emotions could be working overtime. A seemingly innocent remark could lead to a big problem— and possibly a serious rift with someone important. Go slowly, and give yourself the time to absorb all the new events and feelings that seem rather overwhelming now.

*Tuesday, October 14 (Moon in Pisces)*    This is definitely a more lighthearted day. In fact, it may seem as if all kinds of interesting people and experiences are beating a path to your door. Some will have an opportunity to show off their sense of humor and their really sparkling wit. Enjoy being popular! Another Sagittarian could be in the picture.

*Wednesday, October 15 (Moon Pisces to Aries 5:13 p.m.)*    Some really practical stuff will demand your attention today and possibly keep you tied down. It could be as basic as home repairs, security or insurance. For some, a parent, or other older person may need other undivided attention. It is important to live up to your obligations now. Your lucky number is 4.

*Thursday, October 16 (Moon in Aries)*    What a relief! The restrictions are off. For some, there could be some exciting developments—possibly in your love life. For others, a real pleasure trip or other kind of special entertainment is definitely indicated. Be willing to change your schedule at a moment's notice, and you will not regret it. A Gemini or a Virgo could be a sparkling companion.

*Friday, October 17 (Moon in Aries)* Tensions begin to build with the full moon, and you may experience some conflicts. In many cases, there will be a pull between the desire for fun and the necessity to please a love partner. If you are both gentle and tactful, you can smooth the waters. This is one time you probably should curb your Sagittarian desire for a freewheeling life-style. Your lucky number is 6.

*Saturday, October 18 (Moon Aries to Taurus 1:35 a.m.)* For your own health and well-being, you should seek a quiet time away from the ordinary cares of the day. If at all possible, spend them on meditating or at least getting into yourself. It's important to realize that you are a unique individual, and to attempt to understand that mystery. Some simple exercise and fresh air will help a great deal.

*Sunday, October 19 (Moon in Taurus)* Many will have received inspiration yesterday, and can now translate that into practical activity. In some cases, you will have learned how to deal with an older or at least more powerful individual who can help you get ahead. Your course is steady now, and your direction should be right to the top. A Capricorn could easily be involved.

*Monday, October 20 (Moon Taurus to Gemini 12:15 p.m.)* Now's the time to finish off big projects. Then to set your sights on higher goals. Some may be looking for a new job or at least a better shake right where they are; it is important to do some self-promotion, and to show what you have to offer. Keep alert, because someone rather unlikely will step in to help you out. Your lucky number is 9.

*Tuesday, October 21 (Moon in Gemini)* Love and marriage are definitely in the spotlight now. And that means you should be particularly aware of your actions, because you could temporarily forget to see the other person's side of the story. It's great to be an individual, but remember that you've got to live with other people in harmony. It's possible that more cooperation is needed; don't make important decisions alone.

*Wednesday, October 22 (Moon in Gemini)* You are better off listening today than talking. If you must communicate, share your feelings rather than facts. It is not a time to get down to brass tacks or to push or shove anyone. Let things simply move along slowly, and you can have a restful, rejuvenating interlude. Your lucky number is 2.

*Thursday, October 23 (Moon Gemini to Cancer 12:37 a.m.)* This is one of those days when you could easily attract sunshine no matter where you go. People will be rather generous, but there is a cautionary note. Realize that promises made may not be promises kept. In your lighthearted mood, money could easily slip through your fingers. Another Sagittarian could lead you astray. Exercise caution!

*Friday, October 24 (Moon in Cancer)* A solid practical approach to money is absolutely essential now. Rather than thinking about spending, pay your bills and review and revise your budget. In any matter, if you count on someone to take care of the details, you will be disappointed. Realize that you simply must do it yourself.

*Saturday, October 25 (Moon Cancer to Leo 1:02 p.m.)* For many Sagittarians, a romance is intensifying. The reason may be that you have begun to tune in on a much more spiritual level. In all cases, there is much more than simply physical attraction. If you take time for a deep heart-to-heart talk, you will discover this. Your lucky number is 5.

*Sunday, October 26 (Moon in Leo)* A special anniversary or celebration is on many Sagittarian calendars now. For some, the disruption may be a little bit annoying, but in the long run you will love getting together with those you haven't seen for a while. Be willing to listen to and understand ideas that are quite different from your own. You may forget your own problems when you are asked to solve someone else's.

**Monday, October 27 (Moon Leo to Virgo 11:20 p.m.)** If you don't control it, your imagination could easily run wild today. All kinds of flights of fancy are definitely indicated. Force yourself to avoid escapism and to emphasize your spiritual side instead. If you put your mind on "higher things," you will come out way ahead. It is an excellent time to plan travel. Your lucky number is 7.

**Tuesday, October 28 (Moon in Virgo)** Today you will be able to slip back into the world of practical affairs. In fact, you are ready to take some kind of plunge. For some, it is a more serious role in romance. For others, it is a career move. All need stability rather than sensation now and should avoid anything that smacks of the thrills of the moment.

**Wednesday, October 29 (Moon in Virgo)** Don't get shaken up when some kind of break with the past happens. Realize that it is all for the good, and that you will grow and develop through it. Some Sagittarians will get an excellent opportunity to display their talents and to make significant progress in their professional lives. An Aries or a Libra could play a very important role today.

**Thursday, October 30 (Moon Virgo to Libra 6:04 a.m.)** Be as open as possible today—to new friends, ideas, and opportunities. For some, a social occasion will produce a new friend—someone who is drawn by your leadership abilities. Don't be afraid to blow your own horn, no matter where you are. If you express your goals clearly and persuasively, others will back you up. Your lucky number is 1.

*Friday, October 31 (Moon in Libra)*      Someone older
or at least supportive, enters the picture with advice
and aid. You should be in a receptive mood, which is
all to the good. You may be feeling the need for some
special TLC; watch your weight, because you could be
tempted to overeat. The lucky number today is 2.

# NOVEMBER 1986

*Saturday, November 1 (Moon Libra to Scorpio 9:1*
*a.m.)*      Some of you will be thoroughly fed up with
limiting conditions and small minds. Use that feeling to
get yourself up and out—and expand your viewpoint.
With little trouble, you will meet people with new ideas
and dynamic personalities. If necessary, join a new
group or organization. The lucky number is 9.

*Sunday, November 2 (Moon in Scorpio)*      Spend some
quiet time today, but use it to prepare your case for a
coming confrontation. In some cases, your ideas may
simply be too ahead of your time, and others may not
be ready for them. Avoid controversy by playing your
cards close to the vest.

*Monday, November 3 (Moon Scorpio to Sagittarius*
*10:19 a.m.)*      Someone desperately needs your attention and affection now. It is your role to counsel, listen,
and try to lay someone's fears to rest. In the course of
it, you may hear a secret—and you must resolve to
keep it. Important decisions should be avoided today,
and you should do a lot more looking for inner answers than dealing with outward events.

*Tuesday, November 4 (Moon in Sagittarius)*      This
should be a banner day, no matter what you find yourself involved in. Some Sagittarians will be feeling rather
adventurous, and maybe tempted to plunge into new
and different situations. You can without hesitating

Your best buddy today—or traveling companion—would be another Sagittarian.

*Wednesday, November 5 (Moon Sagittarius to Capricorn 10:49 a.m.)* Try to maintain a steady pace, and you will accomplish an incredible amount of work. You may be tempted to break away from obligations, but realize that you are going through a necessary period of self-discipline that will leave you with a definite glow of accomplishment. Your lucky number today is 4.

*Thursday, November 6 (Moon in Capricorn)* Get set for some high times—possibly with members of the opposite sex. Someone will let you know that he/she loves you, in no uncertain terms. The proof could be a generous gift or romantic words. You can be sure they are sincere.

*Friday, November 7 (Moon Capricorn to Aquarius 12:29 p.m.)* All of a sudden you will be able to prove that you really do have a green thumb as far as money is concerned. A windfall or additional source of income could suddenly appear—and it could be connected with your own very special talents. It is an excellent day to shop for something very special, possibly something that will make life a little bit more luxurious for everybody. Your lucky number is 6 today.

*Saturday, November 8 (Moon in Aquarius)* Don't take anything for granted today. And be sure you make yourself clear when you speak. If you believe everything you hear, you could be headed for trouble. It is important to postpone signing an important agreement; you could be far too trusting today. Let a Pisces show you how to be subtle.

*Sunday, November 9 (Moon Aquarius to Pisces 4:30 p.m.)* You will gain far more today by taking a definite stand than by trying to evade a commitment. That applies to both love and money. Your integrity is at stake now, and you should not take a verbal agreement lightly. The lucky number is 8.

**Monday, November 10 (Moon in Pisces)**    You may feel rather overburdened by the cares of others now, particularly family members. However, it is important to recognize the difference between real obligations and simply being used. Refuse to be a crutch for those who refuse to help themselves. An Aries could play a key role.

**Tuesday, November 11 (Moon Pisces to Aries 11:14 p.m.)**    Now you can assert your rights, and get yourself free of former limitations. Some Sagittarians may be getting a new enterprise off the ground, particularly if they believe in themselves. It is important not to hang on to past security blankets; don't be afraid to move forward. Romance could be a big factor today.

**Wednesday, November 12 (Moon in Aries)**    Your intuition is right on target and could lead you to profit—particularly in a speculative venture. However, emotionally you may feel pulled in a couple of different directions. Realize that you may be clinging to memories that are no longer valid. You have outgrown things now. Your lucky number is 2.

**Thursday, November 13 (Moon in Aries)**    Now you should be back to your easygoing self, and be in a much more lighthearted mood. Your casual approach attracts people, and you should have an absolutely glorious day full of a lot of different kinds of activities. Freedom is the goal for you now, and you can grab it if you reach for it. A Gemini could be stimulating.

**Friday, November 14 (Moon Aries to Taurus 8:24 a.m.)**    Come back down to earth and resolve to dig in and follow through on a project you have been postponing. You can easily devise some workable methods that can cut through a lot of roadblocks. Younger people may require your attention now, and you should give it with good grace. Your lucky number is 4.

**Saturday, November 15 (Moon in Taurus)**    You should find yourself on the same wavelength with people around you today. Though you are ready for a change, and possibly travel, you should be able to keep your mind on things that need to be done. And do them joyfully with someone else. Don't be afraid to suggest some rather unorthodox ways of doing things.

**Sunday, November 16 (Moon Taurus to Gemini 7:26 p.m.)**    This full moon threatens conflict in your home sphere, but it needn't get the better of you. The key is to clearly divide your responsibilities from someone else's and to take on your fair share. If you are tactful and loving and show some appreciation, you will come through with flying colors.

**Monday, November 17 (Moon in Gemini)**    You could easily be disappointed by someone today; however, it is important to realize that your expectations may be too high. Don't make too big an issue out of it. If you see others more realistically, you will understand—and will stop feeling sorry for yourself. Your lucky number is 7.

**Tuesday, November 18 (Moon in Gemini)**    Once again your closest relationships are the focus of attention. Don't neglect them, but do follow the lead of someone who has a proven track record and can make very significant things happen for you. If it's a choice between love and business, realize that you have to be practical. Progress is realized through cooperative joint efforts.

**Wednesday, November 19 (Moon Gemini to Cancer 7:46 a.m.)**    Your love life could be rather stormy and dramatic today; jealousy may be the reason. In another scenario, it is possible you will attract someone who is fiercely competitive and rather childish at the same time. It's important for you to be mature, and to take stock of the situation. Perhaps you should demand that someone else grow up.

**Thursday, November 20 (Moon in Cancer)** If you let yourself get depressed today, you will not see the opportunities that are at hand. For one thing, do not allow yourself to be confined by old ways of doing things. If you are willing to take a chance, there is every possibility of greater prosperity. In some cases, marriage has become an issue. Let a Leo tell you how to handle a romantic situation. Your lucky number is 1.

**Friday, November 21 (Moon Cancer to Leo 8:25 p.m.)** Security may be very much on your mind today, and you could be investigating ways to improve the status of joint finances. Good work! Trust a first impression you get today—whether it has to do with love, money, or your career. It probably has a great deal of validity. Someone is prepared to be very generous with you, if you ask.

**Saturday, November 22 (Moon in Leo)** Try to focus your energies on a definite goal. If you scatter your wits or your attention now, it could really stand in the way of progress. Set your sights on something that you really want, and follow through on it. Don't be afraid to expand your mental horizons. Your lucky number is 3.

**Sunday, November 23 (Moon in Leo)** Today you've got to slow down. Realize that you've got to master the details of one thing before you seek new fields to conquer. It is important not to waste time or money now, and not to do anything halfway. You will simply limit yourself if you don't throw your whole heart into everything you do. An Aquarian or a Leo could be a good role model.

**Monday, November 24 (Moon Leo to Virgo 7:46 a.m.)** There are people around you today who are full of very valuable information; don't hesitate to ask a lot of questions. They will be welcomed and answered better than you expect. In some cases, a change of routine will bring an exciting contact with a very stimulating new person. He/she could be very significant in your life in the coming weeks. Your lucky number is 5.

**Tuesday, November 25 (Moon in Virgo)**     No matter where you find yourself, you will feel like digging in and creating a little home for yourself. That means you benefit most by harmonious surroundings now, and it may require your pacifying someone else. Use all the tact and diplomacy you can muster. For sweet relief, use your artistic or musical talents today.

**Wednesday, November 26 (Moon Virgo to Libra 3:59 p.m.)**     You've got some secret fears about something, and it is important to confront them now. For some, it has to do with your reputation. Do something about it, even if it means changing your ways. If you try being less materialistic and more spiritual, you can lift yourself above circumstances that baffle you now. Your lucky number is 7.

**Thursday, November 27 (Moon in Libra)**     Now you should realize that some past efforts are about to pay off. That means that it's important to keep on plugging away, no matter how tired or put upon you may feel. You may be even asked to take on more responsibility than you have now; accept it with good grace. A Capricorn could show you how to do it.

**Friday, November 28 (Moon Libra to Scorpio 8:52 p.m.)**     There is no way one of your dreams is going to come true if you do not become more aware of your own motives and your fears and limitations. It is highly possible that you are holding yourself back through negative thinking. It is an excellent day to change all that, and to expand your expectations. You will help yourself a great deal by hanging around with more positive people.

**Saturday, November 29 (Moon in Scorpio)**    You may get a pleasant surprise today when you discover that a fun-loving person is more attracted to you than you suspect. The two of you could have an excellent time together. For some, a rather important secret may be revealed. Handle it with care.

**Sunday, November 30 (Moon Scorpio to Sagittarius 9:08 p.m.)**    Some Sagittarians are undergoing profound psychological changes. It could make you a lot more loving—and lovable. Your supersensitive feelings could make you wish for time out today. Accept your need to relax and retire. The lucky number today is 2.

# DECEMBER 1986

**Monday, December 1 (Moon in Sagittarius)**    This is your best Sagittarius moon of the year. For one thing, it will focus greater attention on you, and highlight your ability to express yourself in a very positive and creative manner. Dress the part for making a new start— wear something bright and bold. Say yes to almost everything today including a romantic opportunity. A Leo could be in the picture.

**Tuesday, December 2 (Moon Sagittarius to Capricorn 8:26 p.m.)**    The comfort and security of home and family will be all-important to you today. Trust your intuition in most things, particularly for guiding you toward the right source for greater gain. Don't brood over past mistakes now, particularly in the personal area. Resolve to do better in the future.

**Wednesday, December 3 (Moon in Capricorn)**    You may be in an overly generous mood, and too ready to splurge on holiday gifts. If you go shopping, keep a tight hold on your wallet and don't spread yourself too thin. You may try to set off in too many directions at once. Stay on the straight and narrow!

**Thursday, December 4 (Moon Capricorn to Aquarius 8:23 p.m.)**   You may be willing to take a more serious look at your budget and your expenses now. If you are feeling financially limited, use that feeling in a positive way by planning a realistic schedule for holiday spending. Catch up on all the details of record-keeping and other legally financial details. Your lucky number is 4.

**Friday, December 5 (Moon in Aquarius)**   The sense of community is strong wherever you go today. You should feel very much "in synch" with those around you. Be willing to share your ideas as well as your resources. And prepare for some kind of romantic encounter.

**Saturday, December 6 (Moon Aquarius to Pisces 10:48 p.m.)**   A family gathering or celebration will dominate the scenario today. Unless you play the role of peacemaker, sharp words are likely to disturb the peace. Get everyone to concentrate on good food but hold yourself back from overindulging. It is important for you to learn how to say no. Your lucky number is 6.

**Sunday, December 7 (Moon in Pisces)**   You will be very much in an escapist mood today and anxious to avoid stressful situations. Even if you stay home, you may have to avoid family members who are in a rather contentious mood. If you do get hooked, play a waiting game where important decisions are concerned. A nice quiet Pisces could make good company.

**Monday, December 8 (Moon in Pisces)**   You should start out this day with a fresh surge of optimism. Someone may simply hand you some money that can make the holiday season a whole lot more successful. Or, your own enterprising nature may increase your income. Take that important step toward getting yourself more recognition.

**Tuesday, December 9 (Moon Pisces to Aries 4:49 a.m.)** If you finish off a project that you have been procrastinating about, you will be able to take off for some kind of adventure. Your restless nature may be even more so now, and you may be absolutely propelled to seek new horizons. Someone will encourage you to show your talents to a wider audience; don't be shy! Your lucky number is 9.

**Wednesday, December 10 (Moon in Aries)** Now love takes the spotlight, and it should make for a very pleasant twenty-four hours. In some cases, you will attract the attention of someone who is very generous and fond of splurging. However, this person is a lot more sensitive than you think, so be sure to show your appreciation in no uncertain terms.

**Thursday, December 11 (Moon Aries to Taurus 2:10 p.m.)** If you don't keep a promise—possibly to someone younger—you will disappoint him/her severely. In some cases, it will be an outing you will enjoy just as the other person does. Sagittarians have a special knack for reliving their own childhoods; it is a wonderful trait to have. Be sure to give and receive a lot of affection today.

**Friday, December 12 (Moon Taurus)** It may be very difficult for you to keep your mind on your work today. Not only is the holiday approaching, but you are also thinking about some kind of travel plan—or other significant adventure. Give yourself a break by investigating some new work methods that are a little more stimulating. A Gemini or another Sagittarian could be an excellent co-worker today. Your lucky number is 3.

*Saturday, December 13 (Moon in Taurus)*    If you've been thinking about getting yourself in shape for the holiday, today is an excellent day to start a new regime. You still have got a couple of weeks to diet and your ability to discipline yourself should be rather good now. Your own well-being should be at the top of your mind today, and it is important to spend some time and attention on it.

*Sunday, December 14 (Moon Taurus to Gemini 1:41 a.m.)*    Someone may indicate that he/she wants more "togetherness." You should be receptive to the suggestion. It could be as simple as saying yes to an excursion, or being willing to change your routine to accommodate someone else. This can be both an exciting and a productive day. Your lucky number is 5.

*Monday, December 15 (Moon in Gemini)*    You should be exceptionally able to smooth the ruffled feathers of others today. You should also do well in activities where you are the organizer and the one who makes a special occasion even more special. However, don't get carried away when you are asked to perform; you could all too easily play the clown.

*Tuesday, December 16 (Moon Gemini to Cancer 2:09 p.m.)*    The full moon may bring some storm clouds to your relationship life. A misunderstanding could quickly develop if you are vague about some commitment and appointments. Try to concentrate on the things someone else thinks are important. If you don't, you may end up going one way, while your partner goes the other.

*Wednesday, December 17 (Moon in Cancer)*    Today it is quite apparent that you are more realistic about life, and consequently your situation should be a lot better. That applies to your financial life as well as your personal life. If you ask for what you want in the way of support, others are likely to be very outgoing. In fact, a gift of money is a strong possibility.

**Thursday, December 18 (Moon in Cancer)**    Today a very altruistic mood could take over, but don't go overboard by giving more than is warranted. Someone in your circle is dependent enough, and you could make the situation worse. On the positive side, you will be thinking about those who are less fortunate than yourself. The lucky number is 9.

**Friday, December 19 (Moon Cancer to Leo 2:44 a.m.)**    You should be in excellent spirits today, and ready to break free of routine. You should be able to do it, and you will double your fun if you dress as if you are expecting something interesting to happen. That might mean being a little more daring than usual. But after all, you are definitely an individual. You may fascinate someone fascinating.

**Saturday, December 20 (Moon in Leo)**    Whatever you do today, it will be more fun if you do it with someone else. For one thing, it will provide you with the sense of security you need. In some cases, Sagittarians are entering new and different territories that might seem alien at first. Your intuition is very keen today, and you should use it. Your lucky number is 2.

**Sunday, December 21 (Moon Leo to Virgo 2:30 p.m.)** Today you should be feeling much more ready for a challenge. As a matter of fact, you may be willing to go very far afield for new contacts and new knowledge. No matter what your scenario, you will be the life of the party wherever you go and you will very much enjoy the company you find yourself in. Your lucky number is 3.

**Monday, December 22 (Moon in Virgo)**    You may have to take a very firm hold of yourself to come back down to earth today. Somebody is expecting high performance of you, and you had better come through. There is no way you will be pampered or allowed to take the easy way out. Resolve to plow through a mountain of details that have piled up, no matter how much stern self-discipline it takes.

***Tuesday, December 23 (Moon in Virgo)*** A number of Sagittarians will receive something very interesting in the mail today; in some cases, it is an opportunity that must be acted upon to get the full benefit. You should be well able to analyze it today. Someone whose opinion you respect will come through with a compliment that shows you he/she recognizes how hard you have been trying.

***Wednesday, December 24 (Moon Virgo to Libra 12:05 a.m.)*** Some storm clouds may threaten to gather even on this preholiday day; you are the one who can keep the sun shining. It should not be difficult to maintain a light touch, and to get everyone involved in preparing for a celebration. A Libra, a Scorpio, or a Taurus could be your staunchest ally.

***Thursday, December 25 (Moon in Libra)*** It's possible someone is missing from the circle that gathers today, and you should make a special effort to get in touch with him/her. The emphasis is very much on your close relationships today, and you should have a warm glow when you realize how much someone else really does care. Someone may suspect you of having ESP when you know exactly what he/she is thinking about. Your lucky number is 7.

***Friday, December 26 (Moon Libra to Scorpio 7:06 a.m.)*** Look for stability rather than excitement today. In fact, the backing you need is there for the asking. Realize that it will come from one who is quietly supportive. Your long-range plans should be coming into focus. Your lucky number is 8.

*Saturday, December 27 (Moon in Scorpio)*    Your thoughts are still very much in the giving mode. In fact, today you may feel absolutely compelled to help someone else. It could be through a charity drive or fund-raising effort. Whatever you do, it is a day when you definitely are able to rise above purely personal motives.

*Sunday, December 28 (Moon Scorpio to Sagittarius 8:20 a.m.)*    If you are going to make any New Year's resolutions, this is a good day to do it. You should be rather creative, and full of confidence in your abilities. However, don't set your goals so high that you disappoint yourself later on. You may want to get some privacy to put your thoughts down on paper. Your lucky number is 1.

*Monday, December 29 (Moon in Sagittarius)*    With the moon in Sagittarius, the spotlight is on you. It's time you started taking a close look at your appearance; you may have been rather preoccupied recently and not as careful as you should have been. Some partying that is coming up will require some sprucing up. It's an excellent day to go out and buy something new.

*Tuesday, December 30 (Moon Sagittarius to Capricorn 7:54 a.m.)*    You will probably feel like racing around a lot today, because there are so many things you want to do. It's great to be coming out of an emotional rut, but don't take on more than you can handle. Save some energy for the coming holiday. Another bright person— possibly another Sagittarian—is very much in the picture, and the two of you should laugh it up. The lucky number is 3.

*Wednesday, December 31 (Moon in Capricorn)*    The last day of the year finds your attention focused on money and values. You will be in a much more cautious and conservative mood about spending than usual. Your mind will be very much on future plans rather than passing pleasures. It is an excellent way to end the year. You also will find a sane and sensible way to celebrate.

## About This Series

This is one of a series of
Twelve Day-by-Day Astrological Guides
for the signs in 1986
by Sydney Omarr

## *About the Author*

Born on August 5, 1926, in Philadelphia, Omarr was the only astrologer ever given full-time duty in the U.S. Army as an astrologer. He also is regarded as the most erudite astrologer of our time and the best-known, through his syndicated column (300 newspapers), and his radio and television programs (he is Merv Griffin's "resident astrologer"). Omarr has been called the most "knowledgeable astrologer since Evangeline Adams." His forecasts of Nixon's downfall, the end of World War II in mid-August of 1945, the assassination of John F. Kennedy, Roosevelt's election to a fourth term and his death in office . . . these and many others . . . are on record and quoted enough to be considered "legendary."

# How well do you know yourself?

# Know in advance the changes in your life

Wouldn't it be useful to know when important events in your life are going to happen? How would you respond? What will you experience emotionally, intellectually and psychologically? And how will these experiences affect your life.

Your transits can provide valuable clues to various trends or stages of personal growth. This is especially true for the slower moving outer planets—Jupiter through Pluto. The transits for these planets are long lasting and profound in their psychological consequences. Many occur only once in a lifetime. The Astral Forecast is all about the outer planets.

This horoscope provides a reliable tool for astrological forecasting. The Astral Forecast will show you how the outer transits affect your sense of timing, that is, the times that are appropriate for you to take certain kinds of actions and inappropriate for others. This horoscope includes every significant transit to your outer planets that occurs in a twelve-month period. You can use your Astral Forecast to better understand how the outer planets affect such important life issues as career, child rearing, love, marriage and more.

For example, when Jupiter is in the first house, this transit represents a major growth cycle in your life. This is the best time for you to explore who you really are as an individual. Under this transit, you will feel more secure about yourself and the impression you make on others. Therefore, understanding yourself and your influence on others can make this transit an especially powerful and

important time in your life. This is also a time for learning and gaining new experience. All this is part of your present need for personal growth, which affects not only yourself, but also the way you deal with the world as a whole. This is one time when persons and resources are likely to be drawn to you, and you should take constructive advantage of them.

You can find out in advance what your transits are going to be. But if you do it on your own, you will have to consult several astronomical tables to find the positions of each of the transiting planets every day and then compare them mathematically to the positions of the planets at the time of your birth.

There's an easier way to learn of your transits. Our IBM System/36 computer will handle all the calculations and provide you with information on all your

outer transits based on your exact time and place of birth. With the Astral Forecast you not only receive the most accurate calculation of your personal transits for the next twelve months, you will also receive an extensive printout interpreting the character and significance of your individual transits.

Your Astral Forecast is the most accurate and authoritative guide to the outer transits that you can receive. It is based on the work of Robert Hand, one of America's most famous astrologers, and the author of several astrology books.

Like all Para Research horoscopes, the Astral Forecast is inexpensive. For just $16.00 you can have the same kind of advice that would otherwise cost you hundreds of dollars. This low price is possible because the astrological data is stored in our computer, and can be easily formatted and printed. Also, the mathematical calculations can be done in a matter of minutes. Your only cost is the cost of putting your personal information into the computer, producing one copy and then mailing it.

When you order your Astral Forecast, you receive an unconditional money-back guarantee. This means you can return your Astral Forecast at any time and get a full refund of the purchase price. We take all the risk.

Order your Astral Forecast today. Discover how the transits can bring energy to each part of your personality, fulfill your potential and help you gain more control over your own life.
© 1983 Para Research, Inc.

# "Next to my mother, you have been the greatest inspiration of my life."

**MARGUERITE CARTER**

### You'll be amazed!

When you read what Marguerite Carter has to say about your life in the year ahead you'll be amazed. She delves into the most important areas of your life: romance, money, goals, and significant changes. You'll find out all the wonderful ways you can live a better life when you have your Unitology Forecast prepared for you by Marguerite Carter.

### She'll help you.

Marguerite Carter has counseled thousands of enthusiastic followers around the world for decades. She has been the guiding light and helping hand for people from all walks of life: business leaders, hollywood stars and just everyday folks. There is a good reason why they seek her services year after year. They get the help they need in the most important areas of their lives!

### '. . . it was amazing.'

People write all the time telling about how Marguerite Carter has helped them.

". . . it was amazing. I just can't believe it." W.C., Canada

". . . could not put it down until I read it cover to cover." M.L., Illinois.

"Without a doubt, next to my mother, you have been the greatest inspiration of my life. Many others could probably say the same thing." M.A., PA

In letter after letter people comment on the realistic guidance they've received for getting what they want from life. They've found the help they need in times of decision or resolving personal problems. These are judgments by a caring counselor, not some impersonal computer.

### Hidden Opportunities

The things you want most may not be out of reach. Marguerite Carter says, "Many people are completely unaware that the opportunities for money, love or advancement are passing them by almost daily . . ." Without knowledge of when the conditions are favorable or unfavorable, the chances for success and happiness are greatly diminished.

Get your Unitology Forecast with special notations by Marguerite Carter. It will be prepared to your specific birthdate information. Remember that you will receive a full year of guidance, regardless of when your request is received, and you'll know that your forecast has come from one of the world's most highly respected astrologer-counselors.

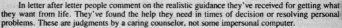

**O-6**

Marguerite Carter • P.O. Box 807 • Indianapolis, Indiana 46206

☐ Yes Miss Carter, Please send me my Unitology Forecast for the year ahead. Enclosed is my remittance of $9.95 plus $1.00 for postage and handling. (First Class $1.30) Make all checks payable in U.S. funds. Allow 4 weeks for delivery.

Name _____

Address _____

City _____ State _____ Zip Code _____

Birthplace _____

Month _____ Day _____ Year _____

Place _____ Hour _____

# ASTROLOGY QUESTIONNAIRE

Help us bring you even better astrology guides by filling out this survey and mailing it today.

A.  Book Title (Sign): _____

B.  Using the scale below how would you rate this astrological guide? (Place one rating from 0–10 in the space provided.)

| Poor | | Not So Good | | | O.K. | | | Good | | Excellent |
|------|---|------|---|---|------|---|---|------|---|------|
| 0 | 1 | 2 | 3 | | 4 | 5 | 6 | | 7 | 8 | 9  10 |

Rating

Overall Opinion of book

Essay On:

1.  Defining Terms _____
2.  Your House of The Sun _____
3.  The Geometry of Relationships _____
4.  Twelve Places at the Table _____
5.  Moods of the Moon _____
6.  Venus and Mars _____
7.  Venus Sign Position Chart _____
8.  Mars Sign Position Chart _____
9.  The Planets as "Stars" _____
10. Astrotrivia _____
11. Sun Sign Changes _____
12. Your Sign: The Big Picture _____
13. Your Sign: Objectives and Obstacles _____
14. Pairing Off With Your Sign _____
15. Your Sign's Sex Role Dilemma _____
16. Your Sign: Female _____
17. Your Sign: Male _____
18. Your Sign: Help Wanted _____
19. How "Pure" a _____ are you? _____
20. Find Your Rising Sign _____
21. Your Sign: Astro-Outlook for '86 _____
22. 15 Months of Day-By-Day Predictions _____

C.  In total about how many astrology guides have you
    purchased for yourself in the past 12 months?
                # of books _____

D.  What topics would you be interested in having Syd-
    ney Omarr write about in the 1987 Astrology Guide?
    _____

    _____

E.  What is your education?

    1( ) High School   3( ) 4 yrs college
    2( ) 2 yrs college  4( ) Postgraduate

F.  What is your occupation? _____

G.  What is your marital status?

    1( ) Single    3( ) Divorced   5( ) Widowed
    2( ) Married   4( ) Separated

H.  Age: _____          I.  Sex: 1( ) Male
                                    2( ) Female

Please Print Name:_____

Address_____

City_____State_____Zip_____

Phone # (    )_____

Thank you. Please send to New American Library,
Research Dept., 1633 Broadway, New York, NY 10019